THEODORE
ROOSEVELT
THE CITIZEN

THEODORE ROOSEVELT
PRESIDENT OF THE UNITED STATES
DRAWN BY GEORGE T. TOBIN

To the Young Men
of America

THEODORE ROOSEVELT
THE CITIZEN

BY
JACOB A. RIIS
AUTHOR OF "THE MAKING OF AN AMERICAN"
"HOW THE OTHER HALF LIVES," ETC.

—

ILLUSTRATED

—

THE
OUTLOOK COMPANY
NEW YORK MCMIV

Republished, 1970
Scholarly Press, 22929 Industrial Drive East, St. Clair Shores, Michigan 48080

Standard Book Number 403-00224-9
Library of Congress Catalog Card Number: 77-108531

This edition is printed on a high-quality,
acid-free paper that meets specification
requirements for fine book paper referred
to as "300-year" paper

CONTENTS

[ix]

CONTENTS

LIST OF ILLUSTRATIONS

[xi]

LIST OF ILLUSTRATIONS

I
BOYHOOD IDEALS

—

I

BOYHOOD IDEALS

ALL summer I have been fighting for leeway to sit down and write about Theodore Roosevelt, and glad am I that I have come to it at last. For there is nothing I know of that I would rather. But let us have a clear understanding about it. I am not going to write a " life " of him. I have seen it said in print that that was my intention. Well, it was. That was the shape it took in my mind at the start; but not for long. Perhaps one of the kindest things the years do for us as they pass is to show us what things we can not do. In that way they have been very kind to me. When I was twenty, there was nothing I could not do. Now I am glad that there are stronger and fitter hands than mine to do many things I had set my heart on. They must do this, then.

THEODORE ROOSEVELT

And, besides, it is both too early and too late for a life of Theodore Roosevelt. Too late for the mere formal details of his career; everybody knows them. Much too early to tell the whole story of what that strong, brave life will mean to the American people, his people of whom he is so proud, when the story is all told. No one can know him and believe in the people without feeling sure of that.

There remains to me to speak of him as the friend, the man. And this is what I shall do, the more gladly because so may it be my privilege to introduce him to some who know him only as the public man, the President, the partisan perhaps—and a very energetic partisan he is—and so really do not know him at all, in the sense which I have in mind. The public man I will follow because he is square, and will do the square thing always, not merely want to do it. With the partisan I will sometimes disagree, at least I ought to, for I was before a Democrat and would be one now if the party would get some sense and bar Tammany out in the cold for its monstrous wickedness.[1] Of the President I am proud with rea-

[1] I am bound to say that I see no signs of it, and also that I am rather relieved, with Roosevelt to run in another year.

son, but the friend I love. And if I can make
you see him so, as a friend and a man, I have
given you the master-key to him as a statesman
as well. You will never need to ask any questions.

For still another reason I am glad that it
is to be so: I shall be speaking largely to the
young whose splendid knight he is, himself yet
a young man filled with the high courage and
brave ideals that make youth the golden age
of the great deeds forever. And I want to show
them the man Roosevelt, who through many a
fight in which hard blows were dealt never once
proved unfaithful to them; who, going forth
with a young man's resolve to try to " make
things better in this world, even a little better,
because he had lived in it," [1] through fair days
and foul, through good report and evil (and of
this last there was never a lack), sounded his
battle-cry, " Better faithful than famous," *and
won*. A hundred times the mercenaries and
the spoilsmen whom he fought had him down
and " ruined " in the fight. At this moment,
as I write, they are rubbing their hands with
glee because at last he has undone himself,

[1] His speech to the Long Island Bible Society, June 11, 1901.

by bidding organized labor halt where it was
wrong.   Last winter, when it was right, he
" killed himself " when he made capital stop
and think.   They were false prophets then as
they are now.   Nothing can ruin Theodore
Roosevelt except his proving unfaithful to his
own life, and that he will never do.   If I know
anything of him, I know this, that he would
rather be right than be President any day, and
that he will never hesitate in his choice.

That is the man I would show to our young
people just coming into their birthright, and
I can think of no better service I could render
them.   For the lying sneers are thick all about
in a world that too often rates success as " what
you can make."   And yet is its heart sound;
for when the appeal is made to it in simple faith
for the homely virtues, for the sturdy manhood, it is never made in vain.   This is Theodore Roosevelt's message to his day, that honor
goes before profit, that the moral is greater
than the material, that men are to be trusted
if you believe in the good in them; and though
it is an old story, there is none greater.   At
least there is none we have more need of learning, since the world is ours, such as it is, to fit

for the kingdom that is to come, and nowhere
is there another plan provided for doing it.

So, then, it is understood that I am absolved
from routine, from chronology, and from sta-
tistics in writing this story. I am to have full
leave to " put things in as I think of them,"
as the critics of my books say I do anyhow.
A more absurd charge was never made against
any one, it has always seemed to me; for how
can a man put things in when he does n't think
of them? I am just to write about Theodore
Roosevelt as I know him, of my own knowledge or through those nearest and dearest to
him. And the responsibility will be mine altogether. I am not going to consult him, even if
he is the President of the United States. For
one thing, because, the only time I ever did,
awed by his office, he sent the copy back unread
with the message that he would read it in print.
So, if anything goes wrong, blame me and me
only.

And now, when I cast around for a starting-
point, there rises up before me the picture of a
little lad, in stiff white petticoats, with a curl
right on top of his head, toiling laboriously
along with a big fat volume under his arm,

THEODORE ROOSEVELT

" David Livingstone's Travels and Researches
in South Africa," and demanding of every
member of the family to be told what were
" the foraging ants " and what they did. It
was his sister, now Mrs. Cowles, who at last
sat down in exasperation to investigate, that
the business of the household might have a
chance to proceed, for baby Theodore held it
up mercilessly until his thirst for information
was slaked. Whereupon it developed that the
supposedly grim warriors of the ant-hill were
really a blameless tribe—" the foregoing ants "
in fact. We are none of us infallible. The
" foraging ants " are a comfort to me when
their discoverer is disposed to laugh at my
ee-wee lamb that but for my foreign speech
should have been a plain ewe. But, then, I
dwelt content in the bliss of ignorance. He,
explorer in baby petticoats, could not be ap-
peased till he found out.

I suppose they called him Ted in those days.
In my own time I have never found any one
to do it who knew him, and the better they
knew him the less liable were they to. You can
tell for a certainty that a man does not know
him when he speaks of him as " Teddy." Not

[8]

that he frowns upon it; I do not believe that he
has often had the chance. But, somehow, there
is no temptation to that kind of familiarity,
which does not imply any less affection, but
just the reverse. He may call me Jake and I
like nothing better. But though I am ten years
older than he, he was always Mr. Roosevelt
with me. His rough-riders might sing of him
as Teddy, but to his face they called him Colonel, with the mixture of affection and respect
that makes troopers go to death as to a dance
in the steps of a leader. The Western plains-
men quickly forgot the tenderfoot in the man
who could shoot and ride though he came out of
the East and wore eye-glasses, and who never
bragged or bullied but knew his rights and
dared maintain them. He was Mister Roosevelt there from the second day on the ranch.
But in those old days at home he was Ted with
the boys, no doubt. For he was a whole boy
and got out of it all that was going, after he
got it going. He has told me that it took
some time, that as a little fellow he was timid,
and that when bigger boys came along and
bullied him he did not know what to do
about it. I have a notion that he quickly

found out and that they did not come back
often.

A woman who lived next door to the Roosevelts in East Twentieth Street told me of how,
passing in the street, she saw young Theodore
hanging out of a second-story window and ran
in to tell his mother.

" If the Lord," said she, as she made off to
catch him, " had not taken care of Theodore,
he would have been killed long ago."

In after years the Governor of New York
told me, with a reminiscent gleam in his eye,
how his boy, the third Theodore in line, had
" swarmed down " the leader of the Executive
Mansion to go and hear the election returns,
rather than go out through the door. There
was no frightened neighbor to betray his exploit then, for it was dark, which made it all
the more exciting. It was the Governor himself who caught him. The evidence is, I think,
that the Theodores were cut out pretty much
on the same pattern.

Of that happy childhood's home, with the
beautiful mother of blessed memory and the
father who rode and played with the children,
and was that, alas! rarest of parents, their

THEODORE ROOSEVELT'S BIRTHPLACE, IN
NEW YORK

DRAWN BY J. CONACHER

chum and companion as well as their just judge when occasion demanded, I have caught many a glimpse I wish I might reveal here, but that shall be theirs to keep. The family romps at home, the strolls on forest paths which their father taught them early to love; their gleeful dashes on horseback, he watchfully leading on, the children scampering after, a merry crew; of how at his stern summons to breakfast, " Children! " they one and all fell downstairs together in their haste to be there, they speak yet with a tenderness of love that discloses the rarely strong and beautiful soul that was his. It was only the other day that, speaking with an old employee of the Children's Aid Society, of which the elder Roosevelt was a strong prop, I learned from him how deep was the impression made by his gentle courtesy toward his wife when he brought her to the lodging-house on his visits. " To see him put on her wraps and escort her from room to room was beautiful," he said. " It seemed to me that I never knew till then what the word gentleman meant." How little we, any of us, know what our example may mean for good or for ill! Here, after thirty years, the recollection of Mr. Roosevelt's simple courtesy was a potent force in one man's life.

With such ties of love binding the home together, the whirlwind of anger and passion that swept over the country in the years of the war had no power to break or to embitter, even though the mother was of the South, with roots that held, while his life and work were given to the Union cause as few men's were. Rather, it laid the foundations broad and deep of that abiding Americanism that is to-day Theodore Roosevelt's most distinguishing trait. It is no empty speech of his that caresses the thought of the men who wore the blue and those who wore the gray standing at last shoulder to shoulder. It was an uncle of Theodore Roosevelt who built the privateer *Alabama,* and another uncle, Irwin S. Bulloch, who fired the last gun aboard her when she went down before the fire of the *Kearsarge,* shifting it from one side of the ship to the other as she sank, to let it have the last word. The while at home his father raised and equipped regiments and sent them to the war, saw to it that they were fed and cared for and that those they left behind did not suffer. I have never been able to make up my mind which was most like the Theodore of to-day. I guess they both were. I know that as he grew, the devotion of the one, the daring of the other, took hold of his soul and together were welded into the man, the patriot, to whom love of country is as a living fire, as the very heart's blood of his being.

For play there was room in plenty in the home in which Theodore grew up; for idleness none. His father, though not rich in the sense of to-day, had money enough to enable them all to live without working if they so chose. That they should not so choose was the constant aim and care of his existence. In his scheme of life the one man for whom there was no room was the useless drone. Whether *he* needed it or not, every man must do some honest, decent work, and do it with his might: the community had a right to it. We catch echoes of this inheritance in his son's writings from the very beginning, and as the years pass they ring out more clearly. I remember his interview with Julian Ralph, when as a Police Commissioner he was stirring New York up as it had not been stirred in many a long day. I can see him now striding up and down the bare gray office.

" What would you say to the young men of our city, if you could speak to them with command this day? " asked Mr. Ralph.

" I would order them to work," said Mr. Roosevelt, stopping short and striking his hands together with quick emphasis. " I would teach the young men that he who has not wealth owes his first duty to his family, but he who has means owes his to the State. It is ignoble to go on heaping money on money. I would preach the doctrine of work to all, and to the men of wealth the doctrine of unremunerative work."

It was hardly unremunerative work that first enlisted young Theodore's energies. Looking at him now, I should think that nothing ever paid a better interest on the investment. He was not a strong child—from earliest infancy liable to asthmatic attacks that sapped his vitality and kept back his growth. Probably that accounts for the temporary indecision in the matter of bullies which he remembers. But in the frail body there lived an indomitable spirit before which had risen already visions of a man with a horse and a gun, of travel and adventure. Mayne Reid's books had found their way to East Twentieth Street, and they went with the lad wherever the family tent was pitched to ease the little sufferer. One winter they spent in Egypt, floating down the Nile amid the ruins of empires dead and gone. But the past and its dead got no grip on the young American. He longed to go back to his own country of the mighty forests and the swelling plains where men worked out their own destiny. He would be a pathfinder, a hunter. But a hunter has need of strong thews; of a sound body. And to become strong became presently the business of his life.

It was one of the things that early attracted me to Theodore Roosevelt, long before he had become famous, that he was a believer in the gospel of will. Nothing is more certain, humanly speaking, than this, that what a man wills himself to be, that he will be. Is he willing to put in all on getting rich, rich he will get, to find his riches turning to ashes in his dead hand; will he have power, knowledge, strength —they are all within his grasp. The question for him to decide is whether they are worth giving up a life to, and, having decided, to give it to his ambition. The boy Theodore saw that to do anything he must first be strong, and chose that. There were many things he might have chosen which would have been easier, but if you are concerned about that, you will not have your way. He was not. He set about resolutely removing the reproach of his puny body, as it seemed to him. He ran, he rode, he swam, he roamed through the hills of his Long Island home, the same to which he yet comes back to romp with his children on his summer holiday. He rowed his skiff intrepidly over the white-capped waters of the Bay—that once, when I had long been a man, carried mine, despite all my struggles, across to Center Island and threw me, skiff and all, upon the beach, a shipwrecked mariner doomed to be ignominiously ferried across on the yacht club's launch. I thought of it the other day when I came ashore from the *Sylph,* and half a mile from shore met young Kermit battling alone with the waves, hatless and with the salt spray in his eyes and hair, tossed here and there as in a nutshell, but laughing and undaunted. I do

not know where he was going. I doubt if he did. His father and mother were ashore and on their way home. He was just having it out and having a good time. It was his father over again, and we cheered him on and let him go. I don't suppose we could have stopped him had we tried.

No more could you have stopped Theodore in his day. What he did he did with the will to win, yet never as a task. He got no end of fun out of it, or it would have been of little use, and one secret of that was that he made what he did serve an end useful in itself. On his tramps through the woods he studied and classified the neighborhood birds. He knew their song, their plumage, and their nests. So he learned something he wanted to know, and cultivated the habits of study, of concentration, at the time when all boys are impatient of these things and most of them shirk them when they can, leaving every task unfinished. And all, as I said, along of a healthy, outdoor, romping life. The reward of that was not long in coming. Presently strong muscles knit themselves about his bones, the frail frame broadened and grew tough. The boy held his own with his fellows. He passed them, and now he led in their games. The horse was his; the gun loomed in the prospect. College was at hand, and then—life. The buffaloes yet roamed the plains. One might unite the calling of a naturalist, a professor, with the interest of a hunter. So ran his dreams. It is the story of one American boy who won against odds, and though he did not become professor he became President; and it is a good story for all American boys to read. For they can do the same, if they choose to. And if they do not all become Presidents, they can all be right, and so be like him in that which is better still.

I said he had his dreams. Every boy has, and if he does not stop at that, it is good for him. Into young Theodore's there had come a new element that spoke loudly for the plains, for the great West. The Leatherstocking stories had been added to his reading. It was with something of fear almost that I asked him once if he liked them. For I loved them. I had lived them all in my Danish home. They first set my eyes toward the west, and in later years, when I have heard it said, and read in reviews that Cooper is out of date; that he

never was a first-class writer, I have felt it
as a personal injury and as if something had
come between me and the day that cannot love
Natty Bumppo and Uncas and Mabel Dun-
ham. And so I say it was with a real pang
that I asked him if he did not also like them.

He whirled round with kindling eyes.

" Like them," he cried, " like them! Why,
man, there is nothing like them. I could pass
examination in the whole of them to-day.
Deerslayer with his long rifle, Jasper and
Hurry Harry, Ishmael Bush with his seven
stalwart sons—do I not know them? I have
bunked with them and eaten with them, and I
know their strength and their weakness. They
were narrow and hard, but they were mighty
men and they did the work of their day and
opened the way for ours. Do I like them?
Cooper is unique in American literature, and
he will grow upon us as we get farther away
from his day, let the critics say what they will."
And I was made happy.

Afterward I remembered with sudden ap-
prehension that he had spoken only of the white
men in the books, for it came to me that he had
lived in the West, where the only good Indian is

esteemed to be the dead Indian. But it was needless treachery of my thought. The red man has no better friend than the Great White Father of to-day, none who burns with hotter indignation at the shame our dealings with him have brought upon the American name. Uncas and Chingachgook, beloved friends of my boyhood, were safe with him.

I have told you of Theodore Roosevelt's boyhood as from time to time I have gathered glimpses of it from himself and from his sister, and as I like to think of it. I did not meet him till long after both horse and gun had become living realities. When he was drifting and dreaming on the Nile I was sailing across the Atlantic to have my first tussle with the slum which in after years we fought together. And now you know one reason why I love him: it was when that same strong will, that honest endeavor, that resolute purpose to see right and justice done to his poorer brothers—it was when they joined in the battle with the slum that all my dreams came true, all my ideals became real. Why should I not love him?

The boy had grown into a man. Since I have here spoken to the boys of his country and, thank God, of mine, let him speak now, and judge yourself how performance has squared with promise, practice with preaching:

"Of course what we have a right to expect of the American boy is that he shall turn out to be a good American man. Now, the chances are strong that he won't be much of a man unless he is a good deal of a boy. He must not be a coward or a weakling, a bully, a shirk, or a prig. He must work hard and play hard. He must be clean-minded and clean-lived, and able to hold his own under all circumstances and against all comers. It is only on these conditions that he will grow into the kind of a man of whom America can really be proud.

"In life, as in a football game, the principle to follow is: Hit the line hard; don't foul and don't shirk, but hit the line hard."

II

WHAT HE GOT OUT OF
COLLEGE

—

II

WHAT HE GOT OUT OF COLLEGE

RATHER a delicate-looking young fellow yet, not over a hundred and thirty pounds on the scales, slender of frame and slim of waist, was the Theodore Roosevelt who made his entry into Harvard while the country yet rang with the echoes of the Electoral Commission and of the destructive railroad riots of the summer that followed. They were troublous times to begin life in, and one would naturally think that they would leave their mark upon a spirit like Roosevelt's. I know that they did, but the evidence of it does not lie on the surface. Neither in the memory of his classmates nor in his record as an editor of the " Advocate " is there anything to suggest it. I was in Pennsylvania during those riots, when militiamen were burned like

rats in a railroad round-house. I saw what
they meant, and I have no difficulty in making
out their stamp upon his ardent spirit when I
read such comments as this on the draft riots
in his history of New York, though written
more than a dozen years after:

" The troops and police were thoroughly
armed, and attacked the rioters with the most
wholesome desire to do them harm; . . . a
lesson was inflicted on the lawless and disor-
derly which they never entirely forgot. Two
millions of property had been destroyed and
many valuable lives lost. But over twelve hundred rioters were slain—an admirable object-
lesson to the remainder."

Perhaps they had more to do with shaping
his later career, those cruel riots, than even he
has realized, for I should not be surprised if,
unconsciously, he acted upon their motion in
joining the militia in his own State, and so
got the first grip upon the soldiering that stood
him in such good stead in Cuba. " I wanted,"
he said to me after he had become President,
" to count for one in the fight for order and for
the Republic, if the crisis were to come. I
wanted to be in a position to take a man's stand

in such a case, that was why." Counting for one in the place where he stood, when that was the thing to do, then and always, he has got to the place where he counts for all of us, should such days come back, as please God they will not; and nowhere, I think, in the land is there any one who doubts that " order and the Republic " are safe in his hands.

But in his youthful mind these things were working yet, unidentified. His was a healthy nature without morbid corners. The business of his boyhood had been to make himself strong that he might do the work of a man, by which he had in mind chiefly, no doubt, the horse and the gun—the bully, perhaps, whom he had not forgotten—but the hunt, the life in the open. Now, among his fellows, it was to get the most out of what their companionship offered. He became instantly a favorite with his class of a hundred and seventy-odd. They laughed at his oddities, at his unrepressed enthusiasm, at his liking for Elizabethan poetry, voted him " more or less crazy " with true Harvard conservatism, respected him highly for his scholarship on the same solid ground, and fell in even with his notions for his own sake, as afterward

some of them fell in behind him in the rush
up San Juan hill, leaving lives of elegance and
ease to starve with him in the trenches and do
the chores of a trooper in camp under a tropi-
cal sun. It is remembered that Theodore
Roosevelt set Harvard to skipping the rope,
a sport it had abandoned years before with
knickerbockers; but it suited this student to
keep up the exercise as a means of strengthen-
ing the leg muscles, and rope-skipping became
a pastime of the class of 1880. In the gym-
nasium they wore red stockings with their
practice suits. Roosevelt had happened upon
a pair that were striped a patriotic red and
white, and he wore them, at first to the amazement of the other students. He did not even
know that they had attracted attention, but
when some one told him he laughed and kept
them on. It was what the legs could do in the
stockings he was there to find out. Twenty
years after I heard a policeman call him a dude
when he walked up the steps of police headquarters with a silk sash about his waist, something no man had been known to wear in Mulberry Street in the memory of the oldest there;
and I saw the same officer looking after him

WHAT HE GOT OUT OF COLLEGE

down the street, as long as he was in sight, the day he went, and turn back with a sigh that made him my friend forever: " There won't such another come through that door again in my time, that there won't." And there did not. The old man is retired long since.

He joined the exclusive " Pork " Club, and forthwith smashed all its hallowed traditions and made the Porcellian blood run cold, by taking his fiancée to lunch where no woman ever trod before. He simply saw no reason why a lady should not lunch at a gentlemen's club; and when the shocked bachelor minds of the " Pork " Club searched the horizon for one to confront him with, they discovered that there was none. Accordingly the world still stood, and so did the college. He played polo, did athletic stunts with the fellows, and drove a two-wheeled gig badly, having no end of good times in it. When he put on the boxing-gloves, he hailed the first comer with the more delight if he happened to be the champion of the class, who was twice his size and heft. The pummeling that ensued he took with the most hearty good will; and though his nose bled and his glasses fell off, putting him at a disadvantage, he refused grimly to cry quarter, and pressed the fight home in a way that always reminds me of that redoubtable Danish sea-fighter, Peter Tordenskjold, who kept up the fight, firing pewter dinner-plates and mugs from his one gun, when on his little smack there was left but a single man of the crew, " and he wept." Tordenskjold killed the captain of the Swedish frigate with one of his mugs and got away. Roosevelt was bested in his boxing-matches often enough, but, however superior, his opponents bore away always the impression that they had faced a fighter.

But the battle was not always to the strong in those days. I have heard a story of how Roosevelt beat a man with a reputation as a fighter, but not, it would appear, with the instincts of a gentleman. I shall not vouch for it, for I have not asked him about it; but it is typical enough to be true, except for the wonder how the fellow got in there. He took, so the story runs, a mean advantage and struck a blow that drew blood before Roosevelt had got his glove on right. The bystanders cried foul, but Roosevelt smiled one of his grim smiles.

THEODORE ROOSEVELT AS A HARVARD SENIOR
PHOTOGRAPH BY PACH BROTHERS

WHAT HE GOT OUT OF COLLEGE

" I guess you made a mistake. We do not do that way here," he said, offering the other his gloved hand in formal salutation as a sign to begin hostilities. The next moment his right shot out and took the man upon the point of the jaw, and the left followed suit. In two minutes he was down and out. Roosevelt was " in form " that day. All the fighting blood in him had been roused by the unfairness of the blow. I have seen him when his blood was up for good cause once or twice, and I rather think the story must be true. If I were to fight him and wanted to win, I should shun a foul blow as I would the pestilence. I am sure I would not run half the risk from the latter.

Play was part of the college life, and he took a hand in it because it belonged. Work was the bigger part, and he did not shirk it, or any of it. I am not sure, but I have a notion that he did not like arithmetic. I feel it in my bones, somehow. Perhaps the wish is father to the thought. I know I hated it. But I will warrant he went through with it all the same, which I did not. I think he was among the first twenty in his class, which graduated a hundred and forty. He early picked out as his specialties the history of men and things, animals included. The ambition to be a naturalist and a professor clung to him still, but more and more the doings of men and of their concerns began to attract him. It was so with all he did in college, whether at work or play—it was the life that moved in it he was after. Unconsciously yet, I think, his own life began to shape itself upon its real lines. He read the " Federalist " with the entire absorption that was and is his characteristic, and lived and thought with the makers of our government. There are few public men to-day who are more firmly grounded in those fundamentals than he, and the airy assumption of shallow politicians and critics who think they have in Roosevelt to do with a man of their own kind sometimes makes me smile. The faculty of forgetting all else but the topic in hand is one of the great secrets of his success in whatever he has undertaken as an official. It is the faculty of getting things done. They tell stories yet, that go around the board at class dinners, of how he would come into a fellow-student's room for a visit, and, picking up a book, would become immediately and wholly absorbed in its con-

tents, then wake up with a guilty start to confess that his whole hour was gone and hurry
away while they shouted after him. It was the
student in him which we in our day are so apt.
to forget in the man of action, of deeds. But
the two have always gone together in him; they
belong together. In all the wild excitement
of the closing hours of the convention that set
him in the Vice-President's chair he, alone in
an inner room, was reading Thucydides, says
Albert Shaw, who was with him. He was resting. I saw him pick up a book, in a lull in the
talk, the other day, and instantly forget all
things else. He was not reading the book as
much as he was *living* it. So, men get all there
is out of what is in hand, and they are few who
can do it. However, of that I shall have more
to say later, when I have him in Mulberry
Street, where he was mine for two years.

His college chums, sometimes, seeing the
surface drift and judging from it, thought him
" quite unrestrained," as one of them put it to
me, meaning that he lacked a strong grip on
himself. It was a natural mistake. They saw
the enthusiasm that gave seemingly full vent
to itself and tested men by the contact, not

the cautious, almost wary, deliberation which
in the end guided action, though he himself
but half knew it. They laughed a little at his
jump at the proposition to go to Greenland
with a classmate and study the fauna there—he
was planning the trip before it had been fairly
suggested—and at the preparations he made
for a tiger-hunting expedition to India with his
brother Elliott. The fact that in both cases he
acted upon the coolest judgment and stayed
home occurred to them only long afterward.
To me at this end, with his later life to interpret
its beginning, it seems clear enough that already the perfect balance that has distinguished his mental processes since was beginning to assert itself. However he might seem
to be speeding toward extremes, he never got
there. He buried himself in his books, but he
woke up at the proper seasons, and what he
had got he kept. He went in for the play,
all there was of it, but he never mistook the
means for the end and let the play run away
with him. Long years after, when the thing
that was then taking shape in him had ripened,
he wrote it down in the record of his Western
hunts: "In a certain kind of fox-hunting lore

there is much reference to a Warwickshire
squire who, when the Parliamentary and Roy-
alist armies were forming for the battle at
Edgehill, was discovered between the hostile
lines, unmovedly drawing the covers for a fox.
Now, this placid sportsman should by rights
have been slain offhand by the first trooper who
reached him, whether Cavalier or Roundhead.
He had mistaken means for ends, he had confounded the healthful play which should fit
a man for needful work with the work itself,
and mistakes of this kind are sometimes criminal. Hardy sports of the field offer the best
possible training for war; but they become con-
temptible when indulged in while the nation
is at death-grips with her enemies."

One factor in this mental balance, his unhesitating moral courage which shirked no disagreeable task and was halted by no false pride
of opinion, had long been apparent. He was
known as a good hand for a disagreeable task
that had to be done, a reproof to be adminis-
tered in justice and fairness—I am thinking
of how the man kept that promise of the youth,
before Santiago, when for the twentieth time
he " wrecked a promising career " with his fa-

mous round-robin—and also for the generous
speed with which he would hasten to undo a
wrong done by word or act. There were no
half-way measures with him then. He owned
right up. " He was fair always," said one of
his classmates who was close to him. " He
never tried to humbug others, or himself either,
but spoke right out in meeting, telling it all."
No wonder some within reach thought him
erratic. There has never been a time in the
history of the world when such a course would
commend itself to all men as sane. It com-
mended itself to him as right, and that was
enough.

A distinguishing trait in his father had been
—he died while Theodore was at college—
devotion to duty, and the memory of it and
of him was potent with the son. He tried
to walk in his steps. " I tried faithfully to do
what father had done," he told me once when
we talked about him, " but I did it poorly. I
became Secretary of the Prison Reform Association (I think that was the society he spoke
of), and joined this and that committee. Father had done good work on so many; but in
the end I found out that we have each to work

WHAT HE GOT OUT OF COLLEGE

in his own way to do our best; and when I
struck mine, though it differed from his, yet
I was able to follow the same lines and do
what he would have had me do."

It was thus natural that Theodore Roosevelt
should have sought out a Sunday-school and a
chance to teach as soon as he was settled at
Harvard, and that his choice should have fallen
upon a mission school. He went there in pur-
suit of no scheme of philanthropy. Providence had given him opportunities and a training that were denied these, and it was simple
fairness that he should help his neighbor who
was less fortunate through no fault of his own.
The Roosevelts were Dutch Reformed. He
found no Dutch Reformed church at Cam-
bridge, but there were enough of other denom-
inations. The handiest was Episcopal. It
happened that it was of high church bent.
Theodore Roosevelt asked no questions, but
went to work. With characteristic directness
he was laying down the way of life to the
boys and girls in his class when an untoward
event happened. One of his boys came to
school with a black eye. He owned up that
he had got it in a fight, and on Sunday. His

teacher made stern inquiry. "Jim" some-
body, it appeared, who sat beside his sister, had
been pinching her all through the hour, and
when they came out they had a stand-up fight
and he punched him good, bearing away the
black eye as his share. The verdict was prompt.

"You did perfectly right," said his teacher,
and he gave him a dollar. To the class it was
ideal justice, but it got out among the officers
of the school and scandalized them dreadfully.
Roosevelt was not popular with them. Unfamiliar with the forms of the service, he had
failed at times to observe them all as they
thought he should. They wished to know if he
had any objection to any of them. No, none
in the world; he was ready to do anything
required of him. He himself was Dutch Reformed—he got no farther. The idea of a
" Dutch Reformed " teaching in their school,
superimposed upon the incident of the black
eye, was too much. They parted with somewhat formal expressions of mutual regard.
Roosevelt betook himself to a Congregational
Sunday-school near by and taught there the
rest of his four years' course in college. How
it fared with Jim's conqueror I do not know.

WHAT HE GOT OUT OF COLLEGE

Before he had finished the course, Roosevelt had started upon his literary career. It came in the day's work, without conscious purpose on his part to write a book. They had at his Club James' history, an English work, and he found that it made detailed misstatements about the war of 1812. Upon looking up American authorities, it turned out that they gave no detailed contradictions of these statements. The reason was not wholly free from meanness: in nearly all the sea-fights of that war the American forces had outnumbered the British, often very materially; but the home historians, wishing not to emphasize this fact, had contented themselves with the mere statement that the " difference was trifling," thus by their foolish vaunts opening the door to exaggeration in the beaten enemy's camp. The facts which Roosevelt brought out from the official files with absolute impartiality grew into his first book, " The Naval War of 1812," which took rank at once as an authority. The British paid the young author, then barely out of college, the high compliment of asking him to write the chapter on this war for their monumental work on " The

Royal Navy," and there it stands to-day, unchallenged.

So with work and with play and with the class politics in which Theodore took a vigorous hand, the four years wore away as one. He was, by the way, not a good speaker in those days, I am told; but such speeches as he made —and he never farmed the duty out when it was his to do—were very much to the point. One is remembered yet with amusement by a distinguished lawyer in this city. He had been making an elaborate and as he thought lucid argument in class-meeting, and sat down, properly proud of the impression he must have made; when up rose Theodore Roosevelt.

" I have been listening, Mr. Chairman," he spoke, " and, so far as I can see, not one word of what Mr. —— has said has any more to do with this matter than has the man in the moon. It is—" but the class was in a roar, and what " it was " the indignant previous speaker never learned.

But, as I said, the years passed, and, having graduated, Roosevelt went abroad to spend a year with alternate study in Germany and mountain-climbing in Switzerland by way of letting off steam. Probably the verdict men might have set down against his whole college career would have been that it was in no way remarkable. Here and there some one had taken notice of the young man, as having quite unusual powers of observation and of concentration, but nothing had happened of any extraordinary nature, though things enough happened where he was around. Later on, when the fact had long compelled public attention, I asked him how it was. His answer I recommend to the close attention and study of young men everywhere who want to get on.

" I put myself in the way of things happening," he said, " and they happened."

It may be that the longer they think of it, like myself, the more they will see in it. A plain ˙and homely prescription, but so, when you look at it, has been the man's whole life so far—a plain talk to plain people, on plain issues of right and wrong. The extraordinary thing is that some of us should have got up such a heat about it. Though, come to think of it, that is n't so extraordinary either; the issues are so very plain. " Thou shalt not steal " is not exactly revolutionary preaching, but it is apt to stir up feelings when it means what it says. No extraordinary ambitions, no other thought than to do his share of what there was to do, and to do it well, stirred in this young student now sailing across the seas to begin life in his native land, to take up a man's work in a man's country. None of his college chums had been found to predict for him a brilliant public career. Even now they own it.

What, then, had he got out of his five years of study? They were having a reunion of his class when he was Police Commissioner, and he was there. One of the professors told of a student coming that day to bid him good-by. He asked him what was to be his work in the world.

" Oh! " said he, with a little yawn. " Really, do you know, professor, it does not seem to me that there is anything that is much worth while."

Theodore Roosevelt, who had been sitting, listening, at the other end of the table, got up suddenly and worked his way round to the professor's seat. He struck the table a blow that was not meant for it alone.

WHAT HE GOT OUT OF COLLEGE

" That fellow," said he, " ought to have been knocked in the head. I would rather take my chances with a blackmailing policeman than with such as he."

That was what Theodore Roosevelt got out of his years at Harvard. And I think, upon the whole, that he could have got nothing better, for himself, for us, or for the college.

III

EARLY LESSONS IN POLITICS

—

III

EARLY LESSONS IN POLITICS

I N the year when President Garfield died,
New York saw the unusual sight of two
young " silk-stockings," neither of whom
had ever been in politics before, running for
office in a popular election. One was the representative of vast inherited wealth, the other
of the bluest of the old Knickerbocker blood:
William Waldorf Astor and Theodore Roosevelt. One ran for Congress, pouring out
money like water, contemptuously confident
that so he could buy his way in. The newspapers reported his nightly progress from saloon to saloon, where " the boys " were thirstily
waiting to whoop it up for him, and the size
of " the wad " he left at each place, as with ill-
suppressed disgust he fled to the next. The
other, nominated for the State Legislature on

an issue of clean streets and clean politics, though but a year out of college, made his canvass squarely upon that basis, and astounded old-time politicians by the fire he put into the staid residents of the brownstone district, who were little in the habit of bothering about elections. He, too, was started upon a round of the saloons, under management. At the first call the management and that end of the canvass gave out together. Thereafter he went it alone. He was elected, and twice re-elected to his seat, with ever-increasing majorities. Astor was beaten, and, in anger, quit the country. To-day he lives abroad, a self-expatriated American. Theodore Roosevelt, who believes in the people, is President of the United States.

There was no need of my asking him how he came to go into politics, for how he could have helped it I cannot see; but I did. He thought awhile.

" I suppose for one thing ordinary, plain, every-day duty sent me there to begin with. But, more than that, I wanted to belong to the governing class, not to the governed. When I said that I wanted to go to the Republican Association, they told me that I would meet the groom and the saloon-keeper there; that politics were low, and that no gentleman bothered with them. ' Then,' said I, ' if that is so, the groom and the saloon-keeper are the governing class and you confess weakness. You have all the chances, the education, the position, and you let them rule you. They must be better men; ' and I went.

" I joined the association, attended the meetings, and did my part in whatever was going. We did n't always agree, and sometimes they voted me down and sometimes I had my way. They were a jolly enough lot and I had a good time. The grooms were there, some of them, and some of their employers, and we pulled together as men should if we are to make anything out of our country, and by and by we had an election."

There had been a fight about the dirty streets. The people wanted a free hand given to Mayor Grace, but the machine opposed. The Assemblyman from Roosevelt's district, the old Twenty-first, was in disgrace on that account. The Republican boss of the district, " Jake " Hess, was at odds with his lieutenants, " Joe " Murray and Major Bullard, and in making up the list of delegates to the Assembly Convention they outgeneraled him, naming fifteen of the twenty-five. Thus they had the nomination within their grasp, but they had no candidate. Roosevelt had taken an active part in opposing the machine man, and he and Murray had pulled together. There is something very characteristic of Theodore Roosevelt in this first political alliance as related by Murray. " When he found we were on the same side, he went to Ed Mitchell, who had been in the Legislature, and asked what kind of a man I was, and when he was told *he gave me his confidence.*" It is another of the simple secrets of his success in dealing with men: to make sure of them and then to trust them. Men rarely betray that kind of trust. Murray did not.

Presently he bethought himself of Theodore Roosevelt, who was fighting but didn't yet quite know how. As a candidate he might bring out the vote which ordinarily in that silk-stocking district came to the polls only in a Presidential year. He asked him to run, but Roosevelt refused. It might look as if he had come there for his personal advantage. Murray reasoned with him, but he was firm. He suggested several candidates, and one after another they were turned down. Roosevelt had another batch. Murray promised to look them over.

" And if I can't find one to suit, will you take it then? " he asked. Yes, he would do that, as a last resort.

" But I did n't look for no other candidate when I had his promise," says " Joe," placidly, telling of it. " Good reason: I could n't find any better, nor as good."

" Joe " Murray is a politician, but that day he plotted well for his country.

Roosevelt was nominated and began the canvass at once. The boss himself took him around to the saloons that night, to meet " the people." They began at Valentine Young's place on Sixth Avenue. Mr. Hess treated and introduced the candidate. Mr. Young was happy. He hoped he was against high license; he, Young, hated it. Now, Roosevelt was attracted by high license and promptly said so and that he would favor it all he could. He gave his reasons. The argument became heated, the saloon-keeper personal. The boss looked on, stunned. He did not like that way of making votes.

Neither did Mr. Roosevelt. He sent "Jake" Hess home and quit the saloon canvass then and there. Instead he went among his neighbors and appealed to them. The "brownstone" vote came out. "Joe" Murray rubs his hands yet at the thought of it. Such a following he had not dreamed of in his wildest flights. Men worth millions solicited the votes of their coachmen and were glad to get them. Dean Van Amringe peddled tickets with the Columbia professors. Men became suddenly neighbors who had never spoken to one another before, and pulled together for the public good. Murray was charged with trading his candidate off for Astor for Congress; but the event vindicated him triumphantly. Roosevelt ran far ahead of the beaten candidate for Congress. He took his seat in the Legislature, the youngest member in it, just as he is now the youngest President.

He was not received with enthusiasm by the old wheel-horses, and the fact did credit to their discernment, if not to their public spirit. I doubt if they would have understood what was meant by this last. They were there on the good old plan—good so far always for the purpose it served—that was put in its plainest, most brutal form, years after, by the champion of spoilsmen forever: " I am in politics working for my own pocket all the time—same as you." The sneer told of their weak spot. The man who has lost faith in man has lost his grip. He may not know it, but he has. I fancy they felt it at the coming of this young man who had taught the Commandments in Sunday-school because he believed in them. They laughed a little uneasily and guessed he would be good, if he were kept awhile.

Before half the season had passed he had justified their fears, if they had them. There was an elevated railroad ring that had been guilty of unblushing corruption involving the Attorney-General of the State and a Judge of the Supreme Court. The scandal was flagrant and foul. The people were aroused, petitioned respectfully but chafed angrily under the yawn with which their remonstrances were received in the Assembly. The legislators " referred " the petition and thought it dead. But they had forgotten Roosevelt.

He had been watching and wondering. To him an unsullied judiciary was the ground fabric of society. Here were charges of the most serious kind against a judge smothered unheard. He asked his elders on the Republican benches what was to be done about it. Nothing. Nothing? Then he would inquire publicly. They ran to him in alarm. Nothing but harm could come of it, to him and to the party. He must not; it was rank folly. The thing was loaded.

" It was," wrote an unnamed writer in the " Saturday Evening Post," whose story should be framed and hung in the Assembly Chamber as a chart for young legislators of good intentions but timid before sneers, " it was obviously the counsel of experienced wisdom. So far as the clearest judgment could see, it was not the moment for attack. Indeed, it looked as if attack would strengthen the hands of corruption by exposing the weakness of the opposition to it. Never did expediency put a temptation to conscience more insidiously.

" It was on April 6, 1882, that young Roosevelt took the floor in the Assembly and demanded that Judge Westbrook, of Newburg, be impeached. And for sheer moral courage that act is probably supreme in Roosevelt's life thus far. He must have expected failure. Even his youth and idealism and ignorance of public affairs could not blind him to the apparently inevitable consequences. Yet he drew his sword and rushed apparently to destruction—alone, and at the very outset of his career, and in disregard of the pleadings of his closest friends and the plain dictates of political wisdom.

" That speech—the deciding act in Roosevelt's career—is not remarkable for eloquence. But it is remarkable for fearless candor. He called thieves thieves regardless of their millions; he slashed savagely at the Judge and the Attorney-General; he told the plain, unvarnished truth as his indignant eyes saw it.

" When he finished, the veteran leader of the Republicans rose and with gently contemptuous raillery asked that the resolution to take up the charges be voted down. He said he wished to give young Mr. Roosevelt time to think about the wisdom of his course. ' I,' said he, ' have seen many reputations in the State broken down by loose charges made in the

Legislature.' And presently the Assembly gave ' young Mr. Roosevelt time to think ' by voting not to take up his ' loose charges.'

" Ridicule, laughter, a ripple—apparently it was all over, except the consequences to the bumptious and dangerous young man which might flow from the cross set against his name in the black books of the ring.

" It was a disheartening defeat—almost all of his own party voted against him; the most earnest of those who ventured to support him were Democrats; perhaps half of those who voted with him did so merely because their votes were not needed to beat him.

" That night the young man was once more urged to be ' sensible,' to ' have regard to his future usefulness,' to ' cease injuring the party.' He snapped his teeth together and defied the party leaders. And the next day he again rose and again lifted his puny voice and his puny hand against smiling, contemptuous corruption. Day after day he persevered on the floor of the Assembly, in interviews for the press; a few newspapers here and there joined him; Assemblymen all over the State began to hear from their constituents. Within a week

his name was known from Buffalo to Montauk
Point, and everywhere the people were ap-
plauding him. On the eighth day of his bold,
smashing attack the resolution to take up the
charges was again voted upon at his demand.
And the Assemblymen, with the eyes of the
whole people upon them, did not dare longer
to keep themselves on record as defenders of a
judge who feared to demand an investigation.
The opposition collapsed. Roosevelt won by
104 to 6."

In the end the corruptionists escaped. The
committee made a whitewashing report. But
the testimony was damning and more than vindicated the attack. A victory had been won;
open corruption had been driven to the wall.
Roosevelt had met his party on a moral issue
and had forced it over on the side of right.
He had achieved backing. Out of that fight
came the phrase " the wealthy criminal class "
that ran through the country. In his essay on
" true American ideals " he identifies it with
" the conscienceless stock speculator who ac-
quires wealth by swindling his fellows, by de-
bauching judges and legislatures," and his
kind. " There is not," he exclaims, " in the

world a more ignoble character than the mere
money-getting American, insensible to every
duty, regardless of every principle, bent only
on amassing a fortune, and putting his fortune
only to the basest uses—whether these uses be
to speculate in stocks and wreck railroads himself, or to allow his son to lead a life of foolish
and expensive idleness and gross debauchery,
or to purchase some scoundrel of high social
position, foreign or native, for his daughter."

" Young Mr. Roosevelt " went into the next
Legislature re-elected with a big majority in
a year that saw his party go down in defeat all
along the line, as its leader on the floor of the
house. At twenty-four he was proposed for
Speaker. Then came his real test. Long after,
he told me of it.

" I suppose," he said, " that my head was
swelled. It would not be strange if it was.
I stood out for my own opinion, alone. I took
the best mugwump stand: my own conscience,
my own judgment, were to decide in all things.
I would listen to no argument, no advice. I
took the isolated peak on every issue, and my
people left me. When I looked around, before
the session was well under way, I found my-

self alone. I was absolutely deserted. The
people did n't understand. The men from
Erie, from Suffolk, from anywhere, would not
work with me. ' He won't listen to anybody,'
they said, and I would not. My isolated peak
had become a valley; every bit of influence I
had was gone. The things I wanted to do I
was powerless to accomplish. What did I do?
I looked the ground over and made up my
mind that there were several other excellent
people there, with honest opinions of the right,
even though they differed from me. I turned
in to help them, and they turned to and gave
me a hand. And so we were able to get things
done. We did not agree in all things, but we
did in some, and those we pulled at together.
That was my first lesson in real politics. It
is just this: if you are cast on a desert island
with only a screw-driver, a hatchet, and a chisel
to make a boat with, why, go make the best one
you can. It would be better if you had a saw,
but you have n't. So with men. Here is my
friend in Congress who is a good man, a strong
man, but cannot be made to believe in some
things which I trust. It is too bad that he
does n't look at it as I do, but he *does not,* and

we have to work together as we can. There is a point, of course, where a man must take the isolated peak and break with it all for clear principle, but until it comes he must work, if he would be of use, with men as they are. As long as the good in them overbalances the evil, let him work with that for the best that can be got."

One can hardly turn a page of his writings even to this day without coming upon evidence that he has never forgotten the lesson of the isolated peak.

The real things of life were getting their grip on him more and more. The old *laissez faire* doctrine that would let bad enough alone because it was the easiest way still pervaded the teaching of his college days, as applied to social questions. The day of the Settlement had not yet come; but his father had been a whole social settlement and a charity organization society combined in his own person, and the son was not content with the bookish view of affairs that so intimately concerned the welfare of the republic to which he led back all things. The bitter cry of the virtually enslaved tenement cigarmakers had reached Albany,

THEODORE ROOSEVELT AS CANDIDATE FOR
MAYOR OF NEW YORK CITY

PHOTOGRAPH BY FALK

and Roosevelt went to their rescue at once. He was not satisfied with hearsay evidence, but went through the tenements and saw for himself. The conditions he found made a profound impression upon him. They were afterward, when I wrote " How the Other Half Lives," an introduction to him and a bond of sympathy between us. He told the Legislature what he had seen, and a bill was passed to stop the evil, but it was declared unconstitutional in the courts. The time was not yet ripe for many things in which he was afterward to bear a hand. A dozen years later, as Health Commissioner, he helped destroy some of the very tenements in which at that earlier day industrial slavery in its worst form was intrenched too strongly to be dislodged by law. The world " do move," with honest hands to help it.

It was so with the investigation of the city departments he headed. There was enough to investigate, but we had not yet grown a conscience robust enough to make the facts tell. Parkhurst had first to prepare the ground. The committee sat for a couple of weeks, perhaps three, at the old Metropolitan Hotel, and

it was there I first met Theodore Roosevelt,
when the police officials were on the stand. I
remember distinctly but one incident of that
inquiry. It was when lawyer George Bliss,
who could be very cutting when it suited his
purpose, made an impertinent remark, as counsel for the Police Commissioners. I can see
" young " Mr. Roosevelt yet, leaning across
the table with the look upon his face that always compelled attention, and saying with
pointed politeness: " Of course you do not
mean that, Mr. Bliss; for if you did we should
have to have you put out in the street." Mr.
Bliss did not mean it.

It was at that session, too, I think, that he
struck his first blow for the civil service reform which his father contended for when it
had few friends; for which cause the Republican machine rejected his nomination for Collector of the Port of New York. I know how
it delighted the son's heart to carry on his father's work then and when afterward as Governor he clinched it in the best civil service law
the State has ever had. But, more than that,
he saw that this was one of the positions to be
rushed if the enemy were to be beaten out.

EARLY LESSONS IN POLITICS

Another was the power of confirmation the
Aldermen had over the Mayor's appointments
in New York. Thus even the best administration would be helpless with a majority of Tammany members on the Board of Aldermen.
Such a thing as the election of a reform Board
of Aldermen was then unthinkable. He
wrested that power from them and gave it to
the Mayor, and, in doing it, all unconsciously
paved the way for himself to the office in which,
under Mayor Strong, he leaped into National
importance. There are many striking coinci-
dences of the kind in Theodore Roosevelt's
career. I have noticed that they are to be
found in the life of every man who goes straight
ahead and does what he knows is right, taking
the best counsel he can and learning from life
as it shapes itself under his touch. All the
time he is laying out grappling-hooks, without
knowing it, for the opportunity that comes
only to the one who can profit by it, and, when
it passes, he lays hold of it quite naturally. It
is only another way of putting Roosevelt's philosophy that things happen to those who are
in the way of it. It is the idlers who prate
of chance and luck. Luck is lassoed by the

masterful man, by the man who knows and who can. And it is well that it is so, or we should be in a pretty mess.

I have spoken at considerable length about Theodore Roosevelt's early legislative experience because I am concerned about showing how he grew to what he is. Men do not jump up in a night like mushrooms, some good credulous people to the contrary notwithstanding, or shoot up like rockets. If they do, they are apt to come down like sticks. At least Mr. Roosevelt stays up a long time, they will have to admit. I have heard of him being " discovered " by politicians as Civil Service Commissioner, as Police Commissioner, as fitter-out of the navy for the Spanish fight, as Rough-Rider—almost as often as he has been ruined by his vagaries which no one could survive; and I have about made up my mind that politicians are the most credulous of beings, instead of the reverse. The fact is that he is a perfectly logical product of a certain course of conduct deliberately entered upon and faithfully adhered to all through life, as all of us are who have any character worth mentioning. For that is what character means, that a man will

do so and so as occasions arise demanding
action. Now here is a case in point. When
President Roosevelt speaks nowadays about
the necessity of dropping all race and creed dis-
tinctions, if we want to be good Americans,
some one on the outskirts of the crowd winks
his left eye and says " politics." When he
promoted a Jew in the Police Department or
in his regiment, it was politics, politics. Well,
this incident I am going to tell you about he
had himself forgotten. When I asked him
about it, he recalled it slowly and with difficulty, for it happened in the days before he had
entered the Legislature. I had it from a friend
of his, the head of one of our great institutions
of learning, who was present at the time.

It was at the Federal Club, a young Republican club started to back up the older organization and since merged with it. A young
Jew had been proposed for membership. He
was of good family, personally unobjection-
able, had no enemies in the club. Yet it was
proposed deliberately to blackball him. There
was no pretense about it; it was a perfectly
bald issue of Gentile against Jew in a club
where it was easy to keep him out, at least so

they thought—till Roosevelt heard of it at the meeting. Then and there he got up and said what he thought of it. It was not complimentary to the conspirators. They were there as Republicans, as American citizens, he said, to work together for better things on the basis of being decent. The proposition to exclude a man because he was a Jew was not decent. For him, the minute race and creed were brought into the club, he would quit, and at once.

" He flayed them as I never heard a body of men flayed in my life," said my informant. " Roosevelt was pale with anger. The club sat perfectly still under the lashing. When he sat down amid profound silence, the vote was taken. There were no black balls. The Jew never knew how narrowly he missed getting in." He had a chance to vote for Roosevelt three times for the Legislature in settlement of the account he did not know he owed, and I hope he did.

When Mr. Roosevelt's third term was out, he had earned a seat in the National council of his party. He went to Chicago in 1884 as a delegate to the convention which nominated

Blaine. He was strongly in opposition, and fought hard to prevent the nomination. The outcome was a sore thrust to him. Some of his associates never forgave him that he did not bolt with them and stay out. Roosevelt came back from the far West, where he had gone to wear off his disappointment, and went into the fight with his party. His training was bearing fruit. " At times," I read in one of his essays, " a man must cut loose from his associates and stand for a great cause; but the necessity for such action is almost as rare as the necessity for a revolution." He did not join in the revolution; the time had not come, in his judgment, to take the isolated peak.

There came to me just now a letter from one of his classmates in college who has heard that I am writing about Mr. Roosevelt. He was one of those who revolted, but I shall set his testimony down here as quite as good an explanation of Theodore Roosevelt's course as Mr. Roosevelt could furnish himself.

" He was," he writes, speaking of his college friend, " next to my own father, the purest-minded man I ever knew. . . . He was free from any tinge of self-seeking. Indeed, he was free, as I knew him, from self-consciousness. What he said and did was simply the unstudied expression of his true self. . . . Although I very rarely see him, I have naturally followed his career with close interest. I am convinced that the few of his acts that I find it hard to condone (*e.g.*, his advocacy of Mr. Blaine's election to the Presidency, and his own acceptance of nomination for the Vice-Presidency) are explained by the fact that he has from the start been a party man, not merely a believer in party government and a faithful party member, but a devout believer, apparently, in the dogma that the success of his party is essential to the welfare of the country."

At that convention George William Curtis was also a delegate from New York. In a newspaper I picked up the other day were some reminiscences of the great fight by a newspaper man who was there. He told of meeting the famous Easy Chair at luncheon when the strife was fiercest. He expressed some surprise at the youth of Mr. Roosevelt, of whom the West then knew little. What followed sounds so like prophecy that I quote it here. The reporter wrote it down from memory that night, so he says, and by accident came across his notes, hence the item:

Mr. Curtis moved his chair back from the table, threw his napkin beside his plate, and was silent for a few seconds. Then he said, in his quiet, modulated tones:

"You'll know more, sir, later; a deal more, or I am much in error. Young? Why, he is just out of school almost, yet he is a force to be reckoned with in New York. Later the Nation will be criticising or praising him. While respectful to the gray hairs and experience of his elders, none of them can move him an iota from convictions as to men and measures once formed and rooted. He has integrity, courage, fair scholarship, a love for public life, a comfortable amount of money, honorable descent, the good word of the honest. He will not truckle nor cringe, he seems to court opposition to the point of being somewhat pugnacious. His political life will probably be a turbulent one, but he will be a figure, not a figurehead, in future development—or, if not, it will be because he gives up politics altogether."

Such a verdict from such a man upon three years of the strife and sweat of very practical politics I should have thought worth all it cost, and I know so does Mr. Roosevelt.

IV

THE HORSE AND THE GUN
HAVE THEIR DAY

—

IV

THE HORSE AND THE GUN
HAVE THEIR DAY

PERHAPS no more striking description of a landscape was ever attempted than when Mr. Roosevelt said that in the Bad Lands he always felt as if they somehow looked just as Poe's tales and poems sound. It is with this as I said before: we sometimes forget the man of words in the man of deeds. Mr. Roosevelt's writings occasionally suffer from a lack of patience to edit and to polish, but they are always full of vigor and directness; in other words, he is himself when he writes as when he talks; and never more so than when he writes of the great West to which I often think he belongs more than to the East where he was born. His home ranch in western North Dakota was among the Bad Lands of the Little Missouri. To grasp fully the meaning of the comparison with Poe, read this from his account of an elk-hunting trip out there:

" The tracks led into one of the wildest and most desolate parts of the Bad Lands. It was now the heat of the day, the brazen sun shining out in a cloudless sky and not the least breeze stirring. At the bottom of the valley, in the deep narrow bed of the winding watercourse, lay a few tepid little pools, almost dried up. Thick groves of stunted cedars stood here and there in the glen-like pockets of the high buttes, the peaks and sides of which were bare, and only their lower, terrace-like ledges thinly clad with coarse, withered grass and sprawling sagebrush; the parched hillsides were riven by deep, twisted gorges, with brushwood on the bottoms; and the cliffs of coarse clay were cleft and seamed by sheer-sided, cañon-like gullies. In the narrow ravines, closed in by barren, sunbaked walls, the hot air stood still and sultry; the only living things were the rattlesnakes, and of these I have never elsewhere seen so many. Some basked in the sun, stretched out at their ugly length of mottled brown and yellow. Others lay half under stones or twined

THE HORSE AND THE GUN

in the roots of the sage-brush, and looked
straight at me with that strange, sullen, evil
gaze, never shifting or moving, that is the
property only of serpents and of certain men;
while one or two coiled and rattled menacingly
as I stepped near."

Fit setting, that kind of a landscape, for a
man who had come out of the sort of fight he
had just been in, and lost. Many of those who
had fought with him went out of the Republican party and did not return. Roosevelt had
it out with the bucking bronchos on his ranch
and with the grizzlies in the mountains, and
came back to fight in the ranks for the man
he had opposed and to go down with him to
defeat. He had come to the bitter waters of
which men must drink to grow to their full
stature—his most ambitious defeat, that of
the Mayoralty campaign of 1886, was yet to
come—and, according to his sturdy way, he
looked the well through and through, and
drank deep.

There stands upon a shelf in my library a
copy of the " Wilderness Hunter," which he
gave me when once I was going to the woods.
On the fly-leaf he wrote: " May you enjoy the

north woods as much as I enjoyed the great plains and the Rockies." It was during that fall that I received the first news from him, up there in the Canadian wilderness, of the sad and terrible doings at Buffalo, when William McKinley was already in his grave. I read in that letter that had been waiting many days for our canoe to come down the lake, even though he wrote hopefully of the President's recovery; that a shadow had fallen across his path, between him and those youthful days, through which he would never cross again the same man. He was himself going away to the woods, he wrote, with the children. The doctors had assured him all was well. There was even a note of glad relief that the dreadful suspense was over. Yet with it all there was a something, undefinable, that told me that the chase he loved so well, the free wild life of the plain, had lost one that understood them as few did; and the closing words of the preface of the book, on which the ink of his name was hardly yet dry, sounded to me like saddening prophecy:

"No one but he who has partaken thereof can understand the keen delight of hunting in lonely lands. For him is the joy of the horse well ridden and the rifle well held; for him the long days of toil and hardship, resolutely endured, and crowned at the end with triumph. In after years there shall come forever to his mind the memory of endless prairies shimmering in the bright sun; of vast snow-clad wastes lying desolate under gray skies; of the melancholy marshes; of the rush of mighty rivers; of the breath of the evergreen forest in summer; of the crooning of ice-armored pines at the touch of the winds of winter; of cataracts roaring between hoary mountain masses; of all the innumerable sights and sounds of the wilderness; of its immensity and mystery; and of the silences that brood in its still depths."

So all things pass. To the careless youth succeeds the man of the grave responsibilities. He would not have it different, himself. But out there, there are men to-day who cannot forgive the White House for the loss of the ranch; who camp nightly about forgotten fires with their lost friend, the hunter and ranchman, Theodore Roosevelt.

When the world was young he came among them and straightway took their hearts by storm, as did they his, men " hardy and self-

reliant, with bronzed, set faces and keen eyes
that look all the world straight in the face without flinching." I know how it is. You cannot help taking to them, those Western fellows, and they need not be cowboys either.
The farther you go, the better you like them.
My oldest son, who spent a year on a ranch,
never wanted to come back. He was among
Roosevelt's men, whose talk was still of his
good-fellowship in camp and on the hunting
trail, his unflinching courage, his even-handed
justice that arraigned the sheriff of the county
as stoutly before his fellows when he failed in
his duty, as it led him in the bitter winter wea-
ther on a month's hunt down-stream through
the pack-ice after cattle thieves—a story that
reads like the record of an Arctic expedition.
But he got the thieves, and landed them in jail,
much to the wonderment of the ranchman at
Killdeer Mountains, who was unable to understand why all this fuss " instead of hanging
them offhand." The vigilantes had just had
a cleaning up in the cattle country, and had
despatched some sixty-odd suspects, some of
them, Mr. Roosevelt says, through misappre-
hension or carelessness. One is reminded of

the apology of the captain of such a band to the widow of a victim of their " carelessness "; " Madam, the joke is on us."

Every land has its ways. They have theirs out there, and if they are sometimes a trifle hasty, life bowls along with them at a pace we do not easily catch up with. On his recent trip across the continent, the President was greeted in a distant State by one of his old men, temporarily out of his latitude. He explained that he had had " a difficulty "; he had " sat into a poker game with a gentleman stranger," who raised a row. He used awful language, and he, the speaker, shot him down. He had to.

" And did the stranger draw? " asked the President, who had been listening gravely.

" He did not have time, sir."

The affair with the sheriff sounds as though it were a chapter of Mulberry Street in his later years. It was the outcome of the struggle to put law and order in the place of the rude lynch justice of the frontier. There was reason to believe that the sheriff leaned toward the outlaws. Men talked of it in bar-rooms; the cattle-thieves escaped. A meeting was called of ranch-owners, the neighbors for half a hundred miles around, and in the meeting Mr. Roosevelt rose and confronted the sheriff squarely with the charges. He looked straight at him through his gold-rimmed eye-glasses, himself unarmed, while from the other's pockets stuck out the handles of two big six-shooters, and told him without mincing words that they believed the charges to be true and that he had forfeited their confidence and good will. A score of grave frontiersmen sat silently expectant of the reply. None came. The man made no defense. But he was not without sympathizers, and his reputation would have made most men think twice before bearding him as Roosevelt did. I asked him once why he did it.

" There was no other way," he said, " and it had exactly the effect we desired. I do not think I was in any danger. I was unarmed, and if he had shot me down he knew he could not have escaped swift retribution. Besides, I was right, and he knew it! "

How often since have I heard him weigh, with the most careful scrutiny of every argument for and against, some matter to be de-

cided in the public interest, and wind up with
the brisk " There is no other way, and it is
right; we will do it; " and heard his critics,
who had given the matter no attention or the
most superficial, and were taking no risks, cry
out about snap judgments, while Roosevelt
calmly went ahead and brought us through.

Whether it was over this cattle matter or
some other local concern that his misunder-
standing with the Marquis de Mores arose, of
which there have been so many versions, I have
forgotten. It does not matter. In the nature
of things it would have come sooner or later,
on some pretext or another. The two were
neighbors, their ranches being some ten or fifteen miles apart. The Marquis was a gallant
but exaggerated Frenchman, with odd feudal
notions still clinging in his brain. He took it
into his head to be offended by something
Roosevelt was reported to have said, before he
had yet met him, and wrote him a curt note
telling him what he had heard and that " there
was a way for gentlemen to settle their differences," to which he invited his attention. Mr.
Roosevelt promptly replied that he had heard
a lie; that he, the Marquis, had no business to

believe it true upon such evidence, and that he
would follow his note in person within the hour.
He despatched the letter to Medora, where the
Marquis was, by one of his men, and, true to
his word, started himself immediately after.
Before he came in sight of the little cow-town
he was met by a courier traveling in haste from
the Marquis with a gentleman's apology and
a cordial invitation to dine with him in town.
And that was all there was of the sensational
" duel " with the French nobleman.

How small this world is, to be sure, that we
make so much of! It was only yesterday that
a woman whom I had never seen spoke to me
on a Third Avenue street-car and told me that
she had been in the house of the Marquis de
Mores at that very time. She was a Mrs. Price,
a nurse, she told me. Of course she knew
Roosevelt. " The cowboys loved him," she
said, and added: " Poor Marquis, he was a nice
gentleman, but he was not so level-headed a
man as Mr. Roosevelt."

The physical vigor for which he had longed
and labored had come to him in full measure
now, and with it the confidence that comes of
being prepared to defend one's rights. The

bully and the brawler knew well enough that they had small chance against such an equipment, and kept out of the way. In all Mr. Roosevelt's life on the frontier, sometimes in unfamiliar towns keyed up to mischief, he was molested but once, and then by a drunken rowdy who took him for a tenderfoot and with a curse bade him treat, at the point of his two revolvers, enforcing the invitation with a little exhibition of " gun-play," while a roomful of men looked stolidly on. Roosevelt was a stranger in the town and had no friends there. He got up apparently to yield to the inevitable, practicing over mentally the while a famous left-hander that had done execution in the old Harvard days. The next instant the bully crashed against the wall and measured his length on the floor. His pistols went off harmlessly in the air. He opened his eyes to find the " four-eyed tenderfoot " standing over him, bristling with fight, while the crowd nodded calmly, " Served him right." He surrendered then and there and gave up his guns, while Mr. Roosevelt went to bed unmolested. Such things carry far on the plains. No one was ever after that heard to express a wish to

fill this tenderfoot " full of holes," even though
he did wear gold spectacles and fringed angora
" chaps " when on a hunt.

And now that I have made use of my privilege to put things in as I think of them, let
me say that brawling was no part of his life in
the West. I thought of it first partly because of
some good people who imagine that there was
nothing else on the frontier; partly because it
was a test the frontier life put to a man, always
does, that he shall not be afraid, seeing that in
the last instance upon his personal fearlessness
depends his fitness to exist where at any moment that alone may preserve his life and the
lives of others. There was room in plenty for
that quality in the real business that brought
him West, the quest of adventure. It was the
dream of the man with the horse and the gun
that was at last being realized. There was yet a
frontier; there were unknown wilds. The very
country on the Little Missouri where he built
his log house was almost untrodden to the
north of him. Deer lay in the brush in the
open glade where the house stood, and once
he shot one from his door. The fencing in of
cattle lands had not begun. The buffalo

grazed yet in scattered bands in the mountain
recesses far from beaten trails; the last great
herd on the plains had been slaughtered, but
five years later Mr. Roosevelt tracked an old
bull and his family of cows and calves in the
wilderness on the Wisdom River near where
Idaho, Wyoming, and Montana come together.
He trailed them all day and at last came upon
them in a glade shut in by dark pines. As
he gazed upon the huge, shaggy beasts, behind
which towered the mountains, their crests crim-
soned by the sinking sun, there mingled with
the excitement of the hunter a " half-melan-
choly feeling at the thought that they were the
last remnant of a doomed and nearly vanished
race." It did not prevent him, however, from
eating the grilled meat of the old bull that
night at the camp-fire, with a hungry hunter's
relish. The great head of the mighty beast
hangs over the fire-place at Sagamore Hill,
an object of shuddering awe to the little ones.
None of them will in their day ever bring home
such a trophy from the hunt.

I looked past it into the room where the piano
stands, the other day, and saw two of them
there, Ethel giving Archie, with the bewitching

bangs and the bare brown boyish legs, his music lesson. One groping foot—for the lesson would n't come—dangled within reach of the ugliest grizzly's head a distorted fancy could conceive of. I know it, for I stumble over it regularly when I come there, until I have got it charted for that particular trip. The skin to which it is attached is one Mr. Roosevelt sets great store by. It is a memento of the most thrilling moment of his life, when he was hunting alone in the foothills of the Rockies. He had made his camp " by the side of a small, noisy brook with crystal water," and had strolled off with his rifle to see if he could pick up a grouse for supper, when he came upon the grizzly and wounded it. It took refuge in a laurel thicket, where Roosevelt laid siege to it. While he was cautiously skirting the edge, peering in, in the gathering dusk, the bear suddenly came out on the hillside: " Scarlet strings of froth hung from his lips; his eyes burned like embers in the gloom."

Roosevelt fired, and the bullet shattered the point of the grizzly's heart. " Instantly the great bear turned with a harsh roar of fury and challenge, blowing the bloody foam from his mouth, so that I saw the gleam of his white fangs; and then he charged straight at me, crashing and bounding through the laurel bushes, so that it was hard to aim. I waited until he came to a fallen tree, raking him as he topped it with a ball which entered his chest and went through the cavity of his body, but he neither swerved nor flinched, and at the moment I did not know that I had struck him. He came steadily on, and in another second was almost upon me. I fired for his forehead, but my bullet went low, entering his open mouth, smashing his lower jaw, and going into his neck. I leaped to one side almost as I pulled the trigger, and through the hanging smoke the first thing I saw was his paw as he made a vicious side blow at me. The rush of his charge carried him past. As he struck, he lurched forward, leaving a pool of bright blood where his muzzle hit the ground; but he recovered himself, and made two or three jumps onwards, while I hurriedly jammed a couple of cartridges into the magazine—my rifle holding only four, all of which I had fired. Then he tried to pull up, but as he did so his muscles seemed suddenly to give way, his head drooped,

and he rolled over and over like a shot rabbit.
Each of my first three bullets had inflicted a
mortal wound."

That was hunting of the kind that calls for a
stout heart. When I think of it, there comes
to me by contrast the echo of the laugh we had,
when he lay with his Rough-Riders at Montauk Point, over my one unlucky experience
with a " silver-tip." I have a letter yet, dated
Camp Wikoff, Montauk, September 9, 1898,
in which he has scribbled after the business on
hand, an added note: " Good luck on your
hunt! Death to grizzly-bear cubs." I can
hear his laugh now. I am not a mighty hunter,
but I know a bear when I see it—at least so I
thought—and when, wandering in the forest
primeval, far from camp, with only a fowling-
piece, I beheld a movement in the top of a big
pine, I had no difficulty in making out a bear-
cub there with the last rays of the sun silvering
the tip of its brief tail—a " silver-tip " then;
and likewise my knowledge of the world in
general, if not of wood-craft, told me that
where the cub was the mamma bear would not
be far away. It was therefore, I insist, proof
of fearless courage that I deliberately shot

down the cub with one of my two No. 12 cartridges, even if I made great haste to pick it up and carry it away before Madam Bruin should appear. It is all right to be bold, but when it comes to maddened she-bears— I made a wild grab for my cub, and had my hand impaled upon a hundred porcupine quills. It was that kind of a cub. It is well enough to laugh, but it took me a little while before I could join in, with all those quills sticking in my fist, just like so many barbed fish-hooks.

I remember we shot together once at the range, and that I made nearly as good a score as he. It was in the beginning of our acquaintance, when I had been staying at Sagamore Hill and the question was put by Mrs. Roosevelt at the breakfast-table whether I would rather go driving with her or " go with Theodore on the range." And I remember the perfidious smile with which he repeated the question, as if he should be *so* glad to have me go driving when he really wanted to try the new rifle on the range. He cannot dissemble worth a cent, and Mrs. Roosevelt laughed and sent us away, to my great relief; for going driving with her is a privilege one might well be proud of, and I—well, we had looked at the rifle together the night before. Really, it is no use for me to try, either.

But about the score; that was shooting at a target. Hitting a running animal is a different story, as I know to my sorrow. Though Mr. Roosevelt is near-sighted and wears glasses, and though his hand, he says himself, is none too steady, yet he has acquired a very formidable reputation as a hunter, and this, he adds with characteristic touch, because he has " hunted very perseveringly, and by much practice has learned to shoot about as well at a wild animal as at a target." It is the story of everything he undertook: his opportunities were in nothing unusually great, except in his marvelous mastery over his own mind, his rare faculty of concentration; sometimes he was at a clear disadvantage, as in the matter of physical strength and promise at the outset; yet he won by sheer perseverance. He has killed in his day every kind of large game to be found on the North American continent.

The " horse and the gun " were having their day. And while he hunted, with the instinct of the naturalist, who lets nothing escape that

THEODORE ROOSEVELT JUMPING HURDLES AT
CHEVY CHASE CLUB, WASHINGTON
COPYRIGHT 1902 BY CLINEDINST

can contribute to our knowledge of the world about us, he made notes of the habits and habitats of the game he hunted. His hunting-books have been extensively quoted by the scientific periodicals. Which brings to my mind another Presidential sportsman who occasionally makes notes of his exploits with the rod. He will forgive me for telling of it, for never did man draw a clearer picture of himself than did Mr. Cleveland when over the dinner-table in a friend's house he told the story of the egg the neighbor's hen laid in his yard. We had been discussing the way of conscience—whether it was born in men, or whether it grew, and he supported his belief that it was born with the child by telling of how when he was a little chap the hen made the mistake aforesaid.

"I could n't have been over five or six at most," said Mr. Cleveland, "but I remember the awful row I made until they brought back that egg to the side of the fence where it belonged."

That was Grover Cleveland, sure enough. My own conscience suffered twinges he knew not of during the recital, for I also had an egg to my account, but on the other side of the ledger, though it was never laid. I remembered well the half of an idle forenoon I spent, when I was nearer fifteen than five, treacherously trying to decoy my neighbor's hen across the fence to lay her egg in my yard. The doorknob I polished a most alluring white and hid in some hay for a nest-egg, and the trail of corn I made—they all rose up and spurned me. Who says the world is not getting better? Look upon this picture and upon that. No one would ever think of making me President. And when I thought of Mr. Roosevelt's probable action with the hen cackling on his side of the fence, who can doubt that he would return the egg with a stern reprimand to its owner not to lead his neighbor into temptation again? Mr. Cleveland might have registered the weight of the egg before returning it; the fisherman would not be denied. Mr. Roosevelt, had the hen been a wild fowl, would have taken note of its plumage and its futile habit of hiding its nest from mankind, even righteous mankind.

A cat may look at a king. One may have a joke even with a President. I know they won't mind. They are two men alike in the best there is in man, sturdy, courageous, splendid types of American manhood, however they differ. And though they do differ, Cleveland gave Roosevelt his strongest backing in the civil service fight, while the younger man holds the ex-President, even though his political opponent, in the real regard in which one true man holds another. And I who write this have had the good luck to vote for them both. The Republic is all right.

But I was speaking just now of the western land he loved; whether in the spring, when " the flowers are out and a man may gallop for miles at a stretch with his horse's hoofs sinking at every stride into the carpet of prairie roses, . . . and where even in the waste places the cactuses are blooming, . . . their mass of splendid crimson flowers glowing against the sides of the gray buttes like a splash of flame "; when " the thickets and groves about the ranch house are loud with bird music from before dawn till long after sunrise and all through the night "; or in the hot noontide hours of midsummer, when the parched land lies shimmering in the sunlight and " from the upper branches of the cottonwoods comes

every now and then the soft, melancholy coo-
ing of the mourning dove, whose voice always
seems far away and expresses more than any
other sound in nature the sadness of gentle,
hopeless, never-ending grief. The other birds
are still. . . . Now and then the black shadow
of a wheeling vulture falls on the sun-scorched
ground; the cattle that have strung down in
long files from the hills lie quietly on the sand-
bars." Whether in the bright moonlight that
" turns the gray buttes into glimmering silver,
the higher cliffs standing out in weird gro-
tesqueness while the deep gorges slumber in
the black shadows, the echoing hoof-beats of
the horses and the steady metallic clank of the
steel bridle-chains the only sounds "; or when
the gales that blow out of the north have
wrapped the earth in a mantle of death; when
" in the still, merciless, terrible cold . . . all
the land is like granite; the great rivers stand
in their beds as if turned to frosted steel. In
the long nights there is no sound to break the
lifeless silence. Under the ceaseless, shifting
play of the Northern Lights the snow-clad
plains stretch out into dead and endless wastes
of glimmering white."

THE HORSE AND THE GUN

So he saw it, and so he loved it; loved it when the work was hard and dangerous; when on the ranchman's occasional holiday he lay stretched before the blazing log-fire reading Shakespeare to the cowboys and eliciting the patronizing comment from one who followed broncho-busting as a trade, that " that 'ere feller Shakespeare saveyed human nature some." Loved the land and loved its people, as they loved him, a man among men. He has drawn a picture of them in his " Ranch Life and the Hunting Trail," from which I have quoted, that will stand as a monument to them in the days that are to come when they shall be no more. In that day we will value, too, the book, as a marvelous picture of a vanished day.

" To appreciate properly his fine, manly qualities, the wild rough-rider of the plains should be seen in his own home. There he passes his days; there he does his life-work; there, when he meets death, he faces it as he faces many other evils, with quiet, uncomplaining fortitude. Brave, hospitable, hardy and adventurous, he is the grim pioneer of our race; he prepares the way for the civilization from before whose face he must himself dis-

appear. Hard and dangerous though his existence is, it has yet a wild attraction that
strongly draws to it his bold, free spirit. He
lives in the lonely land where mighty rivers
twist in long reaches between the barren bluffs;
where the prairies stretch out into billowy
plains of waving grass, girt only by the blue
horizon—plains across whose endless breadth
he can steer his course for days and weeks, and
see neither man to speak to nor hill to break
the level; where the glory and the burning
splendor of the sunsets kindle the blue vault
of heaven and the level brown earth till they
merge together in an ocean of flaming fire."

Working there, resting there, growing there,
in that wonderland under the spell of which
these words of his were written, there came to
him, unheralded, the trumpet call to another
life, to duty. Over the camp-fire he read in a
newspaper sent on from New York that by
a convention of independent citizens he had
been chosen as their standard-bearer in the
fight for the mayoralty, then impending. They
needed a leader. And that night he hung up
the rifle, packed his trunk, and, bidding his
life on the plains good-by, started for the East.

V

THE FAIR PLAY DEPARTMENT

—

V

THE FAIR PLAY DEPARTMENT

THE citizens had picked Roosevelt because they needed a young man with fighting grit, a man with a name to trust, a Republican who was not afraid—of the machine for one thing. The machine took him because there was nothing else left for it to do, and it did that. The thing has happened since: evidence that there is life in our theory and practice of government. When such things cease to happen, popular government will not be much more than a name. The machine is useful—indeed, it is indispensable—as a thing to be run for a purpose. When the purpose becomes merely the running of the machine, however perfect that, the soul is gone out of it. And without a soul a man or a party is dead.

THEODORE ROOSEVELT

Something had occurred in New York fit almost to wake the dead. Henry George had been nominated for Mayor, and the world that owned houses and lands and stocks was in a panic. The town was going to be sacked, at the very least. And, in wild dread of the disaster that was coming, men forsook party, principles, everything, and threw themselves into the arms of Tammany, as babies run in fear of the bogy man and hide their heads in their mother's lap. Nice mother, Tammany! —even with Abram S. Hewitt as its candidate. He lived to subscribe to that statement. I have sometimes wondered what the town thought of itself when it came to, and considered Henry George as he really was. I know what Roosevelt thought of it. He laughed, rather contemptuously, married, and went abroad, glad of his holiday.

But he had contributed something to that campaign that had life in it. Long years after it bore fruit; but at that time I suppose people shrugged their shoulders at it, and ran on to their haven of refuge. It was just two paragraphs in his letter of acceptance to the Committee of One Hundred, the briefest of that kind of documents I ever saw.

THE FAIR PLAY DEPARTMENT

" The worst evils that affect our local government," he wrote to R. Fulton Cutting and his colleagues (even the names sound as if it were yesterday, not nearly twenty years ago), " arise from and are the inevitable results of the mixing up of city affairs with the party politics of the Nation and of the State. The lines upon which National parties divide have no necessary connection with the business of the city; . . . such connection opens the way to countless schemes of public plunder and civic corruption. I very earnestly deprecate all attempts to introduce any class or caste feeling into the mayoralty contest. Laborers and capitalists alike are interested in having an honest and economical city government, and if elected I shall certainly strive to be the representative of all good citizens, paying heed to nothing whatever but the general well-being."

He was not elected, as I said. We were not yet grown to that. Non-partisanship in municipal politics was a poet's dream, nice but so unsubstantial. It came true all the same in time, and it will stay true when we have dozed off a few times more and been roused up with the Tammany nightmare astride of us. Maybe then my other dream will come true, too. It is my own, and I have never told even him of it; but I have seen stranger things hap-- pen. It is this, that Theodore Roosevelt shall sit in the City Hall in New York as Mayor of his own city, after he has done his work in Washington. That would be an object-lesson worth while, one we need and that would show all the world what democracy really means. I shall never be satisfied till I see it. That year I would write the last chapter of my " battle with the slum," and in truth it would be over. For that which really makes the slum is not the foul tenement, not the pestilent alley, not the want and ignorance they stand for; but the other, the killing ignorance that sits in ease and plenty and knows not that it is the brother who suffers, and that, in one way or other, he must suffer with him unless he will suffer for him. Of that there must be an end. Roosevelt in the City Hall could mean only that.

Witness his plea in the letter I quoted: " Laborers and capitalists alike are interested." Of course they are, or our country goes to the dogs. In that day we shall see it, all of us. He saw it always. When I hear any one say that Roosevelt is doing this, or saying that, for effect, I know I have to do with a man who does not read or reason; or he would have made out how straight has been his course from the beginning. What he said then to the electors of New York, he did as President when he appointed the Coal Strike Commission, when he blocked the way of illegal trust combinations, and when he killed the power of " pull " in the Police Department and kept the peace of the city. He said it again the other day in his Labor Day speech at Syracuse.

" They will say, most likely, that it is made up of platitudes," he told me when he had finished it, referring to his newspaper critics; " and so I suppose it is. Only they need to be said just here and now."

They did need to. The Ten Commandments are platitudes, I expect; certainly they have been repeated often enough. And yet even the critics will hardly claim that we have had enough of them. I noticed, by the way, that they were dumb for once. Perhaps it occurred to them that it took a kind of courage to insist, as he did, on the elementary virtues in the dealings of man with man as the basis of all human fellowship, against which their shafts fell powerless. If so, it did more credit to their discernment than I expected ever to have to accord them.

Two years of travel and writing, of working at the desk and, in between, on the ranch, where the cowboys hailed him joyously; of hunting and play which most people would have called hard work; years during which his " Winning of the West " took shape and grew into his great work. Then, in the third, Washington and the Civil Service Commission.

I suppose there is scarcely one who knows anything of Theodore Roosevelt who has not got the fact of his being once a Civil Service Commissioner fixed in his mind. That was where the country got its eye upon him; and that, likewise, was where some good people grew the notion that he was a scrapper first, last, and all the time, with but little regard for whom he tackled, so long as he had him. There was some truth in that; we shall see how much. But as to civil service reform, I have sometimes wondered how many there were who knew as little what it really meant as I did until not so very long ago. How many went about with a more or less vague notion that it was some kind of a club to knock out spoils politics with, good for the purpose and necessary, but in the last analysis an alien kind of growth, of aristocratic tendency, to set men apart in classes. Instead of exactly the reverse, right down on the hard pan of the real and only democracy: every man on his merits; what he is, not what he has; what he can do, not what his pull can do for him. And do you know what first shocked me into finding out the truth? I have to own it, if it does make me blush for myself. It was when I saw a report Roosevelt had made on political blackmail in the New York Custom-House. That was what he called it, and it was meaner than the meanest, he added, because it hit hardest the employees who did n't stand politically with the party in power and were afraid to say so lest they lose their places. Three per cent. of his salary, to a clerk just able to get along, might mean " the difference between having and not having a winter coat for himself, a warm dress for his wife, or a Christmas-tree for his children—a piece of cruel injustice and iniquity." It was the Christmas-tree·that settled it with me. The rest was bad, but I could n't allow that. Not with my Danish pedigree of blessed Christmas-trees reaching 'way back into the day of frocks and rag dolls, and my own children's tree to remind me of it—never!

So I overcame my repugnance to schedules and tables and examinations, and got behind it all to an understanding of what it really meant. And there I found the true view of this champion of civil service reform as I might have expected; fighting the spoilsman, yes! dragging the sting from his kind of politics; hitting him blow after blow, and with the whole pack of politicians, I came near saying good and bad together, in front hitting back for very life. That was there, all of it. But this other was there too: the man who was determined that the fellow with no pull should have an even chance with his rival who came backed; that the farmer's lad and the mechanic's son who had no one to speak for them should have the same show in competing for the public service as the son of wealth and social prestige. That was really what civil service reform meant to Roosevelt. The other was good, but this was the kernel of it, and the kernel was sound. It was, as he said in his first Presidential mes-

THE FAIR PLAY DEPARTMENT

sage, " as democratic and American as the common-school system itself."

And as for the country's end of it: " This is my rule," said he, speaking of it at the time: " if I am in such doubt about an applicant's character and fitness for office as would lead me not to put my private affairs in his hands, then I shall not put public affairs in his hands." Simple and plain enough, is it not?

For all that they called it a " first-class trouble job " and the wise, or those who thought they were wise, laughed in their sleeves when Roosevelt tackled it. For at last they had him where he would be killed off sure, this bumptious young man who had got in the way of the established order in everything. And they wished him luck. President Harrison was in the White House, well disposed, but not exactly a sympathetic court of appeals for a pleader like Roosevelt. In fact, he would have removed him within a year or two of his appointment for daring to lay down the law to a Cabinet officer, had it been expedient. It was not expedient; by that time Theodore Roosevelt had made his own court of appeals —the country and public opinion.

THEODORE ROOSEVELT

Contrary to the general belief, Roosevelt was never President of the Civil Service Commission, though I am strongly inclined to think that where he sat was the head of the table. Until he came the Board had been in hard luck. Unpopular everywhere, it had tried the ostrich game of hiding its head, hoping so to escape observation and the onset of its enemies. Things took a sudden turn with Roosevelt in the Board. He was there to do a work he thoroughly believed in, that was one thing. In the Legislature of New York he had forced through a civil service law that was substantially the same as he was here set to enforce; hence he knew. And when a man knows a thing and believes in it, and it is the right thing to do anyway, truly "thrice armed is he." The enemies of the cause found it out quickly. For every time they struck, the Commission hit back twice. Nor was the new Commissioner very particular where he hit, so long as the blow told. "The spectacle," wrote Edward Cary in reviewing his work when it was done, "of a man holding a minor and rather nondescript office, politically unimportant, taking a Cabinet officer by the neck and exposing him to the amused contempt of all honest Americans, was what the late Horace Greeley would have called ' mighty interesting.' It was also very instructive."

It was that. The whole country took an interest in the show. Politics woke right up and got the ear of the White House. Mr. Roosevelt respectfully but firmly refused to back down. He was doing his sworn duty in enforcing the law. That was what he was there for. He urged his reform measures once, twice, three times, then went to the people, telling them all about it. The measures went through. Surveying the clamoring crowd that railed at him and his work, he flung this challenge to them in an address in the Madison Street Theater in Chicago in March, 1890, the year after he was appointed:

" Every ward heeler who now ekes out a miserable existence at the expense of office-holders and candidates is opposed to our policy, and we are proud to acknowledge it. Every politician who sees nothing but reward of office in the success of a party or a principle is opposed to us, and we are not sorry for it. . . . We propose to keep a man in office as long as

he serves the public faithfully and courteously.
. . . We propose that no incumbent shall be
dismissed from the service unless he proves un-
trustworthy or incompetent, and that no one
not specially qualified for the duties of the position shall be appointed. These two statements we consider eminently practical and
American in principle."

Again, a year later, when the well-worn lies
that still pass current in certain newspapers
had got into the Senate, this was his answer:

" One of the chief false accusations which
are thrown at the Commission is that we test
applicants by puzzling questions. There is a
certain order of intellect—sometimes an order
of Senatorial intellect—which thinks it funny
to state that a first-class young man, thoroughly qualified in every respect, has been
rejected for the position of letter-carrier because he was unable to tell the distance from
Hongkong to the mouth of the Yangtsekiang,
or answer questions of similar nature.

" I now go through a rather dreary, monotonous illustration of how this idea becomes
current. A Senator, for instance, makes statements of that character. I then write to him,

and ask him his foundation for such an asser-
tion. Presumably, he never receives my letter,
for he never answers it. I write him again,
with no better results. I then publish a contra-
diction in the newspapers. Then some enter-
prising correspondent interviews him, and he
states the question is true, but it is below his
dignity to reply to Mr. Roosevelt. As a matter
of fact, he either does know or ought to know
that no such question has ever been asked."

I wonder now, does any one of the editors
who loudly wail over the "weak surrender"
of the President, these days, to malign forces
of their imagination, really believe that of the
man who single-handed bade defiance to the
whole executive force of the Government,
when the knowledge that he was right was his
only weapon; or is it just buncombe like the
Senator's dignity?

And yet, on the other hand, when he had to
do with a different element, honest but not yet
persuaded, note the change from blow to argument. I quote from a speech he made to a club
of business men in the thick of the fight:

"We hear much of the question whether
the Government should take control of the

telegraph lines and railways of the country. Before that question can be so much as discussed, it ought to be definitely settled that, if the Government takes control of either telegraph line or railway, it must do it to manage it purely as a business undertaking, and must manage it with a service wholly unconnected with politics. I should like to call the special attention of the gentlemen in bodies interested in increasing the sphere of State action—interested in giving the State control more and more over railways, over telegraph lines, and over other things of the sort—to the fact that the condition precedent upon success is to establish an absolutely non-partisan governmental system. When that point is once settled, we can discuss the advisability of doing what these gentlemen wish, but not before."

Single-handed, I said. At least we heard from him only in those days. But afterward there came to join him on the Commission a Kentuckian, an old Confederate veteran, a Democrat, and withal as fine a fellow as ever drew breath—John R. Procter—and the two struck hands in a friendship that was for life.

THE FAIR PLAY DEPARTMENT

" Every day," said Mr. Procter as we lay in the grass up in the Berkshires last summer and looked out over the peaceful valley, " every day I went to the office as to an entertainment. ·I knew something was sure to turn up to make our work worth while, with him there. When he went away, I had heart in it no longer."

The thing that turned up at regular intervals was an investigation by Congress. Sometimes it was charges of one kind or another; sometimes the weapon was ridicule; always at the bottom the purpose was the same: to get rid of this impudent thing that was interposing itself between the legislator and the patronage that had been to him the sinews of war till then, costly sinews as he often enough had found out, but still the only ones he knew how to use. Mr. Roosevelt met every attack with his unvarying policy of candor; blow for blow where that was needed; at other times with tact so finished, a shrewdness of diplomacy at which the enemy stared in helpless rage. For the country was visibly falling in behind this wholesome, good-humored fighter. I remember yet with amusement the " withering charge," as he called it, which one of the Washington

papers brought against him. It published
one of his letters in facsimile and asked scornfully if this man could pass an examination in
penmanship for the desk of a third-rate clerk
in his own office; yet he sat in judgment on the
handwriting of aspirants. Now, I have always
thought Mr. Roosevelt's handwriting fine. It
is n't ornate. Indeed, it might be called very
plain, extra plain, if you like. But his character is all over it: a child could read it. There
can never be any doubt as to what he means,
and that, it seems to me, is what you want
of a man's writing. Here is a line of it now
which I quoted before, still lying on my table.
Squeezed in between lines of typewriting it is
not a fair sample, but take it as it is:

I haven't heard a word about it from my superior officers, who have
the complete say-so.

Good luck on your hunt! Dear th to Buzzy - dear cubs! Warm regards to Mrs. Ris. and, Cordially yours,

Theodore Roosevelt

However, Roosevelt made no bones about it.
He owned up that he could n't pass for a clerkship, which was well, he said, for he would have
made but a poor clerk, while he thought he

could make a good Commissioner. "And," he added, "there it is. Under our system of civil service examinations I could n't get in, whereas under the old spoils system you advocate I would have had pull enough to get the appointment to the clerkship I was n't fit for. Don't you see?"

I presume the editor saw, for nothing more was said about it.

In the hottest of the fighting, Mr. Roosevelt executed a flank movement of such consummate strategic skill and shrewdness that it fairly won him the battle. He ordered examinations for department positions at Washington to be held in the States, not at the Capital. When the successful candidates came to take the places they had won—when Congressman Smith met a young fellow from his county whom he knew in Washington, holding office under an administration hostile in politics as he knew, a great light dawned upon him. He felt the fetters of patronage, that had proved a heavier and heavier burden to him, falling from his own limbs, and from among the Congressmen who had hotly opposed Roosevelt came some of the warmest advocates of the new salvation. The policy of fairness, of perfect openness, had won. But it *was* a fight, sure enough. Mr. Roosevelt's literary labors in the cause alone were immense. Besides the six annual reports of the Commission during his incumbency—the sixth to the eleventh, inclusive—which were written largely by him, his essays and papers in defense of the reform covered a range that would give a clerk, I was told at the Congressional Library, a good week's work if he were to make anything like a complete list of them.

There never yet was a perfect law, and the civil service law was no exception. It did not put saints in office. It gave men a fair show, helped kill political blackmail, and kept some scoundrels out. Sometimes, too, it kept the best man out; for no system of examination can be devised to make sure he gets in. Roosevelt was never a stickler for the letter of anything. I know that perhaps better than anybody. If I were to tell how many times we have sat down together to devise a way of getting through the formal husk, even at the risk of bruising it some, to get at the kernel, the spirit of justice that is the soul of every law,

THE FAIR PLAY DEPARTMENT

however undeveloped, I might frighten some good people needlessly. I think likely it was the recognition of this quality in the man, the entire absence of pedantry in his advocacy of the reform, that won the people over to him as much as anything. Some good stories are told about that, but perhaps one he told himself of his experience as a regimental commander in the Spanish war sheds more light on that side of him than anything else. He had a man in his regiment, a child of the frontier, in whom dwelt the soul of a soldier—in war, not in peace. By no process of reasoning or discipline could he be persuaded to obey the camp regulations, while the regiment lay at San Antonio, and at last he was court-martialed, sentenced to six months' imprisonment—a technical sentence, for there was no jail to put him in. The prison was another Rough-Rider following him around with a rifle to keep him in bounds. Then came the call to Cuba, and the Colonel planned to leave him behind as useless baggage. When the man heard of it, his soul was stirred to its depths. He came and pleaded as a child to be taken along. He would always be good; never again could he show up in Kansas if the regiment went to the war without him. At sight of his real agony Mr. Roosevelt's heart relented.

"All right," he said. "You deserve to be shot as much as anybody. You shall go." And he went, flowing over with gratitude, to prove himself in the field as good a man as his prison of yore who fought beside him.

Then came the mustering out. When the last man was checked off and accounted for, the War Department official, quartermaster or general or something, fumbled with his papers.

"Where is the prisoner?" he asked.

"The prisoner?" echoed Colonel Roosevelt; "what prisoner?"

"Why, the man who got six months at a court-martial."

"Oh, he! He is all right. I remitted his sentence."

The official looked the Colonel over curiously.

"You remitted his sentence," he said. "Sentenced by a court-martial, approved by the commanding general, you remitted his sentence. Well, you 've got nerve."

THE FAIR PLAY DEPARTMENT

Perhaps the Civil Service Commissioner's "nerve" had something to do with winning his fight. I like to think it had. With that added, one could almost feel like hugging civil service reform.

One phase of this " Six Years' War " I cannot pass by, since it may serve as a chart to some inquiring minds much troubled to find out where the President will stand in matters of recent notoriety. They may give up their still-hunt for information and assume with perfect confidence that he will stand where he always has stood, on the square platform of fair dealing between man and man. Here is the letter that made me think of it. It was written to the Chairman of the Committee on Reform in the Civil Service of the Fifty-third Congress, in the spring of 1894, the year before he left the Commission:

Congressman Williams, of Mississippi, attacked the Commission in substance because under the Commission white men and men of color are treated with exact impartiality. As to this, I have to say that so long as the present Commissioners continue their official existence they will not make, and, so far as in their power lies, will refuse to allow others to make, any discrimination whatsoever for or against any man

THEODORE ROOSEVELT

because of his color, any more than because of his politics or religion. We do equal and exact justice to all, and I challenge Mr. Williams or any one else to show a single instance where the Commission has failed to do this. Mr. Williams specified the Railway Mail Service in Missouri as being one in which negroes are employed. The books of the Railway Mail Service for the division including South Carolina, Florida, Georgia, Alabama, and Mississippi were shown me yesterday, and according to these books about three-fourths of the employees are white and one-fourth colored. Under the last administration it was made a reproach to us that we did full and entire justice to the Southern Democrats, and that through our examinations many hundreds of them entered the classified service, although under a Republican administration. Exactly in the same way, it is now made a reproach to us that under our examinations honest and capable colored men are given an even chance with honest and capable white men. I esteem this reproach a high compliment to the Commission, for it is an admission that the Commission has rigidly done its duty as required by law without regard to politics or religion and without regard to color.   Very respectfully,

THEODORE ROOSEVELT.

"You cannot change him unless you convince him," said Mr. Procter to me, as we got up to go down into the valley, whence the gray evening shadows were reaching up toward us.

THEODORE ROOSEVELT
FROM THE PORTRAIT BY JOHN S. SARGENT
PHOTOGRAPHED BY FRANCES B. JOHNSTON

THE FAIR PLAY DEPARTMENT

If you think you can convince Theodore Roosevelt that a square deal is not the right thing, you can look for a change in him when he has taken a stand on a moral question; else you need n't trouble.

President Cleveland was in office by that time, and the Democratic party was in. But Roosevelt stayed as Civil Service Commissioner, and abated not one jot of his zeal. I do not know what compact was made between the two men, but I can guess from what I knew of them both. An incident of the White House shows what kind of regard grew up between them as they came to know one another. It was the day President McKinley was buried. President Roosevelt had come in alone. Among the mourners he saw Mr. Cleveland. Now, the etiquette of the White House, which is in its way as rigid as that of any court in Europe, requires that the President shall be sought out; he is not to go to any one. But Mr. Roosevelt waved it all aside with one impulsive gesture as he went straight to Mr. Cleveland and took his hand. An official who stood next to them, and who told me, heard him say:

THEODORE ROOSEVELT

" It will always be a source of pride and pleasure to me to have served under President Cleveland." Mr. Cleveland shook hands, mute with emotion.

I learned afterward that among all the countless messages of sympathy and cheer that came to him in those hard days, the one of them all he prized highest and that touched him most deeply was from Grover Cleveland.

The Six Years' War was nearly over when the summons came to him to take the helm in the Police Department in New York City, the then storm-center in the fight for civic regeneration. He and his colleague, Mr. Procter, had their first and only falling out over his choice to go into the new fight. They quarreled over it until Roosevelt put his arm over the other's shoulder and said: " Old friend! I have made up my mind that it is right for me to go."

Mr. Procter shook him off almost roughly, and got up from the table. " All right," he said, " go! You always would have your way, and I suppose you are right, blank it and blank blank it! " and the grizzled old veteran went out and wept like a child.

THE FAIR PLAY DEPARTMENT

The outcome of it all? Figures convey no idea of it. To say that he found 14,000 government officers under the civil service rules, and left 40,000, does not tell the story; not even in its own poor way, for there are 125,000 now, and when the ransomed number 200,000 it will still be Roosevelt's work. President Cleveland put it more nearly right in his letter to Mr. Roosevelt regretfully accepting his resignation.

"You are certainly to be congratulated," he wrote, "upon the extent and permanency of civil service reform methods which you have so substantially aided in bringing about. The struggle for its firm establishment and recognition is past. Its faithful application and reasonable expansion remain, subjects of deep interest to all who really desire the best attainable public service."

That was what the country got out of it. The fight was won—wait, let me put that a little less strongly: the way to the victory is cleared. Just now, as I was writing that sentence, a man, an old friend, a teacher in Israel, came into my office and to him I read what I had just written. "That's right," he said; "I

came in to ask you if you would n't help a
young man who wants to get into the public
employment. He is a fine fellow, has got all
the qualifications. All he needs is influence to
get him a place. Without influence you cannot
do anything."

The fight will be over the day the American
people get that notion out of their heads, not
before. They can drop it now, for it is all that
really is left. Roosevelt won them the right to
do that. He won his father's fight that he had
made his own. I know how much that meant
to him.

The country got more out of it: it got a man
to whom great tasks and great opportunities
were to come with the years, trained in the
school of all schools to perfect skill in dealing
with men, in making out their motives and
their worth as fighting units. The devious
paths of diplomacy have no such training-
school for leadership as he found in Washington fighting for a great principle, touching elbows every day with men from all over the
country, with the leaders in thought and action,
in politics, in every phase of public life. He
went there, a fearless battler for the right, and

came away with all his ideals bright and unsullied. It was in the Civil Service Commission's office the cunning was fashioned which, without giving offense, put the Kishineff petition into the hands of the Czar and his Ministers before they had time to say they would not receive it, and gave notice to the Muscovite world that there was a moral sense across the sea to be reckoned with; of which fact it took due notice.

Still more did the country get out of that Six Years' War: from end to end of the land the men with ideals, young and old, the men and women who would help their fellows, help their cities, took heart from his example and his victory. Perhaps that was the greatest gain, the one that went farthest. It endures to this day. Wherever he fights, men fall in behind and fight on with new hope; they know they can win if they keep it up. And they will, let them be sure of it. All the little defeats are just to test their grit. It is a question of grit, that is all.

VI

IN MULBERRY STREET

—

VI

IN MULBERRY STREET

A DOZEN years had wrought their changes since Roosevelt took his legislative committee down from Albany to investigate the Police Department of New York City. The only change they had brought to Mulberry Street [1] was that of aggravating a hundredfold the evils which had then attracted attention. He had put an unerring finger upon politics as the curse that was eating out the heart of the force once called the finest in the world. The diagnosis was correct; but the prescription written out by the spoilsmen was more politics and ever more politics; and the treatment was about as bad as could have been devised. With the police become an avowedly political body with a bi-par-

---

[1] The Police Headquarters of the city is in Mulberry Street.

tisan in stead of a non-partisan Board of Commissioners, there grew up, primarily through
the operation, or non-operation, of the Sunday
saloon-closing law, a system of police blackmail
unheard of in the world before. It was the
disclosure of its slimy depths through the
labors of Dr. Parkhurst and of the Lexow
Committee which brought about the political
revolution out of which came reform and
Roosevelt. But in Mulberry Street they were
hailed as freaks. The " system " so far had
been invincible. It had broken many men who
had got in its way.

" It will break you," was the greeting with
which Byrnes, the Big Chief, who had ruled
Mulberry Street with a hard hand, but had
himself bowed to " the system," received Mr.
Roosevelt. " You will yield. You are but
human."

The answer of the new President of the
Board was to close the gate of the politicians
to police patronage.

" We want," he said, " the civil service law
applied to appointments here, not because it is
the ideal way, but because it is the·only way
to knock the political spoilsmen out, and you

have to do that to get anywhere." And the Board made the order.

Next he demanded the resignation of the chief, and forbade the annual parade for which preparations were being made. "We will parade when we need not be ashamed to show ourselves." And then he grappled with the saloons.

Here, before we go into that fight, let me turn aside a moment to speak of myself; then perhaps with good luck we shall have less of me hereafter. Though how that can be I don't really know; for now I had Roosevelt at last in my own domain. For two years we were to be together all the day, and quite often most of the night, in the environment in which I had spent twenty years of my life. And these two were the happiest by far of them all. Then was life really worth living, and I have a pretty robust enjoyment of it at all times. Elsewhere I have told how we became acquainted; how he came to my office one day when I was out and left his card with the simple words written in pencil upon it: " I have read your book, and I have come to help." That was the beginning. The book was " How the Other

Half Lives," in which I tried to draw an indictment of the things that were wrong, pitifully and dreadfully wrong, with the tenement homes of our wage-workers. It was like a man coming to enlist for a war because he believed in the cause, and truly he did. Now had come the time when he could help indeed. Decency had moved into the City Hall, where shameless indifference ruled before. His first thought was to have me help there. I preserve two letters from him, from the time between the election in 1894 that put Tammany out and the New Year when Mayor Strong and reform moved in, in which he urges this idea.

" It is very important to the city," he writes, " to have a business man's mayor, but it is more important to have a workingman's mayor, and I want Mr. Strong to be that also. . . . I am exceedingly anxious that, if it is possible, the Mayor shall appoint you to some position which shall make you one of his official advisers. . . . It is an excellent thing to have rapid transit, but it is a good deal more important, if you look at matters with a proper perspective, to have ample playgrounds in the poorer quarters of the city, and to take the children off the streets to prevent them from growing up toughs. In the same way it is an admirable thing to have clean streets; indeed, it is an essential thing to have them; but it would be a better thing to have our schools large enough to give ample accommodation to all should-be pupils, and to provide them with proper playgrounds."

You see, he had not changed. His was the same old plan, to help the man who was down; and he was right, too. It was and is the essential thing in a country like ours: not to prop him up forever, not to carry him; but to help him to his feet so he can go himself. Else the whole machine won't go at length in the groove in which we have started it. The last letter concludes with regret that he had not seen his way clear to accept the street-cleaning commissionership that was offered him by the Mayor, for " I should have been delighted to smash up the corrupt contractors and put the street-cleaning force absolutely out of the domain of politics." No doubt he would; but it was well he did n't, for so Colonel Waring came into our city's life, and he was just such

another, and an engineer besides, who knew
how.

As to the share he wanted me to take in it,
we had it out at the time over that; and, though
we had little tugs after that, off and on, it was
settled then that I should not be called upon
to render that kind of service—to Mayor
Strong's rather bewildered relief, I fancy. I
think, to the end of his official life he did not
get quite rid of a notion that I was nursing
some sort of an unsatisfied ambition and reserv-
ing my strength for a sudden raid upon him.
I know that when I asked him to appoint an
unofficial Small Parks Committee, and to put
me on it, it took him a long time to make up his
mind that there was not a nigger in that wood-
pile somewhere. He was the only man, if I am
right in that, who ever gave me credit for political plotting. For when, afterward, as I recorded in " The Making of an American," I
marched the Christian Endeavorers and the
Methodist ministers to the support of Roosevelt in the fight between him and his wicked
partners in the Police Board, that was not plotting, though they called it so, but just war; a

kind of hold-up, if you like, in the plain interests of the city's welfare.

But " the system " Roosevelt was called to break up. I shall not attempt to describe it. The world must be weary of it to the point of disgust. We fought it then; we fight it now. We shall have to fight it no one can tell how often or how long; for just as surely as we let up for ever so little a while, and Tammany, which is always waiting without, gets its foot between the door and the jamb, the old blackmail rears its head once more. It is the form corruption naturally takes in a city with twelve or thirteen thousand saloons, with a State law that says they shall be closed on Sundays, and with a defiant thirst which puts a premium on violating the law by making it the most profitable day in the week to the saloon-keeper who will take the chances. Those chances are the opportunities of the politician and of the police where the two connect. The politicians use the law as a club to keep the saloons in line, all except the biggest, the keepers of which sit in the inner councils of " the Hall "; the police use it for extorting blackmail. " The result

was," said Roosevelt himself, when he had got
a bird's-eye view of the situation, " that the
officers of the law and the saloon-keepers became inextricably tangled in a network of
crime and connivance at crime. The most pow-
erful saloon-keepers controlled the politicians
and the police, while the latter in turn terror-
ized and blackmailed all the other saloon-keepers." Within the year or two that preceded
Roosevelt's coming to Mulberry Street, this
system of " blackmail had been brought to such
a state of perfection, and had become so oppressive to the liquor-dealers themselves, that
they communicated first with Governor Hill
and then with Mr. Croker." I am quoting now
from a statement made by the editor of their
organ, the " Wine and Spirit Gazette," the
correctness of which was never questioned.
The excise law was being enforced with " gross
discrimination." " A committee of the Central Association of Liquor Dealers took the
matter up and called upon Police Commissioner Martin (Mr. Roosevelt's Tammany pre-
decessor in the presidency of the Board). *An
agreement was made between the leaders of
Tammany Hall and the liquor-dealers, accord-*

ing to which the monthly blackmail paid to the police should be discontinued in return for political support." The strange thing is that they did not put it on the books at headquarters in regular form. Probably they did not think of it.

But the agreement was kept only with those who had " pull." It did not hurt them to see their smaller, helpless rivals bullied and blackmailed by the police. As for the police, they were taking no chances. They had bought appointment, or promotion, of Tammany with the understanding that they were to reimburse themselves for the outlay. Their hunger only grew as they fed, until they blackmailed everything in sight, from the push-cart peddler in the street, who had bought his license to sell, but was clubbed from post to post until he " gave up," to the brothel, the gambling-house, and the policy-shop, for which they had regular rates: so much for " initiation " every time a new captain came to the precinct, and so much per month for permission to run. The total ran up in the millions. New York was a wide-open town. The bosses at " the Hall " fairly rolled in wealth; the police had lost all decency and sense of justice. That is, the men who ran the force had. The honest men on the patrol posts, the men with the night-sticks as Roosevelt called them when he spoke of them, had lost courage and hope.

This was the situation that confronted him in Mulberry Street, and with characteristic directness he decided that in the saloon was the tap-root of the mischief. The thing to do was to enforce the Sunday-closing law. And he did.

The storm that rose lives in my memory as the most amazing tempest—I was going to say in a teapot—that ever was. But it was a capital affair to those whose graft was at stake. The marvel was in the reach they had. It seemed for a season as if society was struck through and through with the rottenness of it all. That the politicians, at first incredulous, took the alarm was not strange. They had an interest. But in their tow came half the community, as it seemed, counseling, praying, beseeching this man to cease his rash upturning of the foundations of things, and use discretion. Roosevelt replied grimly that there was nothing about discretion in his oath of office, and quoted to them Lincoln's words, " Let reverence of law be taught in schools and colleges, be written in primers and spelling-books, be published from pulpits and proclaimed in legislative houses, and enforced in the courts of justice—in short, let it become the political religion of the nation." He was doing nothing worse than enforcing *honestly* a law that had been enforced dishonestly in all the years. Still the clamor rose. The yellow newspapers pursued Roosevelt with malignant lies. They shouted daily that the city was overrun with thieves and murderers, that crime was rampant and unavenged, because the police were worn out in the Sunday-closing work. Every thief, cut-throat, and blackmailer who had place and part in the old order of things joined in the howl. Roosevelt went deliberately on, the only one who was calm amid all the hubbub. And when, after many weeks of it, the smoke cleared away; when the saloon-keepers owned in court that they were beaten; when the warden of Bellevue Hospital reported that for the first time in its existence there had not been a " case," due to a drunken brawl, in the hospital all Monday; when the police courts gave their testimony, while savings-banks recorded increased deposits and pawn-shops hard times; when poor mothers flocked to the institutions to get their children whom they had placed there for safe-keeping in the "wide-open" days—then we knew what his victory meant.

These were the things that happened. They are the facts. Living in this cosmopolitan city, where, year after year, the Sunday-closing law turns up as an issue in the fight for good government,—an issue, so we are told, with the very people, the quiet, peace-loving Germans, upon whom we, from every other point of view, would always count as allies in that struggle, —I find myself impatiently enough joining in the demand for freedom from the annoyance, for a "liberal observance" of Sunday that shall rid us of this ghost at our civic banquet. And then I turn around and look at the facts as they were then; at that Sunday which Roosevelt and I spent from morning till night in the tenement districts, seeing for ourselves what went on; at the happy children and contented mothers we met whose homes, according to their self-styled defenders, were at that very time

being " hopelessly desolated by the enforcement of a tyrannical law surviving from the
dark ages of religious bigotry "; and I ask myself how much of all the clamor for Sunday
beer comes from the same pot that spewed
forth its charges against Roosevelt so venom-
ously. It may be that we shall need another
emancipation before we get our real bearings:
the delivery of the honest Germans from their
spokesmen who would convince us that with
them every issue of family life, of good government, of manhood and decency, is subordinate
to the one of beer, and beer only.

  Blackmail was throttled for a season; but
the clamor never ceased. Roosevelt shut the
police-station lodging-rooms, the story of
which I told in " The Making of an American." Greater service was never rendered the
city by any man. For it he was lampooned and
caricatured. He was cruel!—he who spent his
waking and sleeping hours planning relief
for his brother in distress. So little was he
understood that even the venerable chairman
of the Charter Revision Committee asked him
sternly if he " had no pity for the poor." I
can see him now, bending contracted brows

upon the young man who struck right and left where he saw wrong done. Roosevelt answered patiently enough, with respect for the gray hairs, that it was poor pity for the tramp to enable him to go on tramping, which was all the lodging-houses did; and he went right ahead and shut them up.

We had a law forbidding the sale of liquor to children, which was a dead letter. I stood in front of one East Side saloon and watched a steady stream of little ones with mugs and bottles going through the door, and I told Roosevelt. He gave orders to seize the worst offender, and had him dragged to court; but to do it he had to permit the use of a boy to get evidence, a regular customer who had gone there a hundred times for a bad purpose, and now was sent in once for a good one. A howl of protest arose. The magistrate discharged the saloon-keeper and reprimanded the policeman. Like a pack of hungry wolves they snarled at Roosevelt. He was to be legislated out of office. He turned to the decent people of the city. "We shall not have to employ such means," he said, "once a year, but when we need to we shall not shrink from it. It is idle to ask us to employ against law-breakers only such means as those law-breakers approve. We are not playing ' puss in the corner ' with the criminals. We intend to stamp out these vermin, and we do not intend to consult the vermin as to the methods we shall employ." And the party managers at Albany he warned publicly that an attack upon the Police Board, on whatever pretext, was an attack upon its members because they had done their duty, and that the politicians must reckon with decent sentiment, if they dared punish them for declining to allow the police force to be used for political purposes, or to let law-breakers go unpunished.

Roosevelt won. He conquered politics and he stopped law-breaking; but the biggest victory he won was over the cynicism of a people so steeped in it all that they did not dream it could be done. Tammany came back, but not to stay. And though it may come back many times yet for our sins, it will be merely like the thief who steals in to fill his pockets from the till when the store-keeper is not looking. That was what we got out of having Roosevelt on the Police Board. He could not set us free. We have got to do that ourselves. But he cut our bonds and gave us arms, if we chose to use them.

Of the night trips we took together to see how the police patrolled in the early hours of the morning, when the city sleeps and policemen are most needed, I told in the story of my own life, and shall not here repeat it. They earned for him the name of Haroun-al-Roosevelt, those trips that bore such sudden good fruit in the discipline of the force. They were not always undertaken solely to wake up the police. Roosevelt wanted to know the city by night, and the true inwardness of some of the problems he was struggling with as Health Commissioner; for the President of the Police Board was by that fact a member of the Health Board also. One might hear of overcrowding in tenements for years and not grasp the subject as he could by a single midnight inspection with the sanitary police. He wanted to understand it all, the smallest with the greatest, and sometimes the information he brought out was unique, to put it mildly. I can never think of one of those expeditions without a laugh. We had company that night:

IN MULBERRY STREET

Hamlin Garland and Dr. Alexander Lambert were along. In the midnight hour we stopped at a peanut-stand in Rivington Street for provender, and while the Italian made change Roosevelt pumped him on the economic problem he presented. How could he make it pay? No one was out; it did not seem as if his sales could pay for even the fuel for his torch that threw its flickering light upon dark pavements and deserted streets. The peanut-man groped vainly for a meaning in his polite speech, and turned a bewildered look upon the doctor.

"How," said he, coming promptly to the rescue,—"how you make him pay—cash—pan out—monish?"

The Italian beamed with sudden understanding. "Nah!" he said, with a gesture eloquent of resentment and resignation in one: "W'at I maka on de peanút I losa on de dam' banán'."

Did the police hate Roosevelt for making them do their duty? No, they loved him. The crooks hated him; they do everywhere, and with reason. But the honest men on the force, who were, after all, in the great majority, even if they had knuckled under in discouragement to a system that could break them, but against which they were powerless, came quickly to accept him as their hope of delivery. For the first time in the history of the department every man had a show on his merits. Amazing as it was, " pull " was dead. Politics or religion cut no figure. No one asked about them. But did a policeman, pursuing a burglar through the night, dive running into the Park Avenue railroad tunnel, risking a horrible death to catch his man, he was promptly promoted; did a bicycle policeman lie with broken and bruised bones after a struggle with a runaway horse that meant his life or the lives of helpless women and children if he let go, he arose from his bed a roundsman with the medal for bravery on his breast. Did a gray-haired veteran swim ashore among grinding ice-floes with a drowning woman, he was called to headquarters and made a sergeant. I am speaking of cases that actually occurred. The gray-haired veteran of the Civil War had saved twenty-eight lives at the risk of his own,—his beat lay along the river shore,—had been twice distinguished by Congress with medals for valor, bore the life-saving medal, and had never a complaint against

him on the discipline-book; but about all the
recognition he had ever earned from the Police
Board was the privilege of buying a new uniform at his own expense when he had ruined
the old one in risking his life. Roosevelt had
not been in Mulberry Street four weeks when
the board resolved, on his motion, that clothes
ruined in risking life on duty were a badge of
honor, of which the board was proud to pay the
cost.

That the police became, from a band of
blackmailers' tools, a body of heroes in a few
brief months, only backs up my belief that the
heart of the force, with which my lines were
cast half a lifetime, was and is all right, with
the Deverys and the Murphys out of the way.
Led by a Roosevelt, it would be the most mag-
nificent body of men to be found anywhere.
Two years under him added quite a third to the
roll-of-honor record of forty years under Tammany politics. However, the enemy was quick
to exploit what there was in that. When I
looked over the roll the other day I found page
upon page inscribed with names I did not
know, behind one of a familiar sound, though I
could not quite make it out. Tammany or

Toomany—either way would mean the same thing: it was no longer a roll of honor.

These were some of the things Roosevelt did in Mulberry Street. He did many more, and they were all for its good. He did them all so simply, so frankly, that in the end he disarmed criticism, which in the beginning took it all for a new game, an " honesty racket," of which it had not got the hang, and could not,—confounded his enemies, who grew in number as his success grew and sat up nights hatching out plots by which to trip him. Roosevelt strode through them all, kicking their snares right and left, half the time not dreaming that they were there, and laughing contemptuously when he saw them. I remember a mischief-maker whose mission in life seemed to be to tell lies at headquarters and carry tales, setting people at odds where he could. He was not an official, but an outsider, an idler with nothing better to do, but a man with a " pull " among politicians. Roosevelt came upon some of his lies, traced them to their source, and met the man at the door the next time he came nosing around. I was there and heard what passed.

" Mr. So-and-so." said the President of the

Board, "I have heard this thing, and I am told you said it. You know, of course, that it is a lie. I shall send at once for the man who says he heard you tell it, so that you may meet him; because you know if you did say it we cannot have you around here any more." The man got out at once and never came back while Roosevelt was there.

It was all as simple as that, perfectly open and aboveboard, and I think he was buncoed less than any of his "wise" predecessors. There was that in his trust in uncorrupted human nature that brought out a like response. There always is, thank heaven! You get what you give in trust and affection. The man who trusts no one has his faith justified; no one will trust him, and he will find plenty to try their wits upon him. Once in a while Roosevelt's sympathies betrayed him, but not to his discredit. They laugh yet in the section-rooms at the police stations over the trick played upon him by a patrolman whose many peccadilloes had brought him at last to the "jumping-off place." This time he was to be dismissed. The President said so; there was no mercy. But the policeman had "piped him off." He knew his soft spot. In the morning, when the Commissioner came fresh from his romp with his own babies, there confronted him eleven youngsters of all ages, howling dolefully. The doomed policeman mutely introduced them with a sorrowful gesture,—motherless all.

Mr. Roosevelt's stern gaze softened. What, no mother? all these children! Go, then, and take one more chance, one last chance. And the policeman went out with the eleven children which were not his at all. He had borrowed them, all but two, from the neighbors in his tenement.

But there is no malice in the joking at his expense, rather affection. It is no mean tribute to human nature, even in the policeman's uniform, that for the men who tricked Roosevelt in the Police Board—his recreant colleagues—and undid what they could of his work, there survives in the Department the utmost contempt and detestation, while Roosevelt is held in the heartiest regard that is not in the least due to his exalted station, but to a genuine reverence for the man's character as Mulberry Street saw it when it was put to the severest test.

SAGAMORE HILL.

THEODORE ROOSEVELT'S SUMMER HOME AT OYSTER BAY

PHOTOGRAPH BY ARTHUR HEWITT

IN MULBERRY STREET

I shall have, after all, to ask those who would
know him at this period of his life, as I
knew him, to read " The Making of an American," because I should never get through were
I to try to tell it all. He made, as I said, a
large part of my life in Mulberry Street, and
by far the best part. When he went, I had no
heart in it. Of the strong hand he lent in the
battle with the slum, as a member of the Health
Board, that book will tell them. We had all
the ammunition for the fight, the law and all,
but there was no one who dared begin it till he
came. Then the batteries opened fire at once,
and it is largely due to him and his unhesitating courage that we have got as far as we have.
And that means something beyond the ordinary, for we were acting under an untried law,
the failure of which might easily involve a man
in suits for very great damages. Indeed, Mr.
Roosevelt was sued twice by landlords whose
tenements he destroyed. One characteristic incident survives in my memory from that day.
An important office was to be filled in the
Health Department, about which I knew.
There were two candidates: one the son of a
janitor, educated in the public schools, faithful

and able, but without polish or special fitness; the other a college man, a graduate of how many foreign schools of learning I don't know, a gentleman of travel, of refinement. He was the man for the position, which included much contact with the outer world,—so I judged, and so did others. Roosevelt had the deciding vote. We urged our man strongly upon him. He saw the force of our arguments, and yielded, but slowly and most reluctantly. His outspoken preference was for the janitor's son, who had fought himself up to the point where he could compete. And he was right, after all. The other was a failure; he was over-educated. I was glad, for Roosevelt's sake as well as for my own, when in after years the janitor's son took his place and came to his own.

One incident, which I have told before, I cannot forbear setting down here again, for without it even this fragmentary record would be too incomplete. I mean his meeting with the labor men who were having constant trouble with the police over their strikes, their pickets, etc. They made me much too proud of them, both he and they, for me ever to forget that. Roosevelt saw that the trouble was in their not understanding one another, and he asked the labor leaders to meet him at Clarendon Hall to talk it over. Together we trudged through a blinding snow-storm to the meeting. This was at the beginning of things, when the town had not yet got the bearings of the man. The strike leaders thought they had to do with an ambitious politician, and they tried bluster. They would do so and so unless the police were compliant; and they watched to get him placed. They had not long to wait. Roosevelt called a halt, short and sharp.

" Gentlemen! " he said, " we want to understand one another. That was my object in coming here. Remember, please, that he who counsels violence does the cause of labor the poorest service. Also, he loses his case. Understand distinctly that order will be kept. The police will keep it. Now, gentlemen! "

There was a moment's amazed suspense, and then the hall rang with their cheers. They had him placed then, for they knew a man when they saw him. And he,—he went home proud and happy, for his trust in his fellow-man was justified.

He said, when it was all over, that there was

no call at all for any genius in the work of administering the police force, nor, indeed, for any unusual qualities, but just common sense, common honesty, energy, resolution, and readiness to learn; which was probably so. They are the qualities he brought to everything he ever put his hands to. But if he learned something in that work that helped round off the man in him,—though it was not all sweetness or light,—he taught us much more. His plain performance of a plain duty, the doing the right because it was the right, taught us a lesson we stood in greater need of than of any other. Roosevelt's campaign for the reform of the police force became the moral issue of the day. It swept the cobwebs out of our civic brains, and blew the dust from our eyes, so that we saw clearly where all had been confusion before: saw straight, rather. We rarely realize, in these latter days, how much of our ability to fight for good government, and our hope of winning the fight, is due to the campaign of honesty waged by Theodore Roosevelt in Mulberry Street.

VII

THE CLASH OF WAR

—

VII

THE CLASH OF WAR

IT sounded like old times, to us who had
stayed behind in Mulberry Street, when,
within a few months after his departure
for Washington, the wail came from down
there that Roosevelt was playing at war with
the ships, that he was spoiling for a row, and
did not care what it cost. It seems he had
been asking a million dollars or so for target
practice, and, when he got that, demanding
more—another half million. I say it sounded
like old times, for that was the everlasting re-
frain of the grievance while he ran the police:
there was never to be any rest or peace where he
was. No, there was not. In Mulberry Street
it was his business to make war on the scoundrels who had wrecked the force and brought
disgrace upon our city. To Washington he

had gone to sharpen the tools of war. War he knew must come. They all knew it; it was his business to prepare for it, since the first and hardest blows must be struck on the sea.

Here let me stop a moment to analyze his attitude toward this war that was looming on the horizon even before he left Mulberry Street. It was perfectly simple, as simple as anything he ever did or said, to any one who had ever taken the trouble to " think him out." I had followed him to Washington to watch events for my paper, and there joined the " war party," as President McKinley called Roosevelt and Leonard Wood, poking fun at them in his quiet way. There was not a trace of self-seeking or of jingoism in Roosevelt's attitude, unless you identify jingoism with the stalwart Americanism that made him write these words the year before:

" Every true patriot, every man of statesmanlike habit, should look forward to the time when not a single European power shall hold a foot of American soil." Not, he added, that it was necessary to question the title of foreign powers to present holdings; but " it certainly will become necessary if the timid and selfish peace-at-any-price men have their way, and if the United States fails to check, at the outset, European aggrandizement on this continent."

That was one end of it, the political one, if you please; the Monroe Doctrine in its briefest and simplest form. Spain had by outrageous mismanagement of its West Indian colonies proved herself unfit, and had forfeited the right to remain. The mismanagement had become a scandal upon our own shores. Every year the yellow fever that was brewed in Cuban filth crossed over and desolated a thousand homes in our Southern States. If proof were wanted that it was mismanagement that did it, events have more than supplied it since, and justified the war of humanity.

Plain humanity was the other end of it, and the biggest. I know, for I saw how it worked upon his mind. I was in Washington when a German cigar-manufacturer, whose business took him once or twice a year to Cuba, came to the capital seeking an interview with Senator Lodge, his home senator, since he was from Boston. I can see him now sitting in the committee-room and telling how on his last trip he had traveled to some inland towns where he was in the habit of doing business, but where now all had been laid waste; how when he sat down in the inn to eat such food as he could get, a famished horde of gaunt, half-naked women, with starving babies at barren breasts, crept up like dogs to his chair, fighting for the crumbs that fell from his plate. Big tears rolled down the honest German's face as he told of it. He could not eat, he could not sleep until he had gone straight to Washington to tell there what he had witnessed. I can see the black look come into Roosevelt's face and hear him muttering under his breath, for he, too, had little children whom he loved. And the old anger wells up in me at the thought of those who would have stayed our hand. Better a thousand times war with all its horrors than a hell like that. That was murder, and of women and innocent children. The war that avenges such infamy I hail as the messenger of wrath of an outraged God.

The war was a moral issue with him, as indeed it was with all of us who understood. It was with such facts as these—and there was no lack of them—in mind and heart that he responded hotly to Senator Hanna pleading for peace for the sake of the country's commerce and prosperity, that much as he appreciated those blessings, the honor of the country was of more account than temporary business prosperity. It has slipped my mind what was the particular occasion,—some club gathering, —but I have not forgotten the profound impression the Naval Secretary's words made as he insisted that our country could better afford to lose a thousand of the bankers that have added to its wealth than one Farragut; that it were better for it never to have had all the railroad magnates that have built it up, great as is their deserving, than to have lost Grant and Sherman; better that it had never known commercial greatness than that it should miss from its history one Lincoln. Unless the moral overbalance the material, we are indeed riding for a fall in all our pride.

So he made ready for the wrath to come. And now his early interest in naval affairs, that gave us his first book, bore fruit. When the work of preparation was over, and Roosevelt was bound for the war to practice what he had preached, his chief, Secretary Long, said, in bidding him good-by, that he had been literally invaluable in his place, and that the navy would feel the stimulus of his personality for a long time. His industry was prodigious. He bought ships for the invasion of Cuba, and fitted them out. He recruited crews and shot away fortunes with the big guns—recklessly shouted the critics. He knew better. His experience as a hunter had taught him that the best gun in the world was wasted on a man who did not know how to use it. The Spaniards found that out later. Roosevelt loaded up with ammunition and with coal. When at last the war broke out, Dewey found everything he needed at Hongkong where he sought it, and was able to sail across to Manila a week before they expected him there. And then we got the interest on the gun-practice that had frightened the economical souls at home.

In Mulberry Street it was corruption that defied him; now it was the stubborn red tape of a huge department that dragged and dragged at his feet, and threatened to snare him up at every second step he took,—the most disheartening of human experiences. The men he came quickly to like. " They are a fine lot of fellows," he wrote to me, " these naval men. You would take to them at sight." Of the other he never spoke, but I can imagine how it must have nagged him. To this day, when I have anything I want to find out or do in the Navy Department, it seems flatly impossible to make a short cut to the thing I want. So many bureaus, so many chief clerks, and so many what-you-may-call-'ems have to pass upon it. It is the way of the world, I suppose, to go on magnifying and exalting the barrel where the staves are men with their little interests and conceits, until what it is made to hold is of secondary importance or less. In the end he burst through it as he did through the jobs the police conspirators tried to put up on him; kicked it all to pieces and went on his way.

A new light shone through the dusty old windows. For generations, since steam came to replace sail, there had been a contention between the line and the engineer corps, as to rank and pay, that cut into the heart of the navy. It was the fight of the old against the new that goes on in all days. The old line-officer was loath to give equal place to the engineer, who, when he was young, was

but an auxiliary, an experiment. The place of
honor was still to be on the deck, though
long since the place of responsibility had
moved to the engine-room. The engineer insisted upon recognition; met the other upon
the floor of Congress and checkmated him in
his schemes of legislation. The quarrel was
bitter, irreconcilable; on every ship there were
hostile camps. Neither could make headway
for the other. Roosevelt, as chairman of a
board to reconcile the differences that were
older than the navy itself as it is to-day,
steered it successfully between the two fatal
reefs and made peace. Under his " personnel
bill " each side obtained its rights, and, with
the removal of the pretext for future quarrels,
the navy was greatly strengthened. Cadets
now receive the same training; the American
naval officer in the next war will be equally
capable of commanding on deck and of mending a broken engine.

When it came to picking out the man who
was to command in the East, where the blow
must be struck, Roosevelt picked Dewey. They
laughed at him. Dewey was a " dude," they
said. It seems the red tape had taken notice of

the fact that the Commodore was always trim
and neat, and, judging him by its own standard, thought that was all. Roosevelt told
them no, he would fight. And he might wear
whatever kind of collar he chose, so long as he
did that. I remember, when Dewey was gone
with his ships, the exultation with which Roosevelt spoke of the choice. We were walking
down Connecticut Avenue, with his bicycle between us, discussing Dewey. Leonard Wood
came out of a side street and joined us. His
mind was on Cuba. Roosevelt, with prophetic
eye, beheld Manila and the well-stocked am-
munition-bins in Chinese waters.

" Dewey," he said, " is the man for the place.
He has a lion heart."

I guess none of us feels like disputing his
judgment at this day, any more than we do
the wisdom of the gun-practice.

When Dewey was in the East, it was Roosevelt's influence in the naval board that kept
his fleet intact. The *Olympia* had been ordered
home. Roosevelt secured the repeal of the
order. " Keep the *Olympia*," he cabled him,
and " keep full of coal." The resistless energy
of the man carried all before it till the day

when orders were cabled under the Pacific to the man with the lion heart to go in and smash the enemy. " Capture or destroy! " We know the rest.

Roosevelt's work was done. " There is nothing more for me to do here," he said. " I 've got to get into the fight myself."

They told him to stay, he was needed where he was. But he was right: his work *was* done. It was to prepare for war. With the fighting of the ships he had, could have, nothing to do. Merely to sit in an office and hold down a job, a title, or a salary, was not his way. He did not go lightly. His wife was lying sick, with a little baby; his other children needed him. I never had the good fortune to know a man who loves his children more devotedly and more sensibly than he. There was enough to keep him at home; there were plenty to plead with him. I did myself, for I hated to see him go. His answer was as if his father might have spoken: " I have done all I could to bring on the war, because it is a just war, and the sooner we meet it the better. Now that it has come, I have no business to ask others to do the fighting and stay at home myself."

THE CLASH OF WAR

It was right, and he went. I have not forgotten that gray afternoon in early May when I went with him across the river to the train that was to carry him and his horse South. He had made his will; the leave-taking was over and had left its mark. There was in him no trace of the " spoiling for a fight " that for the twentieth time was cast up against him. He looked soberly, courageously ahead to a new and untried experience, hopeful of the glad day that should see our arms victorious and the bloody usurper driven from Cuba. " I won't be long." He waved his hand and was gone; and to me the leaden sky seemed drearier, the day more desolate than before.

Two weary months dragged their slow length along. There had been fighting in Cuba. Every morning my wife and I plotted each to waylay the newsboy to get the paper first and make sure he was safe before the other should see it. And then one bright and blessed July morning, when the land was ringing with the birthday salute of the nation, she came with shining eyes, waving the paper, in which we read together of the charge on San Juan Hill; how the Rough-Riders charged, with him at their head, through a hail of Spanish bullets, the men dropping by twos and threes as they ran.

"When they came [1] to the open, smooth hillside there was no protection. Bullets were raining down at them, and shot and shells from the batteries were sweeping everything. There was a moment's hesitation, and then came the order: 'Forward! charge!' Lieutenant-Colonel Roosevelt led, waving his sword. Out into the open the men went, and up the hill. Death to every man seemed certain. The crackle of the Mauser rifles was continuous. Out of the brush came the riders. Up, up they went, with the colored troops alongside of them, not a man flinching, and forming as they ran. Roosevelt was a hundred feet in the lead. Up, up they went in the face of death, men dropping from the ranks at every step. The Rough-Riders acted like veterans. It was an inspiring sight and an awful one.

"Astounded by the madness of the rush, the Spaniards exposed themselves. This was a fatal mistake. The Tenth Cavalry (the col-

[1] This was the account we read in the New York "Sun."

ored troops) picked them off like ducks and rushed on, up and up.

" The more Spaniards were killed, the more seemed to take their places. The rain of shells and bullets doubled. Men dropped faster and faster, but others took their places. Roosevelt sat erect on his horse, holding his sword and shouting for his men to follow him. Finally, his horse was shot from under him, but he landed on his feet and continued calling for his men to advance. He charged up the hill afoot.

" It seemed an age to the men who were watching, and to the Rough-Riders the hill must have seemed miles high. But they were undaunted. They went on, firing as fast as their guns would work.

" At last the top of the hill was reached. The Spaniards in the trenches could still have anni- hilated the Americans, but the Yankees' daring dazed them. They wavered for an instant, and then turned and ran.

" The position was won and the block-house captured. . . . In the rush more than half of the Rough-Riders were wounded."

In how many American homes was that splendid story read that morning with a thrill

never quite to be got over! We read it together, she and I, excited, breathless; and then
we laid down the paper and gave two such
rousing cheers as had n't been heard in Rich-
mond Hill that Fourth of July morning, one
for the flag and one for Theodore Roosevelt.
What was breakfast? The war was won and
over!

We live in a queer world. One man sees the
glorious painting, priceless for all time; the
other but the fly-speck on the frame. A year
or two after, some one, I think he was an editor,
wrote to ask me if the dreadful thing was true
that in the rush up that hill Roosevelt said,
"Hell!" I don't know what I replied—I
want to forget it. I know I said it, anyhow.
But, great Scott! think of it.

Of that war and of his regiment, from the
day it was evolved, uniformed, armed, and
equipped, through "ceaseless worrying of excellent bureaucrats who had no idea how to
do things quickly or how to meet an emergency," [1] all through the headlong race with a
worse enemy than the one in front,—the ma-

---

[1] I am quoting "The Rough-Riders." It seems, then, the
navy has no patent on red tape. I thought as much.

THE CLASH OF WAR

laria, upon which the Spaniards counted openly
as their grewsome ally,—down to the day when,
the army's work done, Colonel Roosevelt
" wrecked his career " finally and for good, by
demanding its recall home, he himself has told
the story in " The Rough-Riders." Every
school-boy in the land knows it. The Rough-
Riders came out of the heroic past of our country's history, held the forefront of the stage
for three brief months, and melted back into
college, and camp, and mine with never a ripple. But they left behind them a mark which
this generation will not see effaced. To those
who think it a sudden ambitious thought, a
" streak of luck," I commend this reference to
the " rifle-bearing horsemen " on page 249
of the second volume of his " Winning of the
West," written quite ten years before: " They
were brave and hardy, able to tread their way
unerringly through the forests, and fond of
surprises; and though they always fought on
foot, they moved on horseback, and therefore
with great celerity. Their operations should
be carefully studied by all who wish to learn the
possibilities of mounted riflemen." Before he
or any one else dreamed of the war, he had

studied and thought it all out, and when the chance came he was ready for it and took it. That is all there ever was in "Roosevelt's luck"; and that is about all there is in this luck business, anyhow, as I have said before.

The chance came to one man beside him who was ready, and the world is the better for it. I saw the growing friendship between the two that year in Washington, and was glad; for Leonard Wood is another man to tie to, as one soon finds out who knows him. They met there for the first time, but in one brief year they grew to be such friends that when the command of the regiment was offered Roosevelt, he asked for second place under Wood; for Wood had seen service in the field, as Roosevelt had not. He had earned the medal of honor for undaunted courage and great ability in the arduous campaigns against the Apaches. Both earned their promotion in battle afterward. I liked to see them together because they are men of the same strong type. When Roosevelt writes of his friend that, " like so many of the gallant fighters with whom it was later my good fortune to serve, he combined in a very high degree the qualities of entire manliness with entire uprightness and cleanliness of character; it was a pleasure to deal with a man of high ideals who scorned everything mean and base, and who also possessed those robust and hardy qualities of body and mind, for the lack of which no merely negative virtue can ever atone "—he draws as good a picture of himself as his best friend could have done. While the Roosevelts and the Woods come when they are needed, as they always have come, our country is safe.

Together they sailed away in the springtime, southward through the tropic seas, toward the unknown. " We knew not whither we were bound, nor what we were to do; but we believed that the nearing future held for us many chances of death and hardship, of honor and renown. If we failed, we would share the fate of all who fail; but we were sure that we would win, that we should score the first great triumph in a mighty world-movement." The autumn days were shortening when I stood at Montauk Point scanning the sea for the vessels that should bring them back. Within the year one was to sit at Albany, the Governor of his own, the Empire State; the other in the palace of the conquered tyrant on the rescued isle. For Roosevelt committees were waiting, honors and high office. The country rang with his name. But when he stepped ashore his concern was for his own at home,—for his wife; and when I told him that I had brought her down to see his triumph, he thanked me with a handshake that told me how glad he was.

I see him now riding away over the hill, in his Rough-Rider uniform, to the hospital where his men lay burning up with the fever. Wherever he came, confusion, incapacity, gave way to order and efficiency. Things came round at once. So did his men. The sight of his face was enough to make them rally for another fight with the enemy. They had seen him walking calmly on top of the earth wall when, in the small hours of the morning, drenched by pouring rains, chilled to the bone, and starving in the trenches, they were roused by the alarm that the Spaniards were coming, and the sight made them heroes. They had heard his cheering voice when the surgeons were dressing the wounded by candle-light, after the fight at Las Guasimas: "Boys, if there is a man at home

who would n't be proud to change places with
you he is not worth his salt, and he is not a
true American "; and the ring of it was with
them yet. So they took heart of hope and got
well, and went back to those who loved them,
even as did he for a little while. Then we
needed him again, and he came when he was
called.

VIII
ROOSEVELT AND HIS MEN

—

VIII

ROOSEVELT AND HIS MEN

THERE was a thunder of hoofs on the road that descends the slope from Camp Wikoff to the Life-Saving Station, and a squad of horsemen swarmed over the hill. A stocky, strongly built man on a big horse was in the lead. In his worn uniform and gray army hat he suggested irresistibly, as he swept by, Sheridan on his wild ride to "Winchester, twenty miles away." They were gone like the wind, leaping the muddy ford at the foot of the hill and galloping madly across the sands. My horse, that had been jogging along sedately enough till then, caught the spirit of the rush and made after them, hard as he could go. On the beach we caught up with them, riding in and out of the surf with shouts of delight, like so many centaurs at play. The salt spray dashed over them in showers of shining white, but they yelled back defiance at the ocean. Their leader watched them from his horse, and laughed loudly at their sport.

They were Roosevelt and his men. " Roosevelt's Rough-Riders " belong to history now, with the war in which they held such a picturesque place. I had seen them go, full of youthful spirits, eager for the fray, and it was my privilege to hear the last speech their Colonel made to them on the night when the news of the disbandment came. He had ridden up from the Commanding General's quarters with the message, and, calling his men about him in the broad street facing the officers' tents, told them of the coming parting.

" I know what you were in the field," he said. " You were brave and strong. I ask now of you that every man shall go back and serve his country as well in peace as he did in war. I can trust you to do it."

They tried to cheer, some of them, but they had no heart in it. The men went quietly to their tents with sober faces, and I saw in them that which warranted the trust their Colonel put in them.

ROOSEVELT AND HIS MEN

The Rough-Riders were not, as many have supposed, a product of the war with Spain. On the contrary, the mounted riflemen were the historic arm of the United States from the earliest days of the Nation. In the War of the Revolution they came out of the West and killed or captured the whole of the British forces at King's Mountain. A descendant of two of the three colonels who commanded them then fought with Roosevelt at Las Guasimas and on the San Juan hill. They furnished the backbone of Andrew Jackson's forces in the War of 1812. As the Texas Rangers they became famous in the troubles with Mexico. They conquered the French towns on the Illinois, and won the West from the Indians in a hundred bloody fights. In the Civil War they lost, to a great extent, their identity, but not their place in the van and the thick of the fight. Theodore Roosevelt as a historian knew their record and value; as a hunter and a plainsman he knew where to find the material with which to fill up the long-broken ranks. It came at his summons from the plains and the cattle-ranges of the great West, from the mines of the Rocky Mountains, from the counting-rooms and col-

leges of the East, and from the hunting-trail of
the wilderness, wherever the spirit of adventure
had sent young men out with the rifle to hunt
big game or to engage in the outdoor sports
that train mind and body to endure uncomplain-
ingly the hardships of campaigning. The
Rough-Riders were the most composite lot that
ever gathered under a regimental standard, but
they were at the same time singularly typical of
the 'spirit that conquered a continent in three
generations, eminently American. Probably
such another will never be got together again;
in no other country on earth could it have been
mustered to-day. The cowboy, the Indian
trailer, the Indian himself, the packer, and the
hunter who had sought and killed the grizzly in
single combat in his mountain fastness, touched
elbows with the New York policeman who, for
love of adventure, had followed his once chief
to the war, with the college athlete, the football-
player and the oarsman, the dare-devil moun-
taineer of Georgia, fresh from hunting moon-
shiners as a revenue officer, and with the society
man, the child of luxury and wealth from the
East, bent upon proving that a life of ease had
dulled neither his manhood nor his sense of our

common citizenship. They did it in a way that was a revelation to some who under other circumstances and in a different environment would have called them " dudes." In the fight they were the coolest and in the camp frequently the handiest of the lot. One whose name is synonymous with exclusiveness in New York's " smart set," and who for bravery in the face of the enemy rose to command of his troop, achieved among his brother officers the reputation of being handiest at " washing up " after " grub," when they had any. And it happened more than once on the long marches through the Cuban jungle, when " Roosevelt's Rough-Riders," compelled to campaign on foot, in humorous desperation had taken the more fitting title of " Wood's Weary Walkers" to themselves, that some Eastern-bred man with normal manners of languid elegance was able to relieve his hardier Western neighbor who had never walked five miles on foot in his life. When at the end of the march the college chap came trudging up cheerfully carrying two packs beside his own and ready for the chores of camp that his tired comrade might rest, a gap was closed then and there in our national life that had yawned wider than it had any right to. More than all political arguments, more than all the preachments of well-meaning sociologists, did this brief summer's campaign contribute to fill out the gap between East and West, between North and South, between " the classes and the masses," unless I greatly mistake. It was not in the contract, but it came out so when once they got a fair look at each other and saw that in truth they were brothers.

There were clergymen in the ranks. I am not referring now to Chaplain Brown, whose stout defense of his Western men,—he was from Prescott, Arizona,—when he thought I was attacking them, I remember with mingled amusement and pleasure. He was an Episcopalian of no special affiliation with high-church or low-church tendencies within his fold. " You see, I don't go much on the fringes of religion," he said simply. He was after the genuine article, and he found it in his cowboy friends—real reverence, and such singing! He was holding forth to me upon this theme as we lay in the long grass, when I ventured to remark that I had heard that his people were given to violence, shooting-matches, and such. He denied it hotly. They were the quietest, nicest fellows; only once in a while, when a fellow was caught cheating at cards, then—

"But," argued the Chaplain, rising on his elbow and earnestly pointing a spear of grass he had been chewing at me, "when a man cheats at cards, he ought to be shot, ought n't he? Well, then, that is all."

I confess to a certain enjoyment in the thought of Chaplain Brown's theology on a background of the Rough-Riders' singing at "meetin'" in the woods. The combination suggests that first funeral on the ridge at Guantanamo, with the marines growling out the responses to the Chaplain's prayer between pot-shots at the enemy, flat on their stomachs under the sudden attack; and, indeed, Colonel Roosevelt himself gave testimony that he had seen Chaplain Brown bring in wounded men from the field under circumstances that were distinctly stirring. But for all that, the Chaplain is a digression. The clergymen I was thinking of wore no shoulder-straps. They carried guns. One of them came up to bid his Colonel good-by when I was sitting with him. He was tall and straight, and of few words.

"That man," said Mr. Roosevelt, as he went across the field back to the camp, "represents probably the very best type of our people. He is a Methodist preacher, of the old circuit-rider's stock, strong, fearless, self-reliant. His people had been in all our wars before him, and he came as a matter of course. You should have seen him one morning sitting in the bomb-proof with his head just below the traverse, where the shrapnel kept cracking over his hat. They could n't touch him, as he knew, and he sat there as unconcerned as if there were no such things as guns and battles, breaking the beans for his coffee with the butt of his revolver. He was n't going into the fight without his coffee. He was a game preacher."

An hour later, when, after a visit to the two mascots of the regiment,—Josie, the mountain lion, and the eagle, Jack,—I was chatting with Lieutenant Ferguson, a young Englishman who won signal distinction in battle, the flap of the tent was raised and a tall trooper darkened the entrance. He came to make a report, and stood silently at attention while the officer examined it. His questions he answered in monosyllables. "That was Pollock," said his superior when he was gone. "He is a full-blooded Pawnee. He has never anything to say, but you should see him in a fight. I shall never forget the ungodly war-whoop he let out when we went up the San Juan hill. I mistrust that it scared the Spaniards almost as much as our charge did. I know that it almost took my breath away."

Such was the material of which the regiment was made. Ninety-five per cent. had herded cattle on horseback, on the great plains, at some time or other. A majority had been under fire. The rifle was their natural weapon. They were not to be stampeded, and they knew how readily to find the range of the enemy's sharpshooters, a fact that rendered them far more effective in a fight than the average volunteer, who had hardly a speaking acquaintance with his gun. Ninety per cent. of the Rough-Riders were Americans born and bred. Perhaps a hundred were of foreign birth—German, Norwegian, English. There were Catholics and Protestants, and they joined with equal fervor in the singing that edified Chaplain Brown.

THEODORE ROOSEVELT

They stood all on the same footing. The old American plan ruled: every one on his merits. In the last batch recommended for promotion by Colonel Roosevelt for gallantry in the field was a Jew. The result of it all was a corps that excited the admiration of the regulars who fought side by side with them.

Of their gameness innumerable stories have been told. The Indian Issbell was shot seven times in the fight at Las Guasimas, but stayed in the firing-line to the end. Private Heffner, shot through the body, demanded to be propped up against a tree and given his rifle and canteen. So fitted out, he fought on until his comrades charged forward and he could no longer shoot without danger of hitting them. They found him sitting there dead after the fight. The cow-puncher Rowland from Santa Fé was shot through the side and ordered to the rear by Colonel Roosevelt, who saw the blood dripping from the wound. He went obediently until he was out of sight, and then sneaked back into the ranks. After it was over they seized him and took him to the hospital, where the surgeons told him he would have to be shipped north. That night he escaped and crawled back to the front as best he could. He fought beside his Colonel all through the Santiago fight.

It was predicted that, with their antecedents, the Rough-Riders could not be disciplined so as to become effective in the field; but exactly the opposite happened. They showed the world the new spectacle of a body of men who could think and yet be soldiers; who obeyed, not because they had to, but because it was right they should, and they liked to. They might not have been perfect in what the Chaplain would have called the fringes of soldiering. The pipe-clay and the regulations, and all that, they knew nothing about. But they kept order in their camp, and they knew the command Forward, when it was given. In their brief campaign they had no opportunity to learn any other. Their soldiers' manual was brief. It forbade grumbling, and there was none. Three days they camped out in the sun and rain on the San Juan hills, fighting by day and digging burrows by night, with little to eat and only the ditches to sleep in, but not a complaint was heard. When the enemy attacked, suddenly and in full force, at three o'clock in the morning, they were there to meet him, and, hungry and shivering, drenched through and through by the rains and by the heavy dews, they drove him back.

"That is the test," said their commander, speaking of it afterward: "to wake up men at three o'clock in the morning who have had nothing to eat, perhaps for days, and nothing to cover them; to wake them up suddenly to a big fight, and have them all run the right way; that is the test. There was n't a man who went to the rear."

The Rough-Riders were natural fighters, from the Colonel down. The science of war as they took it from him and practised it summed itself up in the simple formula to "strike hard, strike quick, and when in doubt go forward." It was so Napoleon won his victories. But the Spaniards complained bitterly. The Americans did not fight according to the rules of war, they wailed. "They go forward when fired upon instead of falling back." Accordingly they, the Spaniards, were compelled to run, which they did, denouncing the irregularity of the preceding. It *was* irregular. It was one of the several things in this extraordi-

THEODORE ROOSEVELT, COLONEL OF THE
ROUGH-RIDERS

PHOTOGRAPH BY PACH BROTHERS

nary war that did violence to all the traditions, and tangled up military precedent and red tape in the field in a hopeless snarl. However, enough remained over in camp, after the fighting was over, to more than make up for it.

The regiment was before the people almost continuously for three months. Raised, organized, equipped, and carried to Cuba within a month by the same splendid energy and executive force that fitted out the navy for its victorious fights in the East and West, it took the field at once and kept it till the army rested upon its arms under the walls of Santiago. All the way up it had been the vanguard. The dispatches from the front dealt daily with the Rough-Riders' exploits. When, at Las Guasimas with General Young's corps, they drove before them four times their number of Spaniards, frightened at their impetuous rush in the face of a withering fire from the shelter of an impenetrable jungle, the croakers said that they were ambushed, and, as in the old days when Roosevelt led the police phalanx, the cry was raised at home that he should be put on trial, court-martialed. The fact was that the Rough-Riders were fighting a most carefully planned battle. It was the way they won that frightened the cravens at home, as it did the Spaniards. The victory cost some precious lives, but it is at such cost that victories are won, and the moral effect of the attack was very great. Beyond a doubt it saved worse bloodshed later on. It has been Theodore Roosevelt's lot often to be charged with rashness, with what his critics in the rear are pleased to call his " lack of tact." It is the tribute paid by timidity to unquestioning courage. The campaign having been carefully planned, and General Wheeler having issued his orders to attack the enemy, the thing left to do was to charge. And they charged. The number of the enemy had nothing to do with it, nor the fact that he was intrenched, invisible, whereas they were exposed, in full sight. He was to be driven out; and he was driven out. That was war on the American plan, as understood by the Rough-Riders.

Ten days of marching and fighting in the bush culminated in the storming of the San Juan hills, with Colonel Roosevelt in full command, Colonel Wood having been deservedly promoted after Las Guasimas. The story of the famous charge up the barren slope, of the splendid bravery of the colored cavalry regiment that had been lying out with the Rough-Riders in the trenches and now came to the support of their chums with a rush, and of the victory wrested from the Spaniards when all depended upon the success of the attack, will be told in years to come at every American fireside. How much of the quick success of the campaign was really due to the Roosevelt Rough-Riders, what fates hung in the balance when their impetuous rush saved the day, when retreat had been counseled and in effect decided, we understood better as we learned the real state of the invading army on the night of June 30. Let it be enough to say that it did save the day. Others fought as valiantly, but the honor of breaking the Spanish lines belongs to the Rough-Riders, as the honor and credit of standing firmly for an immediate advance upon the enemy's works belongs to their Colonel and his bold comrades in the council of the chiefs in that fateful night.

It was one of the unexpected things in that campaign, that out of it should come the appreciation of the colored soldier as man and

brother by those even who so lately fought to
keep him a chattel. It fell to the lot of General
" Joe " Wheeler, the old Confederate warrior,
to command the two regiments of colored
troops, the Ninth and Tenth Cavalry, and no
one will bear readier testimony than he to the
splendid record they made. Of their patience
under the manifold hardships of roughing it in
the tropics, their helpfulness in the camp and
their prowess in battle, their uncomplaining
suffering when lying wounded and helpless,
stories enough are told to win for them fairly
the real brotherhood with their white-skinned
fellows which they crave. The most touching
of the many I heard was that of a negro trooper
who, struck by a bullet that had cut an artery
in his neck, was lying helpless, in danger of
bleeding to death, when a Rough-Rider came
to his assistance. There was only one thing to
be done: to stop the bleeding till a surgeon
came. A tourniquet could not be applied
where the wound was. The Rough-Rider put
his thumb on the artery and held it there while
he waited. The fighting drifted away over the
hill. He followed his comrades with longing
eyes till the last was lost to sight. His place

was there; but if he abandoned the wounded cavalryman, it was to let him die. He dropped his gun and stayed. Not until the battle was won did the surgeon come that way; but the trooper's life was saved. He told of it in the hospital with tears in his voice: " He done that to me, he did; stayed by me an hour and a half, and me only a nigger! "

The colored soldiers had taken a great liking to their gallant side-partners. They believed them invincible, and in the belief became nearly so themselves. The Rough-Riders became their mascot. They would have gone through fire for them, and in sober fact they did. So fighting and burrowing together, holding every foot they gained from the enemy, they came at last to the gates of the beleaguered city, and there were stayed by the white flag of truce. Two weeks they lay in the trenches ready to attack when the word was given, and then came the surrender. Up to that point the Rough-Riders had borne up splendidly. Poor rations had no terrors for them. If " cold hog " was the sole item on the bill of fare, it went down with a toast to better days. Starvation they bore without grumbling while fighting for their lives and their country. The sleepless night, the rain-storms in the trenches, the creeping things that disgust Northern men, the tarantulas and the horrible crabs, they took as they came. It was not until they were fairly back home, in Camp Wikoff, that they rebelled against tainted food sent up from the ship and demanded something decent to eat. But before that they had their dark day, when the fever came and laid low those whom the enemy's bullets had spared.

It was then, when the fighting was over but a worse enemy threatened than the one they had beaten in his breastworks,—an ally on whose aid the Spaniards had openly counted, and, but for the way in which they were rushed from the first, would not have counted in vain, —that the Rough-Riders were able to render their greatest service to their country, through their gallant chief. Until Colonel Roosevelt's round-robin, signed by all the general officers of the army in Cuba, startled the American people and caused measures of instant relief to be set on foot, the fearful truth that the army was perishing from privation and fever was not known. The cry it sent up was: " Take us home! We will fight for the flag to the last man, if need be. But now our fighting is done, we will not be left here to die." It was significant that the duty of making the unwelcome disclosure fell to the Colonel of the Rough-Riders. Of all the officers who signed it he was probably the youngest; but from no one could the warning have come with greater force.

The Colonel of the Rough-Riders at the head of his men on San Juan hill, much as I like the picture, is not half so heroic a figure to me as Roosevelt in this hour of danger and doubt, shouldering the blame for the step he knew to be right. Perhaps it is because I know him better and love him so. Here was this man who had left an office of dignity and great importance in the Administration to go to the war he had championed as just and right; who had left a family of little children to expose his life daily and hourly in the very forefront of battle; whose every friend in political life had blamed him hotly, warning him that he was wrecking a promising career in a quixotic enterprise—apparently justifying their predictions at a critical moment by deliberately shouldering the odium of practically censuring the Administration of which he was so recently a member. For that was what his letter amounted to; he knew it and they knew it. Verily, it is not strange that some who would have shrunk from the duty should call him " rash " for doing what he did. They did not know the man. It was enough for him that it *was* duty, that it was right. He never had other standard than that.

So the army came home, his Rough-Riders with it, ragged, sore, famished, enfeebled, with yawning gaps in its ranks, but saved; they to tell of his courage and unwearying patience; how in the fight he was always where the bullets flew thickest, until he seemed to them to have a charmed life; how, when it was over, as they lay out in the jungle and in the trenches at night, they found him always there, never tiring of looking after his men, of seeing that the wounded were cared for and the well were fed; ready to follow him through thick and thin wherever he led, but unwilling to loaf in camp or to do police duty when the country was no longer in need of them to fight; he to be hailed by his grateful fellow-citizens with the call to "step up higher." Once more the right had prevailed, and the counsel of expediency been shamed. Roosevelt's Rough-Riders had written their name in history.

"They were the finest fellows, and they were dead game. It was the privilege of a lifetime to have commanded such a regiment. It was a hard campaign, but they were beautiful days— and we won."

We were lying in the grass at his tent, under the starry August sky. Taps had been sounded long since. The Colonel's eye wandered thoughtfully down the long line of white tents in which the lights were dying out one by one. From a darker line in front, where a thousand horses were tethered, quietly munching their supper, came an occasional low whinnying. That and the washing of the surf on the distant beach were the only sounds that broke the stillness of the night. A bright meteor shot athwart the sky, leaving a shining trail, and fell far out beyond the lighthouse. We watched it in silence. I know what my thoughts were. He knew his own.

"Oh, well!" he said, with a half-sigh, and arose, "so all things pass away. But they were beautiful days."

I knocked the ashes from my cigar, and we went in.

IX

RULING BY
THE TEN COMMANDMENTS

RULING BY THE TEN COM-
MANDMENTS

THE campaign was over and ended. The morning would break on Election Day. We were speeding homeward in the midnight hour on a special from the western end of the State, where the day had been spent in speech-making, a hurricane wind-up of a canvass that had taken the breath of the old-timers away. Was it the victory in the air, was it Sherman Bell, the rough-rider deputy sheriff from Cripple Creek, or what was it that had turned us all, young and old, into so many romping boys as the day drew toward its close? I can still see the venerable Ex-Governor and Minister to Spain Stewart L. Woodford, myself, and a third scapegrace, whose name I have forgotten, going through the streets of Dunkirk, arm in arm, breasting the crowds and yelling, " Yi! yi! " like a bunch of college boys on a lark, and again and again falling into the line that passed Mr. Roosevelt in the hotel lobby to shake hands, until he peered into our averted faces and drove us out with laughter. And I can see him holding his sides, while the audience in the Opera House yelled its approval of Sherman Bell's offer to Dick Croker, who had called Roosevelt a " wild man ": " Who is this Dick Croker? I don't know him. He don't come from my State. Let him take thirty of his best men, I don't care how well they 're heeled, and I will take my gang and we 'll see who 's boss. I 'll shoot him so full of holes he won't know himself from a honeycomb." And then the wild enthusiasm in the square, where no one could hear a word of what was said for the cheering.

But now it was all over, and we were on the way home to add our own votes to the majority that would carry our Rough-Rider to Albany. We were discussing its probable size over our belated supper,—each according to his experience or enthusiasm. I remember his friendly nod and smile my way when I demanded a

hundred thousand at least. He inclined to ten
or fifteen thousand, as indeed proved quite
near the mark; when there was a rap on the
door, and in came the engineer, wiping his oily
hands in his blouse, to shake hands and wish
him luck. Roosevelt got up from the table,
and I saw him redden with pleasure as he
shook the honest hand and asked his name.

"Dewey," said the engineer, and such a
shout went up! It was an omen of victory,
surely.

"Dewey," said Roosevelt, " I would rather
have you come here as you do to shake hands
than have ten committees of distinguished citizens bring pledges of support "; and I knew he
would. It is no empty form with him when
he shakes hands with the engineer and the fire-
man of his train after a journey. He was ever
genuinely fond of railroad men, of skilled
mechanics of any kind, but especially of the
men who harness the iron steed and drive it
with steady eye and hand through the dangers
of the night. They have something in common with him that makes them kin. The
pilot of the *Sylph* that brought us through the
raging storm in the Sound the other day was

of that class. They sent word from the Navy-Yard to meet the President that on no account must he proceed down the Bay to Ellis Island. No boat could live there, ran the message. The President had the pilot come down and looked him over. He was a bronzed sea-dog, a man every inch of him.

" I have promised to go to Ellis Island; they are waiting for me. Can you get us there? "

The pilot wiped the salt spray from his face. " It can't be worse than we 've had," he said. " I 'll get you there."

" Then go ahead," said Mr. Roosevelt, and to me, " What do you think of him? "

" I would go with him anywhere," said I. " To look at him is to trust him."

The President followed his retreating form up the ladder with a look that, had he seen it, must have made him take his ship through Hades itself had it been between us and Ellis Island. " So do I think," he said. " They are a splendid lot of fellows."

But I am sailing ahead of my time. We were on our train just now. We did n't wake up, any of us, the next morning, till it rolled

THE TEN COMMANDMENTS

over the Hudson at Albany, and there lay the Capitol, with flags flying, in full sight. Just as I put up my curtain and saw it, Roosevelt opened the door of his room and bade us good-morning, and eleven throats sent up three rousing cheers for " the Governor."

At night we shouted again by torch-light, and the whole big State shouted with us. Theodore Roosevelt was Governor, elected upon the pledge that he would rule by the Ten Commandments, in the city where, fifteen years before, the spoils politicians had spurned him for insisting upon doing the thing that was right rather than the thing that was expedient. Say now the world does not move! It strides with seven-league boots where only it has a man who dares to lead the way.

Not necessarily at a smooth or even gait. He knew what was before him, and as for the politicians, they were not appreciably nearer to the Ten Commandments than in the old days. They had not changed. They had fallen in behind Roosevelt because it was expedient, not because it was right. They had to win, and they could win only with him. And yet, when " Buck " Taylor in a burst of fervid frontier

eloquence exhorted his audience to " Follow ma
colonel! follow ma colonel! and he will lead
you, as he led us, like lambs to the slaughter! "
I think not unlikely there mingled with the
cheers and the laughter the secret hope in the
breasts of some that it might be so. It was
but natural. They knew right well, the politicians did, how much they had to expect from
him; it was but a lean two years they were looking forward to with Roosevelt as Governor.
They might have comforted themselves in defeat by the thought that he was killed and out
of the way at last. Who knows?

When I speak of politicians here, I am
thinking of the spoilsmen who played the game
for keeps. They ran the machine, and they
took him, with their eyes open, to save it. And
then we saw the curious sight of the good-gov-
ernment forces, his natural allies, who were
largely what they were because of the example he had all along consistently set, sulking
disconsolate because he, who had always been
a loyal party man without ever surrendering
his conscience to his partisanship, went with
his party; instead of rejoicing, as they might
well have done, that the party had been forced

into making such a choice, that being the very end and aim and meaning of their political existence. They grumbled because he would " see the party bosses." Of course he would— see anybody that could help him get things done; for he had certain definite ends of good government in view, and it was no more to his taste to pose on the solitary peak of abortive righteousness as Governor, than it had been as a legislator. Yes, he would see the bosses, and he went right up to the front door and told the newspaper men his business, though they tried to smuggle him in secretly by the back way, to save his feelings. His feelings were n't hurt a bit. If he could make the machine work with him for good, he had killed two birds with one stone, for so it would be a more effective machine for party purposes as he saw them. As for its working him to its uses—the bosses knew better. The reformers did not. They sat and mourned, needlessly.

For him—I thought more than once in those days of a paragraph he had written about practical politics while he was yet a Civil Service Commissioner practising them with might and main. How much of prophecy there is in his writings, when you look back now! There would be obstacles, he wrote. " Let him make up his mind that he will have to face the violent opposition of the spoils politician, and also, too often, the unfair and ungenerous criticism of those who ought to know better. . . . Let him fight his way forward, paying only so much regard to both as is necessary to help him to win in spite of them. He may not, and indeed probably will not, accomplish nearly as much as he would like to, or as he thinks he ought to; but he will certainly accomplish something." He settled down courageously to the fight that was his own prescription. And when it was over, this was the judgment passed upon his administration in the " Review of Reviews " by Dr. Albert Shaw, than whom there is no fairer, more clear-headed critic of public events in the country: " He found the State administration thoroughly political; he left it business-like and efficient. He kept thrice over every promise that he made to the people in his canvass. Mr. Roosevelt so elevated and improved the whole tone of the State administration and so effectually educated his party and public opinion generally, that future governors will find easy what was before almost impossible."

That was accomplishing something, surely. It worked all right, then. Had some of the solemn head-shakers known how he enjoyed it all, I fear that to the inconsistent charges of bowing down to the idol of party and of wrecking his party, that were flung at him in the same breath, there would have been added the killing one of levity, that was not used up against Abraham Lincoln. I have an amused recollection of one band of visiting statesmen that filed into the Executive Mansion with grave, portentous mien, just as the Governor and I stole down the kitchen stairs to the sub-cellar to visit with Kermit's white rats, that were much better company. The Governor knew their names, their lineage, and all their " points," which were many, according to Kermit. They were fully discussed before we returned to the upper world of stupid politics.

That is my opinion, anyway. I hate politics —I am thinking of the game again—and I am not going to bother with them here, if I can help it, which I suppose I can't since the

THEODORE ROOSEVELT

Governor of the Empire State must needs be in politics up to his neck if he would do his duty; that is, he must be concerned about the welfare of his people rather than about putting his backers into fat jobs and seeing that the " party is made solid " in every county. But then, they are different brands. Roosevelt had his own brand from the start. Long before, he had identified and carefully charted it, lest the party managers make a mistake. " Practical politics," he wrote," must not be construed to mean dirty politics. On the contrary, in the long run, the politics of fraud and treachery and foulness is unpractical politics, and the most practical of all politicians is the one who is clean and decent and upright. The party man who offers his allegiance to party as an excuse for blindly following his party, right or wrong, and who fails to try to make that party in any way better, commits a crime against the country."

To this place had I come when I was asked to go over and tell the Young Men's Christian Association on the West Side what the " battle with the slum " meant to my city. And I did, and when I had told them the story I showed them a picture of Theodore Roosevelt as the man who had done more hard and honest fighting for those who cannot fight for themselves, or do not know how, than any other man anywhere. And a man in the audience—there is always one of that kind in every audience—who could see in the President of the United States only the candidate of his party for the next term, wrote to me of partisanship and of bad taste, and of how he could not stand Roosevelt because as Governor he would " see Platt," and did. I have his letter here before me, and my blood boils up in me whenever I look at it. Not because of the particular man and his letter. I have come across their like before. The thing that angers me is the travesty they make of the real non-partisanship with which we must win our fight for decency in the cities, because national politics in municipal elections are a mere cloak for corruption. How in the world am I to persuade my healthy-minded Democratic neighbor not to listen to Tammany's blandishments when he has this wizened spectacle before him? He is a man with convictions, who understands men and the play of human forces in the world, and can appreciate

Roosevelt for what he is and does, even if he disagrees with him; whereas the other never can. He can only " see Platt." Verily, between the two, give me Platt. If he had horns and a spike-tail painted blue, and all the other parlor furnishings of the evil place, I think I should take my chances with him and a jolly old fight rather than with the shivering visions of my correspondent who is so mortally afraid of the appearance of evil that by no chance can he ever get time to do good.

See Platt! Governor Roosevelt saw no end of people during his two years' term, and from some of them he learned something, and others learned something from him. The very first thing he did when he was in the Capitol at Albany was to ask the labor leaders to come up and see him. There were a lot of labor laws, so called, on the statute-books, designed to better the lot of the workingman in one way or another, and half of them were dead letters. Some of them had been passed in good faith, and had somehow stuck in the enforcement; and then there were others that were just fakes.

" These laws," said the Governor to the la-

bor leaders, " are your special concern. I want
you to look them over with me and see if they
are fair, and, if they are, that they be fairly
enforced. We will have no dead-letter laws.
If there is anything wrong that you know of,
I want you to tell me of it. If we need more
legislation, we will go to the legislature and
ask for it. If we have enough, we will see to
it that the laws we have are carried out, and the
most made of them."

And during two years there was no disagree-
ment in that quarter that was not gotten over
fairly. Sometimes the facts were in dispute.
Then he went to those who were in position
to make them plain and asked them to do it.
On two or three occasions he made me the
umpire between disputing organizations and
the Factory Department, and I had again
a near view of the extraordinary faculty of
judging quickly and correctly which habit and
severe training have developed in this man.
Cases to which I gave weeks of steady endeavor to get at the truth, and then had to bring
to him, still in doubt, he decided almost at a
glance, piercing the husks with unerring thrust
and dragging out the kernel that had eluded

me. I remember particularly one such occasion when I sat on the edge of the bed in his room at the hotel—he had come down to New York to review a militia regiment—while he was shaving himself at the window. I had gone all over the case and told him of my perplexity, when he took it up, and between bubbles of soap he blew at me he made clear what had been dim before, until I marveled that I had not seen it.

There came at last an occasion when nobody could decide. It was the factory law again that was in question—the enforcement of it, that is to say. The claim was made that it was not enforced as it should be. The factory inspectors said they did their best. The registering alone of all the tenement-house workers, as the new law demanded, in a population of over two millions of souls with few enough of their tenements free from the stamp of the sweat-shop, was a big enough task to leave a margin for honest intentions even with poor results. But the Governor was not content to give his inspectors the benefit of the doubt. He wrote to me to get together two or three of the dissatisfied, a list of disputed houses, and the factory inspector of the district, and he would come down and see for himself.

" I think," he wrote, " that perhaps, if I looked through the sweat-shops myself with the inspectors, as well as looked over their work, we might be in a condition to put things on a new basis, just as they were put on a new basis in the police department after you and I began our midnight tours."

I shall not soon forget that trip we took together. It was on one of the hottest days of early summer, and it wore me completely out, though I was used to it. Him it only gave a better appetite for dinner. I had picked twenty five-story tenements, and we went through them from cellar to roof, examining every room and the people we found there. They were on purpose the worst tenements of the East Side, and they showed us the hardest phases of the factory inspector's work, and where he fell short. The rules under which a tenement could be licensed for home work required: absolute cleanliness, that there should be no bed in the room where the work was done, no outsider employed, no contagious disease, and only one family living in the rooms.

THEODORE ROOSEVELT

In one Italian tenement that had room for seventeen families I had found forty-three the winter before on midnight inspection; that is to say, three families in every three-room flat, instead of one, all cooking at the same stove. No doubt they were still there, but the daylight showed us only a few women and a lot of babies whom they claimed as theirs. The men were out, the larger children in the street.

The Governor went carefully through every room, observing its condition and noting the number of the license on the wall, if anything was wrong. Sometimes there was no license. Sometimes one had been issued and revoked, but the women were still at work. They listened to remonstrances unmoved.

" Vat for I go avay? " said one. " Vere I go den? "

It was an intensely practical question with them, but so it was and is with us all; for from those forsaken tenements, where the home is wrecked hopelessly by ill-paid work that barely puts a dry crust into the mouths of the children, stalks the specter of diphtheria, of scarlet fever, and of consumption forth over the city and the land, sometimes basted in the

lining of the coat or the dress that was bought
at the fashionable Broadway counter, proving
us neighbors in very truth, though we deny
the kinship. Roosevelt understood. His in-
vestigations as an assemblyman into the cigarmakers' tenement-house conditions, and, later,
as a member of the Board of Health, had put
him in possession of the facts. He did not
mince matters with the factory inspector when,
after our completed tour, we went to his office
late in the afternoon. There was improvement,
he said, but not enough.

"I do not think you quite understand," he
said, "what I mean by enforcing a law. I
don't want it made as easy as possible for the
manufacturer. I want you to refuse to license
anybody in a tenement that does not come up to
the top notch of your own requirements. Make
the owners of tenements understand that old,
badly built, uncleanly houses shall not be used
for manufacturing in any shape, and that li-
censes will be granted only in houses fulfilling
rigidly the requirements of cleanliness and
proper construction. Put the bad tenement
at a disadvantage as against the well-con-
structed and well-kept house, and make the

house-owner as well as the manufacturer understand it."

We heard the echoes of that day's work in the Governor's emergency message to the legislature the following winter, calling upon it to pass the Tenement House Commission Bill. He summoned " the general sentiment for decent and cleanly living and for fair play to all our citizens " to oppose the mercenary hostility of the slum landlord. And the legislature heard, and the bill became law, to the untold relief of the people. That was a sample of the practical politics in the interest of which he was willing to " see " the party managers, if it was needed. And it usually ended with their seeing things as he did.

It seemed fair and just to the Governor that corporations with valuable franchises should be taxed on these, since they were much more valuable property than their real estate. It was one way, to his mind, of avoiding crank legislation designed merely to " hit money." The party managers disagreed. The Governor had thought it all out; to him it was just, even expedient as a party measure. He invited the corporation people to come and see

MRS. THEODORE ROOSEVELT
FROM THE PORTRAIT BY THEOBALD CHARTRAN
PHOTOGRAPH COPYRIGHT 1902 BY FRANCES B. JOHNSTON

him about it, that they might talk it over. They did n't; they conspired with the party managers to bury the bill in committee in the legislature. When the Governor sent an emergency message to wake it, they tore it up. The next morning another message was laid upon the Speaker's desk.

" I learn," it read, " that the emergency message which I sent last evening to the Assembly on behalf of the Franchise Tax Bill has not been read. I therefore send hereby another. I need not impress upon the Assembly the need of passing this bill at once. . . . It establishes the principle that hereafter corporations holding franchises from the public shall pay their just share of the public burden."

The bill was passed. The party managers " saw." The corporations did, too, and asked to be heard. They were heard. The law was amended at an extra session, but the principle stood unaltered. Since then the Court of Appeals has declared it constitutional and good, and not only the State of New York, but the whole country thanks Governor Roosevelt for a piece of legislation that makes for the permanent peace of our land. There can never

be other basis for that than the absolute assurance that all men, rich and poor, are equal
before the law. Trouble is sure to come,
sooner or later, where money can buy special
privilege. The marvel is that those who have
the money to buy, cannot half the time see it.

I am tempted to tell the story of how Roosevelt appointed the successor of Louis F. Payn,
Superintendent of Insurance, and made one
more mortal enemy. That was one of the times
he " saw " Senator Platt, whose lifelong political friend Payn was. But what would be
the use? None to my correspondent who
knows it all, yet does not understand. All the
rest of us have it by heart. And it would be
politics, which I said I would eschew. It *was*
politics for fair, for all the power of the machine, all of it and more, was opposed to the
Governor in his determination to displace this
man. But Roosevelt was right, and he won.
Let that be the record. When he was
gone from Albany the oldest lobbyist, starved
though he was, had to own that Roosevelt
fought fair, always in the open. His recourse
was to the people, and that was how he
won,—even in the matter of the civil service

bill, in which he trod hard on the toes of the politicians. We had a law, but they had succeeded in " taking the starch out of it." Roosevelt put it back. I think no man living but he could have done it. But they realized that they could not face him before the people on that, of all issues. And to-day my State has a civil service law that is as good as it can well be made, and we are so much better off.

I never liked Albany before, but I grew to be quite fond of the queer old Dutch city on the Hudson in those two years. It is not so far away but that I could run up after office hours and have a good long talk with the Governor before the midnight train carried me back home. Sometimes it was serious business only that carried me up there. I am thinking just now of the execution of Mrs. Place, who had murdered her stepdaughter and tried to brain her husband. It was a very wicked murder, but there was something about the execution of a woman that stirred the feelings of a lot of people, myself included. Perhaps it was largely a survival of the day of public hangings, which is happily past. But, more than

that, I had a notion that it would hurt his career. I think I told of it in " The Making of
an American " when it was all long over. I
certainly did not tell him. I knew better. But
I argued all through a long evening into the
midnight hour, until I had to grab my hat and
run for the train, that he should not permit it.
I argued myself to an absolute stand-still, for
I remember his saying at last impatiently:

" If it had only been a man she killed—but
another woman! " and I, exasperated and il-
logical: " Anyway, you are obliged to admit
that she tried hard enough to kill a man."

After I got back home he sent me a letter
which I may not print here. But I shall hand
it down to my children, and they will keep it as
one of the precious possessions of their father,
long after I have ceased to live and write.
One sentence in it I have no right to withhold,
for it turns the light on his character and way
of thinking as few things do:

" Whatever I do, old friend, believe it will be
because after painful groping I see my duty
in some given path."

So it was always with him. His duty was
made clear when the commission of experts he

had appointed reported that Mrs. Place was as sane and responsible as any of them, and public clamor had no power to move him from it.

I like to set over against her case another in which my argument prevailed, for it shows the man's heart, which he had often no little trouble to hide under the sternness imposed by duty. I knew the soreness of it then by the joy I saw it gave him to make people happy. Policeman Hannigan had been sent to Sing Sing for shooting a boy who was playing football in the street on Thanksgiving Day. He ran, and the policeman, who had been sent with special orders to clear the ball-players out of the block, where they had been breaking windows, ran after him. In the excitement of the chase he fired his pistol, and the bullet struck and slightly wounded the boy in the leg. The policeman was " broken " and sent to the penitentiary, and of the incident we made a mighty lever in the fight for playgrounds where the boys might play without breaking either windows or laws. And then I thought of the policeman in the prison, a young man with a wife and children and a clean record till then, and I asked the Governor to pardon him. Of course he had not meant to shoot; he was carried away, and now he had been punished enough. I have preserved the Governor's answer that came by next day's mail. It was written on the last day of the year 1899:

" DEAR JAKE:

" Happy New Year to you and yours, and as a New Year's gift take the pardon of the policeman Hannigan. The papers were forwarded to the prison this morning.

" Ever yours,

" THEODORE ROOSEVELT."

And so one man who that day was without hope started fair with the new year.

I wish I might go on and write indefinitely of those days and what they were to me: Of that dinner-party to some foreign visitors into which I, taking tea peacefully with Mrs. Roosevelt and the children, was suddenly catapulted by the announcement that through an unexpected arrival there would be thirteen at the table, a fact which would be sure to make some one of the guests uncomfortable, and at which the Governor kept poking quiet fun at me across the table, until I warned him with a look that I might even betray his perfidy, if he kept it up. Of how I kept admiring the Executive Mansion because Cleveland had lived in it, till he took me to the Capitol and showed me there the pictures of all his predecessors except Cleveland, who was stingy, he said, and wouldn't give the State his. Whereat I rebelled loudly, maintaining that it was modesty. Of the mighty argument that ensued, — a mock argument, for in my soul I knew that he thought as much of Cleveland as did I. Of these things I would like to tell, for they make the picture of the man to me, and perhaps I can smuggle it in later. But here, I suppose, I ought to remember the Governor, and therefore I shall not do as I would otherwise.

When I look back now to the day when he stood in the Assembly Chamber, with the oath of office fresh upon his lips, and spoke to his people, there comes to me this sentence from his speech: " It is not given to any man, nor to any set of men, to see with absolutely clear vision into the future. All that can be done is to face the facts as we find them, to meet each difficulty in practical fashion, and to strive steadily for the betterment both of our civil and social conditions."

Truly, if ever man kept a pledge, he kept that. He nursed no ambitions; he built up no machine of his own. He was there to do his duty as it was given to him to see it, and he strove steadily for the betterment of all he touched as Governor of the State that was his by birth and long ancestry, even as his father had striven in his day and in his sphere. He made enemies—God help the poor man who has none; but he kept his friends. When he was gone, a long while after, my way led me to Albany again. I had not cared much for it since he went. And I said so to a friend, an old State official who had seen many governors come and go. He laid his hand upon my arm.

"Yes," said he, "we think so, many of us. The place seemed dreary when he was gone. But I know now that he left something behind that was worth our losing him to get. This past winter, for the first time, I heard the question spring up spontaneously, as it seemed, when a measure was up in the legislature: 'Is it right?' Not 'Is it expedient?' not

THE TEN COMMANDMENTS

' How is it going to help me?' not ' What is it worth to the party?' Not any of these, but ' Is it right?' That is Roosevelt's legacy to Albany. And it was worth his coming and his going to have that."

So that was what we got out of his term as Governor—all of us, for the legacy is to the whole land, not only to my own State. As for him, all unconscious of it, he had been learning to be President, the while he taught us Henry Clay's lesson that there is one thing that is even better than to be President,—namely, to be right.

X

THE SUMMONS ON MOUNT MARCY

—

X

THE SUMMONS ON MOUNT MARCY

ON that summer day, three years ago, when the Republican party nominated Theodore Roosevelt for Vice-President, I was lying on my back, stricken down by sudden severe illness. My wife had telegraphed to him that I longed to see him; but in the turmoil of the convention the message did not get to him till the morning after the nominations were made. He came at once from Philadelphia, and it was then that I, out of pain and peril, heard from his own lips the story of his acceptance of the new dignity his countrymen had thrust upon him. "Thrust upon" is right. I knew how stoutly he had opposed the offer, how he had met delegation after delegation with the frank avowal that he could serve the party and the country better as Governor of New York, and I knew that that was his ambition; for his work at Albany was but half finished. It was his desire that the people should give him another term in his great office, unasked, upon the record of the two years that were drawing to a close. He had built up no machine of his own. He had used that which he found to the uttermost of its bent, and of his ability,—not always with the good will of the managers; but he had used it for the things he had in mind, telling the bosses that for all other legitimate purposes, for organization, for power, they might have it: he should not hinder them. Now, upon this record, with nothing to back him but that, he wished the people to commission him and his party to finish their work. It was thoroughly characteristic of Roosevelt and of his trust in the people as both able and willing to do the right, once it was clearly before them.

He knew well enough what was on foot concerning him. He was fully advised of the plans of his enemies to shelve him in the "harmless office" of Vice-President, and how they were taking advantage of his popularity in the West and with the young men

throughout the land to " work up " a strenuous
demand for him to fill the second place on the
ticket. So, they reasoned, he would be out of
the way for four years, and four years might
bring many things. As Vice-President he
would not be in 1904 anything like the candidate before the people which two years more as
Governor of the Empire State would make
him. Back of the spoils politicians were the
big corporations that had neither forgotten nor
forgiven the franchise-tax law that made them
pay on their big dividend-earning properties,
as any poor man was taxed on his home. Anything to beat him for Governor and for the
Presidency four years hence! The big traction
syndicates in the East made the pace: Roosevelt
for Vice-President! He was not deceived; but
the plotters were. Their team ran away with
them. The demand they desired came from
the West and swept him into the office. From
perhaps one State in the East and one in the
West it was a forced call. From the great
and bounding prairies, from the rugged mountain sides, and from the sunny western slope of
the Rockies, where they knew Roosevelt for
what he was, and loved him; from the young

men everywhere, from the men with ideals, it was a genuine shout for the leader who spoke with their tongue, to their hearts. Senator Wolcott spoke their mind when he brought him the nomination: " You, everywhere and at all times, stood for that which was clean and uplifting, and against everything that was sordid and base. You have shown the people of this country that a political career and good citizenship could go forward hand in hand. . . . There is not a young man in these United States who has not found in your life and influence an incentive to better things and higher ideals." Against such a force traditions went for nothing; it was strong enough to break more stubborn ones than that which made of the Vice-Presidency a political grave. In 1904 it was to be Roosevelt for President.

Roosevelt yielded. His friends were in despair; his enemies triumphed. At last they had him where they wanted him.

Man proposes, but God disposes. Now in joy, and again in tears and sorrow, do we register the decree. One brief year, and the nation wept at the bier of William McKinley. Of his successor the President of Columbia College wrote: " He was not nominated to satisfy or placate, but to succeed. The unspeakably cruel and cowardly assassin has anticipated the slow and orderly processes of law."

He himself, standing within the shadow of the great sorrow—though, light of heart, we knew it not—spoke these brave words to his people: " We gird up our loins as a nation with the stern purpose to play our part manfully in winning the ultimate triumph; and therefore we turn scornfully aside from the paths of mere ease and idleness, and with unfaltering steps tread the rough road of endeavor, smiting down the wrong and battling for the right, as Greatheart smote and battled in Bunyan's immortal story." [1]

The campaign of that year none of us has forgotten. An incident of it lives in my memory as typical of the spirit in which the people took his candidacy, and also with a sense of abiding satisfaction that one thing was done right, and at the right moment, in my sight. I was coming up from Chatham Square one night in the closing days of the canvass, when

[1] The concluding words of Vice-President Roosevelt's speech at the Minnesota State Fair, Minneapolis, Sept. 2, 1902.

a torch and a crowd attracted me to a truck
at the lower end of the Bowery, from which
a man was holding forth on the issues involved
in the national election. He was not an effective speaker, and the place needed that, if any
place did. The block was "the panhandlers'
beat," one of the wickedest spots in the world,
I believe. I stood and listened awhile, and the
desire to say a word grew in me until I climbed
on the wagon and, telling them I was a Roosevelt man, asked for a chance. They were willing enough, and, dropping tariff and the "honest dollar" that had very little to do with that
spot, I plunged at once into Roosevelt's career as Governor and Police Commissioner.
I thought with grim satisfaction, as I went on,
that we were fairly within sight of "Mike"
Callahan's saloon, where the fight over the excise law was fought out by Policeman Bourke,
who dragged the proprietor, kicking and
struggling all the way, to the Elizabeth Street
station. He had boasted that he had thrown
the keys of the saloon away, and that no one
could make him close on Sunday. Bourke was
made a sergeant, and Roosevelt and the law
won.

THE SUMMONS ON MOUNT MARCY

But of that I made no boast then. I told the people what Roosevelt had done and had tried to do for them; how we had traveled together by night through all that neighborhood, trying to enter into the life of the people and their needs. As the new note rose, I saw the tenement blocks on the east of the Bowery give up their tenants to swell the crowd, and was glad. Descrying a policeman's uniform on its outskirts, I reminded my hearers of how my candidate had stood for an even show, for fair play to the man without a pull, and for an honest police. I had got to that point when the drunken rounder who by right should have appeared long before, caromed through the crowd and shook an inebriated fist at me.

" T-tin s-soldier! " he hiccoughed. " Teddy Ro-senfeld he never went to Cu-u-ba, no more 'n, no more 'n—"

Who else it was that had never been to Cuba fate had decreed that none of us should know. There came, unheralded, forth from the crowd a vast and horny hand that smote the fellow flat on the mouth with a sound as of a huge soul-satisfying kiss. He went down, out of sight, without a word. The crowd closed in over him; not a head was turned to see what became of him. I do not know. Who struck the blow I did not see. He was gone, that was enough. It *was* enough, and just right.

Which reminds me of another and very different occasion, when I addressed a Sunday-evening audience in the Cooper Institute at the other end of the Bowery upon my favorite theme. The Cooper Institute is a great place, a worthy monument to its truly great founder. But its Sunday-evening meetings, when questions are in order, have the faculty of attracting almost as many cranks as did Elijah the Restorer to Madison Square Garden. I had hardly finished when a man arose in the hall and, pointing a menacing finger at me, squeaked out:

" You say Theodore Roosevelt is a brave man. How about his shooting a Spaniard in the back? "

I had been rather slow and dull up till then, in spite of my theme; but the fellow woke me right up. My wife, who had come over with me and sat in the audience, said afterward that she never saw a man bristle so suddenly in her life.

THEODORE ROOSEVELT AS VICE-PRESIDENT

COPYRIGHT, 1901, BY ARTHUR HEWITT

THE SUMMONS ON MOUNT MARCY

"The man," I cried out, "who says that is either a fool or a scoundrel. Which of the two are you?"

I don't believe he heard. His kind rarely do. They never by any chance get any other side of a subject than their own, for they never can shake themselves off for a moment. He stood pointing at me still:

"Does not Holy Writ say, 'Thou shalt not kill?'" he went on.

"Yes! and on the same page does it not say that 'Thou shalt not bear false witness against thy neighbor,' even if he is the President of the United States?"

The audience by this time was upon its feet, yelling its delight. It was what it wanted. The crank sat down. In the front row a red-faced Irishman jumped up and down like a jack-in-the-box, wildly excited.

"You let him alone," he shouted to the people, shaking his hat at them; "let Professor Riis alone. He can take care of himself. Teddy Roosevelt is the greatest man in the country"; and, turning half toward me, he shot up a fist like a ham and, grabbing mine, yelled out, "I druv him oncet!"

THEODORE ROOSEVELT

Crank after crank got up with their questions, and as I looked out over them bobbing in the amused crowd like corks on a choppy sea, there came into my head Solomon's precept to answer a fool according to his folly. The President's first message was just out.

" How shall we interpret it? " queried a pedantic spectacled loon, with slow deliberation checking the points off on his fingers; " shall we class it as an economic effort or as a political discourse, as a literary production or as a—"

" The President's message," I interrupted, " has just been rendered into the language of the blind, and *they* don't have any difficulty in making it out."

The meeting broke up in a great laugh, amid a storm of protests from the cranks whose fun was spoiled. They were not looking for information. They had come merely to hear themselves talk.

I guess it is no use beating about the bush, telling stories; I have to come to it. But I have n't got over the shock the news from Buffalo gave me up there in the Canadian wilderness. I hate to think of it.

Roosevelt had gone to join his children in

the Adirondacks, with the assurance of the doctors that President McKinley was mending, and in no danger. He had come straight to Buffalo at the first news of the murderous attempt upon the President's life, thereby giving great offense to the faultfinders, who could see in the Vice-President's solicitude for his friend and chief only a ghoulish desire to make sure of the job. And now, when he went with lightened heart to tell his own the good news, they cried out in horror that he went hunting while the President lay fighting death. They were as far from the truth then as before. He, knowing little and caring less what was said of him, was resting quietly with his wife and the children, who had been sick, at the Upper Tahawus Club on Mount Marcy. No one in that party had thought of hunting or play. Their minds were on more serious matters. It was arranged that they were all to go out of the woods on Saturday, September 14, on which day Mr. Roosevelt had summoned his secretary to meet him at his Long Island home. He had come from Buffalo only two days before. Friday found them all upon the mountain: the Vice-President, Mrs. Roosevelt, and their nephews, the two Robinson boys, and Mr. James McNaughton, their host. Ted, the oldest of the Roosevelt boys, had gone fishing. The rest, with two guides, formed the party.

Far up the mountain side there lies a pretty lake, the "Tear in the Clouds," whence the Hudson flows into the lowlands. There the party camped after a long and arduous tramp over the mountain trail. Mrs. Roosevelt had gone back with the children. From his seat on a fallen log Roosevelt followed the gray outline of Mount Marcy's bald peak piercing mist and cloud. Up there might be sunshine. Where they were was wet discomfort. A desire grew in him to climb the peak and see, and he went up. But there was no sunshine there. All the world lay wrapped in a gray, impenetrable mist. It rained, a cold and chilly rain in the clouds.

They went down again, and reached the wood-line tired and hungry. There they spread their lunch on the grass and sat down to it. Upon the quiet talk of the party there broke suddenly an unusual sound in that quiet solitude, the snapping of a twig, a swift step. A man came out of the woods, waving a yellow envelope in his hand.

Silence fell upon them all as they watched Mr. Roosevelt break it and read the message. It was brief: " The President's condition has changed for the worse.—CORTELYOU." That was all. He read it over once, twice, and sat awhile, the message in his hand, grave shadows gathering in his face. Then he arose, the food untouched, and said briefly: " I must go back at once."

They fell in behind him on the homeward trail. Silent and sad, the little procession wound its way through the gloomy forest. Dusk was setting in when they reached the cottage. No news was there. The Vice-President's secretary, warned in the early morning by despatches from Buffalo, had started for the mountains on a special train, but the road ended at North Creek, more than thirty miles away, and from there he had been telegraphing and telephoning all day that he would wait till Mr. Roosevelt came. Of this nothing was known on the mountain. The telephone line ended at the lower club-house —ten miles farther down, and the messages lay there. No one had thought of sending them up.

Mr. Roosevelt sent runners down at once to find out if there was any summons for him, and made ready for an immediate start before he changed his clothing. He was wet through. The dusk became darkness, and the hours wore far into the evening. He walked up and down alone in front of the cottage, thinking it all over. It could not be. He had arranged to be advised at once of the least change, and no word had come. Up to that morning all the bulletins were hopeful. There must be some awful mistake. Black night sat upon the mountain and no message yet. He went in to snatch such sleep as he could get. Too soon he might need it.

In the midnight hour came the summons. Mr. McNaughton himself brought the message: "Come at once." In ten minutes Mr. Roosevelt threw his grip into the buckboard that was hurriedly driven up, and gave the word to go.

How that wild race with death was run and lost—for before it was half finished President McKinley had breathed his last, and there was no longer any Vice-President hastening to his bedside—will never be told. But for a frightened deer that sprang now and then from the roadside, stopping in the brush to watch wideeyed the plunging team and the swaying lantern disappear in the gloom, no living thing saw it. The two in the wagon—the man on the driver's seat and the silent shape behind him —had other thoughts: the one for the rough trail which he vainly tried to make out through the mist; at any moment the wheels might leave their rut or crash against a boulder, and team and all be flung a hundred feet down a precipice. As for the other, his thoughts were far away at a bedside from which a dying man was whispering words of comfort to his weeping wife. Mechanically, when the driver turned to him with warning of the risks they were taking, he repeated, as if he had scarcely heard: " Go on—go right ahead! "

The new day was an hour old and over when the vehicle stopped at the lower club-house, mud-splashed from hub to hood. Here Mr. Roosevelt heard for the first time from his secretary, who had watched sleepless at the other end of the wire, the tragedy then passing into history in the city of Buffalo. Secretary Loeb knew the dangers of the mountain roads on a dark and rainy night, and pleaded with him to wait till morning.

"I will come right through, as quick as I can," was the answer he received; and before he could ring the telephone bell, Mr. Roosevelt was in his seat again, and the horses were plunging through the night toward the distant railroad.

Down hill and up, through narrow defiles, over bare hillsides where the wheels scraped and slid upon the hard rock and the horses' hoofs struck fire at every jump; on perilous brinks hidden in the shrouding fog, and tenfold more perilous for that; now and then a bog-hole through which the wheels of the buckboard sank to the hubs; past a little school-house where a backwood's dance was just breaking up, the women scattering in sudden fright as the traveler drove by. Then the wayside hotel with waiting horses in relay, and two thirds of the way was covered.

Once more the gloom and the forest; once more the grim traveler gazing ahead, ahead, as if he would pierce the veil of fate and wrest from it its secret, repeating his monotonous " Go on! Keep right ahead!" In the city by the lake William McKinley lay dead. Through the darkness rode the President, clinging obstinately to hope.

So the dawn came. As the first faint tinge of it crept into the night, and trees and rocks whirling past took on dim outlines, the steaming horses drew up at the railroad station at North Creek, where a puffing engine had been in waiting many hours. From the platform Secretary Loeb came down, bareheaded:

" The worst has happened," he said. " The President is dead."

So, to this man, who had been tried and found faithful in much, came the call to take his place among the rulers of the earth.

XI
WHAT HE IS LIKE HIMSELF
—

XI

WHAT HE IS LIKE HIMSELF

NOW that by good luck I have after
all presented in something like orderly
fashion the main facts in Theodore
Roosevelt's career,—of which every one knows
more or less, and which he regards as more or
less significant, according to his attitude toward the old college professor's prediction,
many years ago, that his students might rate
our people's fitness for self-government by the
headway Roosevelt made with his ideals and
ambitions—now that we have got so far, I can
hear my reader ask: "But about himself;
about the man, the friend? You promised to
tell us. We want to know." And so you shall.
I am going to tell you now,—at least, I am going to try. Here, a whole week, have I been
walking about the garden, upon which winter

had laid its rude hand and put all the flowers to sleep; only the wild thyme I brought down from the Berkshire Hills stands green and fragrant, as does the sunny field where I dug it, in my memory ever. A whole week have I walked about among the bare bushes, poking in the dead leaves, trying to think how. Something very learned and grand had come into my head. But how can you analyze your friend? Men's minds and men's motives you may analyze, if you care and have a taste that way,—and a pretty mess you will make of it more than half the time. But resolve a sunbeam, or a tear, into its original elements, and what do you get? So much oxygen, perhaps; so much salt—let the chemist tell in his learned phrase; and when all is told your sunbeam and your tear have escaped you. Whatever else you have, them you have not. No, I shall not try that. I shall tell you of him just as I knew him. I like him best that way, anyhow,—just as he is.

But first let me give fair warning: if there be any among my readers still-hunting for special privilege, let him get off right here; for he won't like him. Whether it be the Trust

that has nothing to conceal,—dear me, no!
—yet most strenuously objects to the public
knowing about its business; the corporation
with franchises paying big dividends but no
taxes; the labor leader who has stared himself
blind upon the dividends, and to whom the
pearly gates shall not swing unless they have
the union label on them; or the every-day dolt
who must have the railroad track between himself and his brother of darker skin, of different
faith or tongue or birthplace; who, like the
woman of the Four Hundred in Philadelphia,
" must be buried in St. Peter's churchyard
because, really, on resurrection day she must
rise with her own set "—whichever his own
particular folly in this land of no privilege
and of an equal chance, and wherever found,
he will be against Roosevelt, instinctively and
always. He will fight him at the polls and in
the convention; he will bet his money against
him, and pour it out like water across every
party line that held him before, and by the
measure of his success we can grade our own
grip on the ideal of the Republic. That was
what the professor I spoke of meant, and he
was right. And so are they, according to their

light. Roosevelt is their enemy, the enemy forever of all for which they stand.

Because he stands for fair play; for an even chance to all who would use it for their own and for their country's good; for a broad Americanism that cares nothing for color, creed, or the wherefrom of the citizen, so that, now he is here, he be an American in heart and soul; an Americanism that reaches down to hard-pan. " Ultimately," he said at Grant's Tomb, when Governor of New York,—" ultimately, no nation can be great unless its greatness is laid on foundations of righteousness and decency." And at Syracuse on Labor Day I saw ten thousand stirred by his words: " If alive to their true interests, rich and poor alike will set their faces like flint against the spirit which seeks personal advantage by overriding the laws, whether that spirit shows itself in the form of bodily violence by one set of men or in the form of vulpine cunning by another set of men." These are his professions. I know how they square with his practice, for I have seen the test put to him a hundred times in little things and in great, and never once did he fail to ask the question, if there was any doubt about it, after all was said and done, " Which is right? " And as it was answered, so was the thing done.

His ambition? Yes, he has that. Is it to be President? He would like to sit in the White House, elected by the people, for no man I ever met has so real and deep a belief in the ultimate righteousness of the people, in their wish to do the thing that is right, if it can be shown them. But it is not that. If I know anything of the man, I know this : that he would fight in the ranks to the end of life for the things worth fighting for, rather than reach out a hand to grasp the Presidency, if it were to be had as the price of one of the principles upon which his life has been shaped in the sight of us all. He might, indeed, quarrel with the party of a lifetime, for he would as little surrender his conscience to a multitude of men as to one,[1] and he has said that he does not number party loyalty with the Ten Commandments, firmly as he holds to it to get things done. Party allegiance is not a compelling force with him; he is the compelling force. " I believe

[1] Gov. Roosevelt's speech to the West Side Republican Club, New York, March, 1899.

very firmly," he said to the State Bar Association in New York, in 1899, " that I can best render aid to my party by doing all that in me lies to make that party responsive to the needs of the people; and just so far as I work along those lines I have the right to challenge the support of every decent man, no matter what his party may be." That is his platform, always was. In matters of mere opinion I can conceive of his changing clear around, if he were shown that he was wrong. I should expect it; indeed, I do not see how he could help it. It was ever more important to him to be right, and to do right, than to be logical and consistent.

And that really is his ambition, has been since the day he rose in the Assembly Hall at Albany and denounced the conspirators of his own party and of the other to their faces: to do the right, and to so do it in the sight of his fellow-men that they shall see that it is the right and follow it; that the young, especially, shall make the high and the right choice at the beginning of life that puts ever more urgent questions to the succeeding generations. That is the mainspring and the motive. " Because

he thinks he is so much better than all the rest?"
I can hear my cynical neighbor ask. No, but
because to him life is duty first, always; because
it gave him certain advantages of birth, of education, of early associations for which he owes
a return to his day and to his people. I wish
to God more of us felt like that; for until we
do our Republic will be more of a name and
of an empty boast than we have any right to
let it be. Sometimes, when, in the effort of
class privilege to assert itself here as everywhere, the fear comes over me that it will not
last, I find comfort in the notion that it has
hardly yet begun, and that it cannot be that
He in whose wise purpose men must grow
through struggling, will let it pass so soon.
A hundred years of the Republic, and we are
only beginning to understand that what it was
meant to mean, and alone can be made to mean,
is opportunity; that the mere fact of political freedom is in itself of little account, but
can be made of ever so much; that different
levels there will be in a democracy as in a mon-
archy, but not of rank nor, indeed, of wealth,
though for a while it may seem so; but according to our grasp of the idea of the respon-

sibilities of citizenship and its duties and standards. There is the cleavage, and his is the highest level who would serve all the rest. Service to his fellow-men: that is the key-note to Roosevelt's life, as faith in the Republic and love of country are its burning fire. Well did President Eliot, when he bestowed upon him the degree of his Alma Mater, call him a " true type of the sturdy gentleman and high-minded public servant in a democracy."

There! I freed my mind, anyhow. I was thinking, when I spoke of consistency, of the fellows who mistake stubbornness for principle, and what a beautiful mess they make of it. There came one of that kind to the Board of Health in Brooklyn, and wanted his landlord compelled to put a broken window-pane in. The landlord said it was not in the lease and he would n't do it. And for two weeks his wife had been sleeping under it, in danger of pneumonia every hour of the night.

" But," said they, " have you let her sleep there all this time without putting in the pane? "

" Yes, sir! " said he. " Yes, sir! I did it on principle! "

WHAT HE IS LIKE HIMSELF

But about himself. You know how he looks. To my mind, he is as handsome a man as I ever saw; and I know I am right, for my wife says so too, and that settles it. Which reminds me of the time I lectured in a New York town with a deaf man in the audience who was no friend of Roosevelt. The chairman introduced me with the statement that he had heard that the Governor called me " the most useful man in New York." My friend with the ear-trumpet did n't quite catch it, and was in high dudgeon after the meeting.

" Did n't I tell you Teddy Roosevelt ain't got no sense? " he cried. " The idea of calling that man Riis the most beautiful man in New York! Why, he is as plain as can be."

By handsome I do not mean beautiful, but manly. Stern he may, indeed, appear at times, though to my mind nearly all his portraits do him hideous injustice in that respect. I have seen but two that were wholly himself. One was a pen sketch of him on horseback at the head of his men, climbing some mountain ridge. There he had on his battle face, the dark look I have seen come in the middle of some pleasant chat with gay friends. I knew then that he was alone and that the burden was upon him, and I felt always as if, upon some pretext, any pretext, I would like to get him away where he could be by himself for a while. The other, curiously, was an old campaign poster from the days when he ran for Governor. It hung over my desk till the boys in the office, who used to decorate the volunteers' slouch-hat with more bows than a Tyrolese swain ever wore to the village fair, made an end of it, to my great grief. For it was the only picture of him I ever saw that had the smile his friends love. There was never another like it. And it is for them only. I have come into a room packed full of people crowding to speak with him, and seen it light up his face as with a ray of sunshine from a leaden sky, and his hand go up in the familiar salute I meet out West nowadays, but nowhere else. Odd how people, even those who should know him well, can misunderstand. " I saw him several times in Colorado," wrote one who likes him, after his recent Western trip, " and he pleased me very much by his growing tenderness toward men and animals. His chief weakness has always seemed to me his almost cruel strength." To me he has always seemed as tender as a woman. Perhaps they had been on the hunting-trail together; or on one of his long Washington walks that were the terror of his friends. I am told they lay awake nights, some of them, trembling for fear he might pick *them* out next.

By contrast there comes to me the recollection of a walk we took together in the woods out at Oyster Bay. It was after I had been sick, and some one had told him that I could not walk very fast, and must not, any more. So I infer; for we had not gone five furlongs at the old clipping gait, he a little ahead, thrashing through the bushes, when he suddenly came back and, taking my arm, walked very slowly, telling me something with great earnestness, to cover up his remorse. I have never anywhere met a man so anxiously considerate of a friend's weakness as he ever was and is, though happily in this instance there was no need of it. I have been learning to ride these days, and ride hard, to show him, and also to have the fun of going out with him again. I cannot think of anything finer.

It seems to me, when I think back now, that

all the time I have known him, with all the
burden and care of such a career as his on his
shoulders, he was forever planning some kind
act toward a friend, carrying him and his concerns with him incessantly amid the crowding
of a thousand things. His memory is something prodigious. I happened once to mention
to him that when next I came to Washington
I would bring my little boy.

" And don't forget," I said, " when you see
him to ask if he goes regularly to Sunday-
school." To his laughing inquiry I made answer that the lad would occasionally be tempted
by the sunshine and some game up by the golf-
grounds, whereupon I would caution him to
keep his record clear against the day when he
would see the President, who, being the boys'
as well as the papas' President, would naturally ask him if he " went regular." And of
course he must back me up in this; for little
boys remember, too. The thing had long since
gone out of my head when I brought Vivi to
the White House; but not so with him. He
took him between his knees and asked him, first
thing, if he went to Sunday-school like a good
boy; and so the day and my reputation were

saved, and the boy made happy; for he *had* kept his slate clean.

It was at that visit that, after a thorough inspection of the premises, the President asked the lad what he thought of the White House.

" Pretty good," said he. " But I like better to ride up and down in the elevator at the hotel." It was his first experience with an elevator, and he made full use of it.

The President considered him thoughtfully a moment. What visions of politicians and delegations passed before his mind's eye I know not; but it was with almost a half-sigh that he said: " So would I, my boy, sometimes."

That slouch-hat of his, by the way, at which some folks took umbrage, at the Philadelphia Convention, I don't believe he gave as much thought to, in all the years he wore it, or one like it, as did those good people in the three or four days of the convention. He did not wear it because the rough-riders did, but because it is his natural head-gear. He began it in Mulberry Street, and he has kept it up ever since. He hates a stovepipe, and so do I; but I thought to honor him especially one day, when I was going traveling with him, by

putting on mine; and all I got for it was, when
General Greene got into the carriage with a
straw hat on, a deep sigh of relief and an
" Oh, I am so glad you did n't come in a
top-hat," with a malicious gleam toward me.
Next time I leave it home. Perhaps it was to
pay me for being late. He had arranged to
pick me up at my home station, when going
through to the city; but his train was a full half-
hour ahead of time, and who could have fore-
seen that? What other President, do you suppose, would have waited fifteen minutes at the
depot with his special train while he sent up
to the house for me, and then received me with
a laugh?

That was characteristic of him, both the
waiting and the being ahead of time. It was
night, and there was nothing on the road to
hinder, so he just slammed through. In that
also he is a typical American in the best
sense: given a thing to be done, he makes sure
of the way and then goes ahead and does it.
" The way to do a thing is to do it," might be
his motto; it certainly is his way. But the man
who concludes from that that he runs at it headlong makes the mistake of his life. I know ab-

solutely no man who so carefully weighs all
the chances for and against, ever with the one
dominating motive in the background—" Is it
right?"—to steer him straight. In the Police
Department he surprised me over and over
again by his quick grasp and mastery of
things until then foreign to his experience.
He would propose some action and turn it over
to me for review because I had been there
twenty years to his one; and I would point out
reefs I thought he had forgotten. But not he;
he had charted them all, thought of every con-
tingency, and done it all in an hour, when I
would be poring over the problem for days,
perhaps weeks. And when it had all been gone
over he would say:

"There! we will do it. It is the best we can
do. If it turns out that there is anything
wrong, we will do it over again." But I do not
remember that he ever had to.

Mere pride of opinion he has none. No one
ever estimated his own powers, his own capa-
cities, more modestly than he. Something I
said one day brought this matter up, and few
things have touched me as did the humility with
which this strong man said: " I know the very

ordinary kind of man I am to fill this great office. I know that my ideals are commonplace. I can only insist upon them as fundamental, for they are that. Not in the least doing anything great, I can try, and I am trying, to do my duty on the level where I am put, and, so far as I can see the way, the whole of it." And I thought of his talk to the New York Chamber of Commerce on the " homely virtues " as a solvent of our industrial and other problems, and his counsel to every good citizen to be able and willing to " pull his own weight." He has to pull the weight of all of us along with his own. If these plain sketches help some who do not know him to make out how patiently, how thoughtfully he labors at it, how steadfastly he is on guard, I shall be glad I wrote them.

As I am writing this now, there comes to mind really the finest compliment I ever heard paid him, and quite unintentionally. The lady who said it was rather disappointed, it seemed. She was looking for some great hero in whom to embody all her high ideals, and, said she, " I always wanted to make Roosevelt out that; but, somehow, every time he did something that

seemed really great it turned out, upon looking at it closely, that it *was only just the right
thing to do."* I would not want a finer thing
said of me when my work is done. I am glad
I thought of it, for I know that he would not,
either. And it comes as near as anything
could to putting him just right.

Perhaps a good reason why he grasps things
so quickly and correctly is that he looks for
and tries to get at the underlying principles of
them; deals with them on the elementary basis
of right and fitness, divested of all the con-
ceit and the flummery which beset so many
things that come to the Executive of a great
nation. I had gone out to see him at Oyster
Bay, heavy with the anxieties of mothers all
over the land who had sons soldiering in the
Philippines. There was news of fighting every
day, but only the names of the killed or
wounded officers came by cable. There was a
War Department order against sending those
of the privates who fell, or who died of cholera;
and it resulted that when, say, Company H
of the Fifteenth Regiment had been in a battle,
every mother who had a boy serving in that
command went shivering with fear for six long

weeks before the mails brought word whether her boy was among the " thirteen private soldiers " who fell, or not. I had been asked to put the case to the President, and get him to cut the red tape, if possible; but, against expectation, I found a tableful of soldiers and statesmen at lunch, and I saw clearly enough that it would be hard to get the President's ear long enough.

But, as luck would have it, I was put beside General Young, fine old warrior, whom I had met before, and I told him of what was on my heart. He knew of no such order when he was in the Philippines, and we got into quite a little argument about it, which I purposely dragged out till there was a lull in the talk at the President's end of the table, and I saw him looking my way. I asked him if he knew of the order.

" What order? " said he; and I told him— told him of the mothers fretting for their boys all over the land. He looked up quickly at Adjutant-General Corbin, who sat right opposite. It was what I wanted. *He* knew.

" General," said Mr. Roosevelt, " is there such an order? "

THEODORE ROOSEVELT AT SAGAMORE HILL
PHOTOGRAPH BY ARTHUR HEWITT

WHAT HE IS LIKE HIMSELF

" Yes, Mr. President," said he; " there is."

" Why? " President Roosevelt wastes few words when in earnest about anything.

General Corbin explained that it was a measure of economy. The telegraph tolls were heavy. An officer had a code word, just one, to pay for, whereas to send the whole name and place of a private soldier under the Pacific Ocean might easily cost, perhaps, twenty-five dollars. The President heard him out.

" Corbin," he said, " can you telegraph from here to the Philippines? "

The General thought he might wait till he got to Washington; he was going in an hour.

" No," said the President; " no, we will not wait. Send the order to have the names telegraphed, now. Those mothers gave the best they had to their country. We will not have them breaking their hearts for twenty-five dollars or for fifty. Save the money somewhere else."

And he sent one of his rare smiles across the table, that made my heart light, and many another, from Maine to Texas. The order went out from the table, then and there, and, before we had finished our luncheon, was speeding under the sea to the far East.

I was an unintentional listener that day to the instructions Generals Young and Corbin received for their interview with Emperor William; they were about to go abroad. I doubt if ever greeting from the Executive of one great country to the head of another was more informal than that, and, equally, if there ever was a heartier.

" Tell him," said the President,—" tell the Emperor that I would like to see him ride at the head of his troops. By George, I would! And give him my hearty regards. Some day we shall yet have a spin together."

I hope they may. Those who know Mr. Roosevelt and have met the Emperor say that in much they are alike: two strong, masterful young men of honest, resolute purpose, and the faith in it that gets things done. But they face different ways: the one toward the past, with its dead rule " by the grace of God "; the other to the light of the new day of the living democracy that in its fullness shall make of the man a king in his own right, by his undimmed manhood, please God.

WHAT HE IS LIKE HIMSELF

I am told that the generals carried out their instructions in the spirit in which they were given, to the great delight of the Emperor, who asked General Corbin if he had ever before been in Germany. The General said not in that part of it.

" Which part, then? " asked the Emperor.

" In Cincinnati and St. Louis, your Majesty," responded the General, and the Emperor laughed till his sides shook. His brother had told him about those cities.

We went home in the same train, and General Young and I sat together in the car. I had been reading the " Sunday-school Times," and it lay on the opposite seat so that the General could read the title. He regarded it fixedly for a while, then poked it cautiously with the end of his stick, as who should say, " I wonder—now—what—" I read him like a book, fighting-man to the finger-tips that he is, but said nothing until curiosity got the better of him and he asked some question about it. Then I reached out for the paper.

" Oh, yes, General! This is the paper for you. See here,"—and I pointed to a column telling of all the big fighters in the Old

Testament, the Maccabees and the rest, with
their battles in chronological order, and what
they were about. The old warrior's eyes
kindled.

"Well, I never!" he said, and took the paper
up with an evident respect that contrasted com-
ically with his gingerly way of before. The
General of the Army will forgive me for telling
on him. He has my heartiest friendship and
regard. I expect to see him yet conduct a
Sunday-school on Maccabean lines, and we
shall all be glad. For that is what we and the
Sunday-school want.

But though ordinarily President Roosevelt
is the most democratic of men, he does not lack
a full measure of dignity when occasion requires it. The man whom I had seen telling
stories of his regiment to a school full of little
Italian boys in the Sullivan Street slum, had,
a little while after the interview with the generals, to receive a delegation from the French
people, and it happened that one of the guests
of that day was present. He told me that he
never was prouder of the President and of his
people than when he saw him meet the distinguished strangers. And so were they. They

spoke of it as the honor of a lifetime to be received by President Roosevelt.

It is just the human feeling that levels all differences and makes kin of all who have claim to the brotherhood; searches out and lays hold of the good streak in man wherever it is found. It accounts for the patience I have known him to exercise where no one would have expected it; and it accounts, to my way of thinking, for the friendships that have existed between him and some men as far from his way of thinking in all other respects as one could well imagine. I know. I ever had a soft spot for "Paddy" Divver, with whom I disagreed in all things that touched his public life as fundamentally as that was possible. But there was a mighty good streak in "Paddy," for all his political ill-doings. As a police judge he came as near doing ideal justice in all matters that had nothing to do with politics as any man who ever sat on the bench, and he was not bothered in his quest by the law half as much. I remember—but no, "Paddy" is dead, and the story shall remain untold. Some would not understand; but I did, for I had in mind the Kadi administering justice in the gate, and this fellow needed that kind if the law *was* powerless to reach him.

I told the President when, at his recent visit to Ellis Island, he had personally heard the case of a woman detained under the rules, but whom my friend on the police bench would have discharged with a ten-dollar bill in her pocket, that his judgment was almost equal to "Paddy's," whereat he laughed in amusement, for our dealings—"Paddy's" and mine—had been the cause of his poking fun at me before. But when I told him of what befell me in Chicago on a visit there, he said he should presently have to cut my acquaintance, and I was bound to agree with him. I had gone to the ball of the Hon. Bath-house John's constituents, to see the show; and when their great leader heard of my being from New York, nothing was too good for me. Evidently, he took me for "one of the b'ys," for when the champagne had opened wide the floodgates of liberality and companionship, he addressed me confidentially in this wise:

"B'y, the town is yours! Take it in. Go where ye like; do with it what ye like. And if ye run up against trouble—ye know, the

b'ys will have their little scrap with the police—
come to me for bail—any crime! any crime!"

Say not that the freedom of the city by the
lake has not been conferred upon me. It has.
Even Mayor Harrison will have to own it.

But this chapter has outrun its space, and I
have n't yet said what I had in mind concerning
Theodore Roosevelt. I will drop reminiscences and settle right down to it now.

XII
THE DESPAIR OF POLITICIANS
—

XII

THE DESPAIR OF POLITICIANS

WE had been summoned to the White
House, my wife and I. I say,
" summoned " on purpose, because
we had carefully avoided Washington; it was
enough for us to know that he was there. But
he would not have it, and wrote threateningly
that he would send a posse if we did n't come.
So we went. I do not think I ever saw a
prouder woman than my wife when the
President took her in to dinner. I heard her
ask him if her·smile reached from ear to ear
because she felt like it. And I was proud
and glad, for so it seemed to me that she had
at last come to her rights, and I where there
was nothing more to wish for. But withal
I felt a bit unhappy. I had thought to do
him the highest honor I could by wearing the

cross King Christian gave me, but it turned out
that among the dozen diplomats and other
guests no one wore any decoration save myself, and I did n't like it. The President saw,
I think, that I was troubled, and divined the
reason in the way he has. He slipped up behind me, at the first chance, and said in my ear:
" I am so much honored and touched by your
putting it on for me." So he knew, and it was
all right. The others might stare.

It is just an instance of the loyalty that is
one of the traits in the man which bind you to
him with hoops of steel once you are close to
him. It takes no account of condition in life:
good reason why his Rough-Riders worshiped
the ground he trod on. When they ate bacon
and hard-tack, that was his fare; and if there
was any better to be had, they shared even. It
was that trait that came out in him the night
a half-witted farmer drove to Sagamore Hill
on purpose to shoot him. He was in the library with Mrs. Roosevelt when the voice of
the fellow, raised in angry contention with the
secret service guard under the trees, attracted
his attention. He knew the officer was alone,
out of ear-shot of the others down at the barn,

and he acted at once upon the impulse to go to his aid. Before Mrs. Roosevelt could put in a word of warning, he was out on the veranda in the moonlight, his white shirt bosom making a broad target for the frenzied man who had a cocked pistol in the buggy. He whipped up his horse when he saw the President, and made straight for him, but before he had gone a step the secret service man had him down and safe. I joined Mrs. Roosevelt the next day in demanding the President's promise that he would not do it again, and he gave it good-humoredly, insisting that he had been in no danger. "But," said he, "he was fighting my fight, and he was alone. Would you have had me hide, with him, perhaps, one against two or three?" It was a hard question to answer. We could only remind him that he was the President, and not simply Theodore Roosevelt, and had the whole country to answer to.

I think I never knew a man who so utterly trusts a friend, once he has taken him to his heart. That he does not do easily or offhand; but once he has done it, there is no reservation or secret drawback to his friendship. It is a splendid testimony to the real worth of human nature that his trust has rarely indeed been betrayed. Once his friend, you are his friend forever. To the infallible test he rings true: those who love him best are those who know him best. The men who hate him are the scalawags and the self-seekers, and they only distrust him who do not know him. He never lost a friend once made. Albert Shaw summed it all up in a half-impatient, wholly affectionate exclamation when he was telling me of a visit he had made to Washington to remonstrate with the President.

"I never knew a man," he said, "to play so into the hands of his enemies. He has no secrets from them; he cannot bear a grudge; he will not believe evil; he is generous and fair to everybody; he is the despair of his friends. And, after all, it is his strength."

And the reason is plain. Had I not known him, I would have found it long ago in his insistence that the America of to-day is better than that of Washington and Jefferson. A man cannot write such things as this he wrote of Lincoln without meaning every word of it and acting it out in his life:

"The old-school Jeffersonian theorists believed in a strong people and a weak government. Lincoln was the first who showed how a strong people might have a strong government and yet remain the freest on earth. He seized, half unwittingly, all that was best in the traditions of Federalism. He was the true successor of the Federal leaders, but he grafted on their system a profound belief that the great heart of the nation beats for truth, honor, and liberty."

Now do you wonder that he is the despairing riddle of the politicians the land over, the enemy, wherever they meet, of all the after-us-the-deluge plotters? They have not the key to the man; and if they had, they would not know how to use it. The key is his faith that the world is growing better right along. In their plan, it may go to the devil when they have squeezed it for what there is in it for them. They can never comprehend that the man who believes in the world growing better helps make it better, and so, in the end, is bound to win; or why he is closer to the people than any man since Lincoln's day. It is all a mystery and a nuisance to them, and I am glad it is.

THEODORE ROOSEVELT

Speaking of Lincoln, one of the few times I have seen Roosevelt visibly hurt was when some yellow newspaper circulated the story that he had had Lincoln's portrait taken from the wall in the White House and hung in the basement, and had his own put up in its place. Ordinarily he takes no notice of attacks of that kind, except to laugh at them if they are funny; but this both hurt and saddened him, for Lincoln is his hero as he is mine. It was at the time the White House was undergoing alterations, and the pictures were hung in the basement to preserve them, or there would have been no pictures by this time. Some of the old furniture was sent away and sold at auction, as it had to be, there being no other legal way of disposing of it. Even the chairs in the cabinet-room his official family had to buy at five dollars each, when they wanted them as keepsakes. Among the things that went to the auction-shop was a sideboard from the dining-room, and promptly the report was circulated that it had been presented by the temperance women of Ohio to Mrs. Hayes, and that President Roosevelt had sold it to a saloon-keeper. Resolutions began to come from Women's Christian Temperance Union branches East and West until Secretary Loeb published the facts, which were these: that no sideboard had ever been presented to Mrs. Hayes, but an ice-pitcher with stand, long since placed in a Cincinnati museum, where it now is. The sideboard was a piece of furniture bought in the ordinary avenues of trade during President Arthur's term, and of no account on any ground. But long after the true story had been told the resolutions kept coming; for all I know, another one is being prepared now in some place which the lie on its travels has just reached.

I know what it was that hurt, for I had seen Roosevelt recoil from the offer to strike an enemy in the Police Department a foul blow, as from an unclean thing, though that enemy never fought fair. He does. "I never look under the table when I play," he said, when the spoilsmen beset him in their own way at Albany; "they can beat me at that game every time. Face to face, I can defend myself and make a pretty good fight, but any weakling can murder me. Remember this, however, that if I am hit that way very often, I will take to the open, and the blows from the dark will only help me in an out-and-out fight." " Clean as a hound's tooth," one of his favorite phrases, fits himself best. It was the showing that an honest man's honest intentions were not accepted at their face value that saddened and hurt, for it smudged the ideal on which he builds his faith in his fellow-man.

It was only yesterday that a friend told me of an experience he had at Albany while Roosevelt was Governor. He was waiting in the Executive Chamber with, as it happened, a man of much account in national politics, a Federal office-holder occupying a position second to none in the land in political influence. The gentleman had come to Albany to press legislation for good roads, being interested in the manufacture of bicycles or automobiles, I forget which. While they waited, in came the Governor. There were but two other persons in the room, an old farmer and his daughter, evidently on a holiday. They were looking at the pictures with much interest. Mr. Roosevelt went over to them and engaged them in conversation, found out where they were from, said he was glad to see them, and pointed out one or two of the portraits especially worth seeing. Then he shook hands and bade them come back as often as they pleased. It was clear that they did not know who the friendly man was. When they went out he came straight across to the Federal official.

"Now, Mr. ——," he said, shaking his finger at him, "the legislature has appropriated every cent it is going to this year for good roads, and nothing you can say will change their minds or mine on that subject. So you can save yourself the trouble. It is no use." And, turning to my friend, "Do you wish to see me?" But his amazement was so great that he said no, making up his mind on the spot to talk to the Governor's secretary. The official had gone away at once.

I recommend this anecdote to the special perusal of the friends who think Roosevelt is playing to the galleries when he hails the plain man cordially. He does it because he likes him. They might have seen him one day in an elevated car, when we were riding together, get up to give his seat to a factory-girl in a worn coat. I confess that I itched to tell her who he was, but he let me have no chance.

THEODORE ROOSEVELT

We were talking about a public institution I wished to see reformed, and he was anxious to know if there was any way in which he could help. " If there is," he said, " let me." But there was not, and I was sorry for it; for the matter concerned the growing youth and the citizenship of to-morrow, and I knew how near his heart that lay.

I have been rambling along on my own plan of putting things in when I thought of them, and I cannot say that I feel proud of the result; but if from it there grows a personality whose dominating note is utter simplicity, I have not shot so wide of the mark, after all. For that is it. All he does and says is to be taken with that understanding. There again is where he unconsciously upsets all the schemes and plots of the politicians. They don't understand that " the game can be played that way," and are forever looking for some ulterior motive, some hidden trap he never thought of. Bismarck, it is said, used to confound his enemies by plumping out the truth when, according to all the rulers of the old-school diplomacy, he should have lied, and he bagged them easily. Roosevelt has one fundamental convic-

tion, that a frank and honest man cannot in the
long run be entangled by plotters, and his life
is proving it every day. To say that the world
can be run on such a plan is merely to own that
the best there is in it, the cynics to the contrary
notwithstanding, is man himself, which is true
and also comforting in the midst of all the
trickery contrived to disprove it.

It was the simplest thing in the world, when
the nation was justly up in arms about the
Kishineff atrocity, to do what Roosevelt did,
and that was why he did it. Friends from all
over wrote to me to warn the President not to
get into trouble with Russia by mixing up in
her domestic troubles. Mischief would be sure
to come of it. The Czar would n't receive the
Jews' petition, in the first place, and we would
have to take a rebuke if we tried to send it.
But the President did not need my advice or
theirs. I laughed when I read in the paper
how he cut that Gordian knot that was so full of
evil omen: merely telegraphed *the whole petition* to the American minister in St. Peters-
burg, with orders to lay it before the Czar and
ask whether he would receive it if transmitted
in the usual way. To which the Czar returned

a polite answer, as he was in duty bound, that
he would not; but *he had received it,* all of it,
and the results were not long in showing themselves.[1] For days the cables had groaned under
guarded threats of what would happen if we
tried to send the petition over, and that was
what happened!

Perhaps it is in a measure this very unex-
pectedness—more pity that it is unexpected—
of method that is no method, but just common
honesty, that has got abroad among people
the notion that he is a man of impulse, not
of deliberate, thoughtful action. More of it,
probably, is due to his quick energy that sizes
things up with marvelous speed and accuracy.
In any event, it is an error which any one can
make out for himself, if he will merely watch
attentively what is going on, and what has been
going on since Roosevelt came prominently
into the public eye. What position did he ever
take hastily that had to be abandoned, ready
as he would have been to quit it had he been
shown that he was wrong? He shut the saloons
as Police Commissioner, since the law he had

---

[1] What they will amount to or how long they will last is another
matter. The Muscovite is a slippery customer.

sworn to enforce demanded it. And though politicians claimed that he alienated support from the administration he stood for, he taught us a lesson in civic honesty that will yet bear fruit; for while politics are allowed to play hide-and-seek with the majesty of the law, that majesty is a fraud and politics will be unclean. As Health Commissioner he gave the push to the campaign against the old murderous rookeries that broke the slum landlord's back; abuse and threats were his reward, but hope came into the lives of two million souls in my city, and all over the land those who would help their fellow-men took heart of hope because of what he did. He offended a thousand spoilsmen as Civil Service Commissioner, and earned the gratitude and confidence of a Democratic President; but who now who has sense would have had him do otherwise?

He compelled the corporations to pay just taxes, and though they swore to knife him for it, the Court of Appeals has said it was fair and just. I have heard some people blaming him hotly for interfering in the anthracite coal strike. Their cellars were full of coal that winter, but their factory bunkers were not;

and, singularly, I remember some of those very men, when their pocket-books were threatened, predicting angrily that "something would happen" if things were not mended. And in that they were right; something would have happened. Perhaps that was a reason why he interfered. However, I shall come back to that yet. But where is there to-day a cloud on the diplomatic horizon because of the "impulsiveness" of the young man in the White House? When were there so cordial relations with the powers before—with England, with France, with Germany that sends the President's personal friend to represent her here? Does any one imagine William of Germany seeks personal advantage in that? Then he is not as smart as the emperor. For the first time in the memory of diplomats, I imagine, they are able to discuss things, up at the White House, just as they are; yet they don't take a trick, and they know it.

Roosevelt is as far as possible from being rash. When people say it I am always reminded of the difference between the Danish word *rask* and the English *rash*. *Rask* means quick, resolute. That is what he is. He arrives at a conclusion more quickly than any one I ever knew; but he never jumps at it. He has learned how to use his mind, and all of it, that is why. " I own," writes a friend to me from Ohio, " that he has been right so far every time. But next time where will we find him? " Learn to think a thing out, as he does; and when you have done it, ask yourself, " Which, now, is right? " and you will know. Watch and you will see that the real difference between his critics and him is this: they chase all round the compass for some portent of trouble " if they do this or do that," and in the end throw themselves headlong on some course that promises safety; whereas, he goes calmly ahead, seeking the right and letting troubles take care of themselves if they must come. That is the quality of his courage which some good people identify as a kind of fighting spunk that must be in a broil at regular intervals. I do not suppose there is a less emotional man in existence than Secretary Root of the War Department. He was the only one, the newspapers said, in the cabinet who would not give five dollars for his chair as a souvenir. He could put the money to better use, and he did n't need the chair. But when he came to take leave of Roosevelt, this is what he wrote: " I shall carry with me unabated loyalty to your administration, confidence in the *sound conservatism* and patriotic unselfishness of your policy, . . . and I shall always be happy to have been a part of the administration directed by your sincere and rugged adherence to right and devotion to the trust of our country." Blame me for partiality, if you will, but against Secretary Root the charge does not justly lie. He just spoke the truth.

Verily, I think that were the country to be called upon to-morrow to vote for peace or for war, his voice would be for peace to the last hour in which it could be maintained with honor. Slower than Lincoln would he be to draw the sword. But once drawn for justice and right, I should not like to be in its way, nor should I be lazy about making up my mind which way to skip. I remember once when I got excited—over some outrage perpetrated upon American missions or students in Turkey, I think. It was in the old days in Mulberry Street, and I wanted to know if our ships could not run the Dardanelles and beard the Turk in his capital.

" Ah," put in Colonel Grant, who was in the Police Board, " but those forts have guns."

" Guns! " said Roosevelt; nothing more. It is impossible to describe the emphasis he put upon the word. But in it I seemed to hear Decatur at Tripoli, Farragut at Mobile. Guns! The year after that he was busy piling up ammunition at Hongkong. They had guns at Manila, too. And Dewey joined Decatur and Farragut on the record.

I said Roosevelt had learned to use all of his mind. To an extraordinary degree he possesses the faculty of concentrating it upon the subject in hand and, when it has been disposed of, transferring it at will to the thing next in order, else he could not have written important historical works while he was Police Commissioner and Governor. Whether this is all the result of training, or a faculty born in him, I do not know. Napoleon had the same gift. I have sat with Mr. Roosevelt in his room at Police Headquarters and seen him finish his correspondence, dispose of routine matters in hand, and at once take up dictation of some magazine article, or a chapter in one of his books where he left off the day before. In five minutes he would be deep in the feudal days, or disentangling some Revolutionary kink in Washington's time, and seemingly had lost all recollection of Mulberry Street and its concerns. In the midst of it there would come a rap at the door and a police official would enter with some problem to be solved. Roosevelt would stop in the doorway, run rapidly over it with him, decide it, unless it needed action by the Board, and after one nervous turn across the floor would resume dictating in the middle of the sentence where he had stopped. I used to listen in amazement. It would have taken me hours of fretting to get back to where I was.

One secret laugh I had at him in those days. The room was a big square one, with windows that had blue shades. When he got thoroughly into his dictation—during which he never permitted me to leave; he would stay any movement of mine that way with a detaining gesture, and go right on—he made, unconsciously, a three-fourths round of the office, and when he passed each window would seize the shade-cord and give a little abstracted pull, bringing it down an inch or so, until by degrees the room was in twilight. By the fourth or fifth round he would acquire a game leg. One of his knees stiffened, and thereafter he would drag around with him a disabled limb to the end of the chapter, when he as suddenly recovered the use of it. I sometimes wonder if his game leg takes part in cabinet discussions. If it does, I will warrant the country will know of it, though it may not be able to identify the ailment. I give it as a hint to nations that may be meditating provocation of Uncle Sam. I should beware of provoking the President's game leg.

Which reminds me of the time we plotted against him in Mulberry Street, putting in quarters at a raffle at an Italian feast. The raffle was for a sheep which we hoped to win, and to lead to Headquarters in procession, headed by the Italian band. We even took Mr. Roosevelt around and made him spend five quarters in his own prospective undoing. But we did n't win the sheep. It was the Widow Motso on the third floor back who did; and when I heard her rapturous cry, and saw her hug the sheep then and there, and kiss its black nose, I was glad the plot miscarried. The widow killed the sheep the next day. Roosevelt never knew what he had escaped. It was all my way of paying him for calling sheep "woolly idiots," whereas they are my special pets. There is no animal I like so much as a sheep. It is so absolutely, comfortably stupid. You don't have to put sense into it, because you can't.

I am tempted to tell you of more jokes, for he loves one dearly so long as it hurts no one's feelings. Two timid parsons found that out who saw Mr. Gilder shake hands with him at a reception and express the hope that "he would not embroil us in any foreign war."

"What," cried the President, "a war? with me cooped up here in the White House! Never, gentlemen, never!" I wonder what the parsons thought when they caught their breath. Perhaps the man I met on a railroad train and told the story to, expressed it. "There, you see," said he; "he says it himself. If he could get away he would start a fight." His fun sometimes takes the form of mock severity with intimate friends. In the swarm of officials that

came to wish the President a happy New Year
were the Civil Service Commissioners, headed
by John R. Procter, his old colleague, all men
after his own heart. Mr. Procter still laughed
at the recollection of that New Year's greeting when I saw him last.[1] The President
drew himself up at their approach and re-
marked with stiff dignity, loud enough for all
to hear:

"The moral tone of the room is distinctly
lowered."

No one need ever have any fear that Roosevelt will get the country into an undignified
position. If unfamiliarity with a situation
should lead him off the track, take my word for
it he will take the straight, common-sense way
out, and get there. The man who in his youth
could describe Tammany as "a highly organized system of corruption tempered with ma-
levolent charity," and characterize a mutual acquaintance, a man with cold political ambitions
whom I deemed devoid of sentiment, as having
both, but "keeping them in different com-

---

[1] Poor friend! As the printer brings me the proof of this, I
hear of his death. There was never a more loyal heart, a more
dauntless soul than his. The world is poorer, indeed, for his
going from us.

partments," can be trusted to find a way out of any dilemma.

If he got into one, that is to say. I know him well enough to be perfectly easy on that score. It seems to me that all the years I have watched him he has tackled problems that were new and strange to him, with such simple common sense that the difficulties have vanished before you could make them out; and the more difficult the problem the plainer his treatment of it. We were speaking about the Northern Securities suits one day.

" I do not claim to be a financial expert," he said; " but it does not take a financial expert to tell that, the law being that two small men shall not combine to the public injury, if I allow two big men to do it I am setting up that worst of stumbling-blocks in a country like ours, which persuades the poor man that if he has money enough the law will not apply to him. That is elementary and needs no training a financier. So in this matter of publicity of trust accounts. Publicity hurts no honest business, and is not feared by the man of straight methods. The man whose methods are crooked is the man whose game I would block. Those who complain know this perfectly well, and their complaining betrays them. Again, with honest money—I did not need any financier to tell me that a short-weight dollar is not an honest dollar to pay full-weight dollar debts with."

I thought of the wise newspaper editors who had been at such pains to explain to us how Roosevelt was responsible for the "unsettled condition" of Wall Street. Their house of cards, built up with such toilsome arguing, was just then falling to pieces, and the news columns in their own papers were giving us an inside view of what it was that had been going on in the financial market, and why some securities remained "undigested." Water and wind are notoriously a bad diet; and what else to call the capitalization of a concern at thirty millions that rated itself at five, would puzzle, I imagine, even a "financial expert."

And has he then no faults, this hero of mine? Yes, he has, and I am glad of it, for I want a live man for a friend, not a dead saint—they are the only ones, I notice, who have no faults. He talks, they say, and I hope he will keep on, for he has that to say which the world needs

to hear and cannot hear too long or too often.
I don't think that he could keep a scrap-book,
if he tried. I am sure he could not. It is not
given to man once in a thousand years to make
and to record history at the same time. But
then it is not his business to keep scrap-books.
I know he cannot dance, for I have seen a
letter from a lady who reminded him of how
he " trod strenuously " on her toes in the old
dancing-school days when the world was
young. And I have heard him sing—that he
cannot do. The children think it perfectly
lovely, but he would never pass for an artist.
And when the recruit in camp accosted him
with " Say, are you the Lieutenant-Colonel?
The Colonel is looking for you," he did not
order him under arrest or jab him with his
sword, but merely told him to " Come with me
and see how I do it "; which was quite irregular, of course, if it did make a soldier out of
a raw recruit. Oh, yes! I suppose he has his
faults, though all these years I have been so
busy finding out good things in him that were
new to me, that I have never had time to look
for them. But when I think of him, gentle,
loyal, trusting friend, helpful, unselfish ever,

champion of all that is good and noble and honest; when I read in an old letter that strays into my hands his brave, patient words: " We have got to march and fight for the right as we see it, and face defeat and victory just as they come "; and in another: " As for what ⸺ say of my standing alone, why, I will if I must, but no one is more heartened by such support as you give than I am "—why, I feel that if that is the one thing I can do, I will do that; that, just as he is, with or without faults, I would rather stand with him and be counted than anywhere else on God's green earth.   For, standing so, I know that I shall count always for our beloved country, which his example and his friendship have taught me to love beyond my own native land.   And that is what I would do till I die.

There is yet one side of Theodore Roosevelt upon which I would touch, because I know the question to be on many lips; though I approach it with some hesitation.   For a man's religious beliefs are his own, and he is not one to speak lightly of what is in his heart concerning the hope of heaven.   But though he is of few public professions, yet is he a reverent man, of practice, in private and public, ever in accord with the highest ideals of Christian manliness. His is a militant faith, bound on the mission of helping the world ahead; and in that campaign he welcomes gladly whoever would help. For the man who is out merely to purchase for himself a seat in heaven, whatever befall his brother, he has nothing but contempt; for him who struggles painfully toward the light, a helping hand and a word of cheer always. With forms of every kind he has tolerant patience—for what they mean. For the mere husk emptied of all meaning he has little regard. The soul of a thing is to him the use it is of. Speaking of the circuit-riders of old, he said once: " It is such missionary work that prevents the pioneers from sinking perilously near the level of the savagery against which they contend. Without it, the conquest of this continent would have had little but an animal side. Because of it, deep beneath and through the national character there runs that power of firm adherence to a lofty ideal upon which the safety of the nation will ultimately depend."

He himself declared his faith in the closing

words of his address to the Young Men's Christian Association in New York City the night before he surrendered his stewardship as Governor into the hands of the people; and so let him stand before his countrymen and before the world:

" The true Christian is the true citizen, lofty of purpose, resolute in endeavor, ready for a hero's deeds, but never looking down on his task because it is cast in the day of small things; scornful of baseness, awake to his own duties as well as to his rights, following the higher law with reverence, and in this world doing all that in him lies, so that when death comes he may feel that mankind is in some degree better because he has lived."

XIII
AT HOME AND AT PLAY
—

XIII

AT HOME AND AT PLAY

THE *Sylph* had weighed anchor and was standing out for the open, sped on her way by a small gale that blew out of a bank of black cloud in the southeast. The sailors looked often and hard over the rail at the gathering gloom, the white-caps in the Sound, and the scudding drift overhead, prophesying trouble. A West Indian cyclone that had destroyed the crops in Jamaica and strewn our coast with wrecks had been lost for two days. It looked very much as if the *Sylph,* carrying the President from Oyster Bay to New York, had found it. And, indeed, before we reached the forts that guard the approach to the city, a furious hurricane churned the waters of the Sound and of the clouds into a maddening whirl in which it seemed as if so small a ship could never live. A tug went down within hail; but only the sailors knew it. The passengers had been cleared from the deck, that the *Sylph* might be stripped of its awnings and every rag of canvas which might help throw it over if the worst happened. We went gladly enough, for the deck had ceased to be a comfortable or even a safe place,—all except the President, who had fallen out of the general conversation and into a corner by himself, with a book. A sailor confronted him with an open knife in his hand.

" Mr. President," he said, " orders are to cut away "; and without any more ado he slashed at the awning overhead, cutting its fastenings. The President woke up and retreated. Following him down into the cabin, I came upon Mrs. Roosevelt placidly winding yarn from the hands of the only other woman passenger. They were both as calm as though Government tugs were not chasing up the river as hard as they could go to the rescue of our boat, supposed to be in peril of shipwreck.

But at the moment I am thinking of, the hurricane was as yet only a smart blow. We were steaming out past Centre Island, under the rugged shore where Sagamore Hill lay hid among the foliage. The President stood at the rail surveying the scenes he loves. Here he had played as a boy, and dreamed a boy's dreams; here he had grown to manhood; here his children were growing up around him, happy and healthy boys and girls. We passed a sandy bluff sloping sheer into the Sound from under its crown of trees.

" See," he said, pointing to it. " Cooper's Bluff! Three generations of Roosevelts have raced down its slope. We did, only yesterday. Good run, that! "

And as the *Sylph* swept by I made out three lines .of track, hugging each other close,—a man's long, sturdy stride and the smaller feet of Archie and Kermit racing their father down-hill. Half-way down they had slipped and slid, scooping up the sand in great furrows. I could almost hear their shouts and laughter ringing yet in the woods.

Sagamore Hill is the family sanctuary, whither they come back in June with one long sigh of relief that their holiday is in sight, in which they may have one another. No longer to themselves, it is true. The President is not permitted to be alone even in his own home.

THEODORE ROOSEVELT

But still they have days of seclusion, and nights,—that greatest night in the year, when the President goes camping with the boys. How much it all meant to him I never fully realized till last Election day, when I went with him home to vote. The sun shone so bright and warm, when he came out from among his old neighbors, who crowded around to shake hands, that a longing came over him for the old place, and we drove out to Sagamore Hill to catch a glimpse of it in its Indian-summer glory. Four dogs came bounding out with joyous barks and leaped upon him, and he caressed them and called them by name, each and every one, while they whined with delight, —" Sailor-boy " happiest of the lot, a big, clumsy, but loyal fellow, " of several good breeds," said the President, whimsically. They followed him around as he went from tree to tree, and from shrub to shrub, visiting with each one, admiring the leaf of this and the bark of that, as if they were personal friends. And so they were; for he planted them all. Seeing him with them, I grasped the real meaning of the family motto, *Qui plantavit curabit,* that stands carved in the beam over the door looking north toward the hill with the cedars, where the soil is warm and full of white pebbles, and it is nice to lie in the grass when strawberries are ripe.

Roses were blooming still, and heliotrope and sweet alyssum, in Mrs. Roosevelt's garden, and down at the foot of the long lawn a wild vine crept caressingly over the stone that marks the resting-place of the children's pets. " Faithful Friends " is hewn in its rough face, with the names of " Susie," " Jessie," and " Boz." How many rabbits, rats, and guinea-pigs keep them company in their ghostly revels I shall not say. No one knows unless it be Kermit, who has his own ways and insists upon decent but secret burial as among the inalienable rights of defunct pets. It was his discovery, one day in the White House, that a rabbit belonging to Archie lay unburied in the garden a whole day after its demise, which brought about a court-martial in the nursery. Ted, the oldest brother, was Judge-Advocate-General, and his judgment was worthy of a Solomon.

" It was Archie's rabbit," he said gravely, when all the evidence was in, " and it is Archie's funeral. Let him have it in peace."

Poor " Susie "—ill named, for " she " was a

he—came nearer to provoking irreverence in
me, by making me laugh in church, than anything that has happened since I was a boy. I
had come out on a Sunday, and finding the
President's carriage at the church, went in to
join in the worship while waiting for him.
" Susie " lay in the vestibule, and at sight of
me manifested his approval by pounding the
floor with his club tail until the sound of it re-
verberated through the building like rolling
thunder. The door opened, and a pale young
man came out to locate the source of the dis-
turbance. Discovering it in " Susie's " tail, he
grabbed him by the hind legs and dragged him
around so that the blows might fall on the soft
door-mat. But " Susie," pleased with the extra attention paid him, hammered harder than
ever, and in his delight stretched himself so far
that his tail still struck the hollow floor. I was
convulsed with laughter, but never a smile
crossed the countenance of the proper young
man. He studied " Susie " thoughtfully, made
a mental diagram of his case, then took a fresh
hold and dragged him around, this time to a
safe harbor, where he might wag as he would
without breaking the Sabbath peace. I am

glad I sat five seats behind Mr. Roosevelt during the rest of the service, and that he knew nothing of " Susie's " doings; for if he had turned his head and given me as much as one look, I should have broken right out laughing and made a scandal.

When we drove back to the village that November day I caught him looking back once or twice toward the house in its bower of crimson shrubs, and I saw that his heart was there. You would not wonder if you knew it. I never go away from Sagamore Hill without a feeling that if I lived there I would never leave it, and that nothing would tempt me to exchange it for the White House, with all it stands for. But then I am ten years older than Theodore Roosevelt; though it isn't always the years that count. For I think if it came to a vote, the children would carry my proposition with a shout. Not that Sagamore Hill has anything to suggest a palace. Quite the contrary: it is a very modest home for the President of the United States. On a breezy hilltop overlooking field and forest and Sound, with the Connecticut shore on the northern horizon, its situation is altogether taking. The house is comfortable,

filled with reminders of the stirring life its
owner has led in camp and on the hunting-trail,
and with a broad piazza on the side that catches
the cool winds of summer. But it is homelike
rather than imposing. It is the people themselves who put the stamp upon it,—the life they
live there together.

Truly, together. The President is boy with
his boys there. He puts off the cares of state
and takes a hand in their games; and if they
lagged before, they do not lag then. It is he
who sets Josiah, the badger, free, and bids all
hands skip, and skip lively; for Josiah's one
conscious aim, when out of his cage, appears to
be to nip a leg,—any leg, even a Presidential
leg, within reach,—and he makes for them all
successively in his funny, preoccupied way. Josiah, then a very small baby badger, was heaved
on board the Presidential train out in Kansas
last year, by a little girl who shouted his name
after the train, and was brought up on a nurs-
ing-bottle till he cut his teeth. Since then he has
been quite able to shift for himself. At present he looks more like a small, flat mattress,
with a leg under each corner, than anything
else. That is the President's description of

him, and it is a very good one. I wish I could
have shown you him one morning last summer
when, having vainly chased the President and
all the children, he laid siege to Archie in his
hammock. Archie was barelegged and pru-
dently stayed where he was, but the hammock
hung within a few inches of the grass. Josiah
promptly made out a strategic advantage there,
and went for the lowest point of it with snapping jaws. Archie's efforts to shift continuously his center of gravity while watching his
chance to grab the badger by its defenseless
back, was one of the funniest performances I
ever saw. Josiah lost in the end.

The President himself teaches his boys how
to shoot; he swims with them in the cove and
goes with them on long horseback rides, start-
ing sometimes before sunrise. On fine days, as
often as he can get away, luncheon is packed in
the row-boat and he takes the whole family
rowing to some distant point on the shore,
which even the secret service men have not discovered, and there they spend the day, the
President pulling the oars going and coming.
Or else he takes Mrs. Roosevelt alone on a little
jaunt, and these two, over whose honeymoon

the years have no dominion, have a day to themselves, from which he returns to wrestle with powers and principalities and postmasters with twice the grip he had before; for she is truly his helpmeet and as wise as she is gentle and good.

When he wants to be alone, he dons a flannel shirt, shoulders an ax, and betakes himself to some secluded spot in the woods where there are trees to fell. Then the sounds that echo through the forest glade tell sometimes, unless I greatly mistake, of other things than lifeless logs that are being smitten,—postmasters let us say. I remember the story of Lincoln, whom one of the foreign ambassadors found pacing the White House garden in evident distress, at a time when Lee was having his own way with the Union armies; whereat the ambassador expressed his regret that the news from the field so distressed the President.

" From the field? " said Mr. Lincoln. " If that were all! No, it is that wretched postmastership of Brownsville that makes life a burden."

I have met Mr. Roosevelt coming in with his ax, and with a look that told of obstinate knots smashed—yes, I think they were smashed. I fancy tougher things than post-masters would have a hard time resisting the swing of that strong and righteous arm bound on hewing its way; wolves howling in the woods would n't stay it, I know,—not for a minute.

The great day is when he goes camping with the boys. The Sagamore Hill boys and their cousins whose summer homes are near plan it for months ahead. A secluded spot alongshore is chosen, with good water and a nice sand beach handy, and the expedition sets out with due secrecy, the White House guards-men being left behind to checkmate the report-ers and the camera fiends. Mr. Roosevelt is sail-ing-master and chief of the jolly band. Along in the afternoon they reach their hiding-place; then bait and fishing-poles are got ready—for they are real campers-out, not make-believes, and though they have grub on board, fish they must. When they have caught enough, the boys bring wood and build a fire. The Presi-dent rolls up his sleeves and turns cook.

" Um-m! " says Archie; " you oughter taste my father's beefsteak! He tumbles them all in together,—meat, onions, and potatoes,—but, um-m! it is good."

I warrant it is, and that they eat their fill!

THEODORE ROOSEVELT

I have n't forgotten the potatoes I roasted by the brook in the wood-lot when I was a boy. No such potatoes grow nowadays.

Afterward, they sit around the fire, wrapped in blankets, and tell bear-stories and ghost-stories, while the children steal furtive glances at the shadows closing in upon the circle of flickering light. They are not afraid, those children. The word is not in the Sagamore Hill dictionary. The spectacle of little Archie, hatless, guiding a stalwart Rough-Rider through the twilight woods, telling him to follow his white head and not be afraid of bogies,—they won't hurt him,—is a joy to me forever. But when owls are hooting in the dark woods I like to hug the fire myself. It feels twice as good then.

When the stars shine out in the sky over-head, they stretch themselves with their feet to the fire, roll up in their blankets, and sleep the untroubled sleep of the woods. The sun, peeping over the trees, finds them sporting in the cool, salt water; and long before the day begins for the world of visitors they are back home, a happy, roistering crew.

The Roosevelts have found (if they have

not always had it; certainly the President's father did) the secret that binds families together with bonds which nothing can break: they are children with their boys and girls. How simple a secret, yet how many of us have lost it! I did not even know I was one of them, or what it was that had come between me and my little lad—the one who figured out after hours of deep study, when our second grandchild was born, that now he was " two uncles " —until one bright day last summer when I went fishing with him. I wanted to know where he went when he disappeared for whole days at a time; and when I volunteered to dig the bait by a new method that made the worms come up of themselves to locate a kind of earthquake I was causing, he took me by many secret paths to a pond hidden deep in the woods a mile away, which was his preserve. There we sat solemnly angling for shiners an inch long, with bent pins on lines of thread, and were nearly eaten up by mosquitoes. But to him it was lovely, and so it was to me, for it gave me back my boy. That evening, on the way home, his boyish hand stole into mine with a new confidence. We were chums now, and all was well.

THEODORE ROOSEVELT

When they were little, the Roosevelt boys and girls went to the Cove school, which is the public school of the district, where the children of the gardener and the groom go, as well as those of their employers if they live there in the school season. Now, in Washington, the Roosevelts follow the same plan. The public school first, as far as it will carry the children to advantage, thereafter the further training for college. It is the thoroughly sound and sensible way in which they do all things in the Sagamore Hill family. So only can we get a grip on the real life we all have to live in a democracy of which, when all is said and done, the public school is the main prop. So, and in no other way, can we hold the school to account, and so do we fight from the very start the class spirit that is the arch enemy of the republic. If it could be done that way, I would have it ordered by law that every American child, be its parents rich or poor, should go certain years to public school. Only it cannot be done that way, but must be left to the citizens' common sense that in the end has to be counted with everywhere.

All real children are democrats if left to their

THEODORE ROOSEVELT, JR.

PHOTOGRAPH BY ARTHUR HEWITT

AT HOME AND AT PLAY

natural bent, and the Roosevelt children are
real children. At Groton I met Ted, the oldest, with his arm in a sling, a token from the
football game and also from a scrap he had had
with another lad who called him " the first boy
in the land " and got a good drubbing for it.
" I wish," said Ted to me in deep disgust, " that
my father would soon be done holding office.
I am sick and tired of it."

It was not long after that that Ted fell ill
with pneumonia, and his brother Archie sent
him his painfully scrawled message of sympathy: " I hop you are beter." His father keeps
it, I know, in that sacred place in his heart
where lie treasured the memories of letters in
childish scrawl that brought home even to the
trenches before Santiago, with the shrapnel
cracking overhead.

There are other lessons than spelling and
grammar to be learned in Washington,—lessons of democracy, too, in their way. I have
heard of the policeman of the White House
Squad who was discharged for cause, and appealed to the little lad who answers roll-call
with the police on holidays and salutes the sergeant as gravely as the men in blue and brass.

Archie heard him out. Appeal to his father direct was cut off—the policeman knew why. But Senator Lodge, who is next friend of the President and is supposed to have a " pull," lives in Massachusetts Avenue, opposite Archie's school. That was it.

" You come around," were Archie's directions to his friend, " to the Force School tomorrow, and we will see what Lodge can do about it."

What " Lodge did " I don't know. I know it would have been hard for me to resist.

It was the privilege of Mr. Roosevelt, when he was nearer home, to give the children at the Cove school their Christmas gifts, and the memory of those occasions is very lively in Oyster Bay. Mr. Roosevelt made a good Santa Claus, never better than when he was just home from the war, with San Juan hill for a background. That time he nearly took the boys' breath away. Nowadays some one else has to take his place; the gifts come, as in the past, and the little " coves " are made happy. But the President comes into their lives only twice or three times a year—at Christmas and when he comes home for his vacation; perhaps on the Fourth of

AT HOME AND AT PLAY

July. Mrs. Roosevelt is part of it all the time, and a very lovely because a loving part of life in the little village. When I hear of her going about among its people, their friend and neighbor in the true sense, I think of her husband's father, the elder Theodore, who systematically took one day out of six for personal visitation among his poor friends; and how near they, both he and she, have come to the mark which the rest of us go all around and miss with such prodigious toil and trouble. Neighborliness,—that covers the ground. It is all that is needed.

They have a sewing-circle in Oyster Bay, the St. Hilda chapter of the Society of Christ Church, which the Roosevelts attend; and of its twenty-odd members, embracing the wives of the harness-maker, the conductor, the oyster-man,—the townspeople whom she has known all her married life,—there is no more faithful attendant at the Thursday-afternoon meetings than Mrs. Roosevelt. She brings her own thimble and cotton, and hems and sews with the rest of them the little garments of outing-flannel or unbleached muslin that are worn by the child cripples in the House of St. Giles,

Brooklyn, the while she gossips with them and tells all about the fine doings in Washington. I saw not long ago in a newspaper that some thoughtless woman who had demanded of Mrs. Roosevelt a gift for a church fair, and had received a handkerchief hemmed by herself, had sent it back with the message that something better was wanted. I hope this which I am writing here will come under her eye and make her sorry for what she did. At that very time the President's wife, with six children whose bringing up she supervises herself, and with all the social burdens of the mistress of the White House upon her shoulders, was patiently cutting and sewing a half-dozen nightgowns for the little tortured limbs of her crippled friends, and doing it all herself for love's sake. She had brought them with her from Oyster Bay and finished them in the White House, where, I suppose, the church-fair woman thought she was being amused to keep from perishing of ennui.

They recall in that sewing-circle the days of the war, when Mrs. Roosevelt, walking down from the hill every Thursday to their meeting, and never betraying by word or look the care that gnawed at her heart, grew thin and pale as the days went by with news of fighting and her husband in the thick of it; till on the day of San Juan hill the rector's wife caught her impetuously into her embrace before them all, and told her that Colonel Roosevelt was a hero, without doubt, " but you are three."

And they tell, while they wipe a tear away with the apron corner, of the consumptive girl lying in her bed longing for the bright world which she would never see, to whom the then Vice-President's wife brought back from the inauguration ball her dance-card and her bouquet, and all the little trinkets she could gather for her in Washington, to make her heart glad. No wonder they think her a saint. There are those in Washington, in need and in sorrow, I am told, who would think so, too, did they know the whence of the helping hand that comes just in time. It was so in Albany, I know. No one ever appealed to the Governor's wife without having his case intelligently and sympathetically inquired into, so that she might know exactly how to help. Mrs. Roosevelt does not believe in wasting anything, least of all sweet charity. With her husband she wisely maintains that the poorest service one can render his neighbor is to carry him when he ought to walk.

As for the St. Hilda circle, its measure was full last summer when Mrs. Roosevelt took it out in a body on the *Sylph* to the naval review in the Sound, and the great ships gave them the Presidential salute,—or the *Sylph,* anyway, which was the same thing. Were they not on board, its honored guests?

The same simple way of living that has always been theirs at home, they carried with them to the White House. I do not know how other Presidents lived, for I was never there before, but I imagine no one ever led a more plain and wholesome life than the Roosevelts do. I cannot think that there was ever a family there that had so good a time. The children are still the mother's chief care. They have their hour that is for them only, when she reads to them or tells them stories in her room, and at all other hours they are privileged to intrude except when, on Tuesday, their mother entertains the cabinet ladies in the library. She is never too busy to listen to their little stories of childish pleasure and trouble, and they bring

to her everything, from the first dandelion
Quentin found in the White Lot to the latest
prank of Algonquin, the calico pony that was
smuggled up in the elevator to Archie when
he was sick with the measles. Algonquin is
about the size of a big Newfoundland dog,
but twice as lively with his heels. That was a
prank of the stable-boy, aided and abetted, I
imagine, by the doorkeeper, who had been a
boy himself, and to whom the swiftly flashing
legs of Archie in the corridors of the old building are like spring come again. They all love
him; no one can help it.

But I must not be tempted to write about
the children, since then there would be no end,
and this is a story of their father.

I might even be led to betray the secret of
the morning battles with pillows when the
children, in stealthy, night-robed array, am-
bush their father and compel him to ignomin-
ious surrender if they catch him " down."
That is the rule of the game. I remember
the morning when they came swarming down
about him, rejoicing in their victory, and his
sober counsel to them to go slow thenceforth,
for Rose, their maid, whom they brought with

them from Oyster Bay, and whom wild horses could n't drag away from the Roosevelts, had protested that they mussed the beds too much. I have read of President Jackson making an isolated ward of the White House, and himself nursing a faithful attendant who was stricken with the smallpox, when his fellow-servants had run away; and of Lincoln laughingly accepting General Grant's refusal of the dinner Mrs. Lincoln had planned in his honor, because he had " had enough of the show business." The Colonel of the Rough-Riders bowing obediently before the law of the household, and retreating before Rose where she was rightfully in command, belongs with them in my gallery of heroes; and not a bit less hero does he seem to me, but more.

The White House in its new shape—or, rather, as restored to the plan that was in the minds of the builders—is in its simple dignity as beautiful a mansion as any land has to show, altogether a fitting residence for the President of the American Republic. The change is apparent to the casual visitor as soon as he enters the great hall, where the noble white pillars have been set free, as it were, from their hideously incongruous environment of stained glass and partition, and stand out in all their massive beauty. Really, the hall is as handsome a place as I have ever seen. Upstairs, where the public does not come, a wide corridor, I should think quite twenty feet, that is in itself a cozy living-room, with its prevailing colors dark green and gray, runs the whole length of the building from east to west, and upon it open the family rooms and the guest-rooms. The great hall makes a splendid ball-ground, as I know from experience, for I joined Ethel and Archie in a game there, which they would have won by about 99 to 0, I should say, if there had been any score, which there was n't. At the east end of the hall is the President's den, where the lamp burns late into the small hours many a night when the world sleeps without. There he keeps the swords and the sticks with which he takes vigorous exercise when he cannot ride. The woodman's ax he leaves behind at Oyster Bay.

The day begins at exactly 8:30 at the White House. The President himself pours the coffee at breakfast. It is one of his privileges, and he looks fine as host. I can almost hear my woman reader say, " What do they eat at a White House breakfast? " Oatmeal, eggs and bacon, coffee and rolls—there is one morning's menu. I don't think they would object to my telling, and I like to think that in thousands of homes all over our land they are sharing the President's breakfast, as it were. It brings us all so much nearer together, and that is where we belong. That was why I told of the children's play. And if there is any who thinks that his sporting with the little ones when it is the hour of play makes him any less fitted for the work he has to do for all of us,—why, he never made a bigger mistake. Ask the politicians and the place-seekers who come to see him in the early hours of the afternoon, and hear what they think of it.

From breakfast to luncheon the President is in his office, seeing the people who come from everywhere to shake hands, or with messages for the Chief Magistrate.

Along in the afternoon the horses are brought up and the President goes riding with Mrs. Roosevelt or alone. Once I heard him tempt Secretary Root to go, and the Secretary agreed if he would guarantee that Wyoming, the horse he offered him, would not kneel. He was averse to foreign customs, he said.

" Yes," laughed the President, " you are a good American citizen, and home ways are good enough for you."

I have a ride on Wyoming coming to me, and I am glad. I was cheated out of it the last time, because Washington had so tired me out that the President would not take me. And Wyoming can kneel if he wants to. I think I would let him jump a fence with me where his master led. I guess I know how his Rough-Riders felt.

That was the only time Washington tired me out. I had come to help tackle its slums, for it has them, more 's the pity. Ordinarily it is one of my holiday cities: I have three, Washington, Boston, and Springfield, Massachusetts. As to Boston and Springfield, I suppose it is just because I like them. But Washington is a holiday city to me because he is there. When he was in Albany that was one. To Washington I take my wife when we want to be young again, and we go and sit in the theater and weep over the miseries of the lovers, and rejoice

with them when it all comes right in the end.
There should be a law to make all lovers happy
in the end, and to slay all the villains, at least
in the national capital. And then, nowadays,
we go to the White House, and that is the best
of all. I shall never forget the Christmas before last, when I told the President and Mrs.
Roosevelt at breakfast of my old mother who
was sick in Denmark and longing for her boy,
and my hostess's gentle voice as she said,
" Theodore, let us cable over our love to her."
And they did. Before that winter day was
at an end (and the twilight shadows were steal-
ing over the old town by the bleak North Sea
even while we breakfasted in Washington) the
telegraph messenger, in a state of bewilder-
ment,—I dare say he has not got over it yet,—
brought mother this despatch:

" THE WHITE HOUSE, Dec. 20, 1902.
" MRS. RIIS, RIBE, DENMARK:
" Your son is breakfasting with us. We send
you our loving sympathy.
" THEODORE AND EDITH ROOSEVELT."

Where is there a mother who would not get
up out of a sick-bed when she received a mes-

sage like that, even though at first she would not believe it was true? And where is the son who would not cherish the deed and the doer forever in his heart of hearts? But it is the doing of that sort of thing that is their dear delight, those two; and that is why I am writing about them here, for I would like every one to know them just as they are. Here is a friend 'way out in Kansas, whose letter came this minute, writing, " the President who walks through your pages is a very heroic and kingly figure, a very Arthur among his knights at the round table." Truly the President is that. I think we can all begin to make it out, except those who are misled and those in whose natures there is nothing to which the kingly in true manhood appeals. But could I show you him as he really is, as husband, father, and friend, you would have to love him even if you disagreed with him about everything. You just could n't help it any more than could one of the old-time employés in the White House who stopped beside me as I stood looking at him coming across from the Executive Office the other day.

" There he is," said he, and his face lighted up. "I don't know what there is about that man to make me feel so. I have seen a good many Presidents come and go in this old house, and I liked them all. They were all good and kind; but I declare I feel as if I could go twice as far and twice as quick when he asks me to, and do it twice as gladly."

I guess he knows, too, how his Rough-Riders felt about their Colonel.

XIV
CHILDREN TRUST HIM

—

XIV

CHILDREN TRUST HIM

WHEN the President came back from his long Western trip, I went to meet him on the Long Island ferry. I had myself returned from the Western country a little while before, a very tired man, though I had only to lecture once each night; and when I remembered his experience on that record-breaking journey I expected to meet a jaded, worn-out man. But his powers of physical endurance are truly marvelous. I found him as fresh, to all appearances, as if he had been off in the woods on a hunt instead of shaking hands with and being entertained by half the nation. No doubt going home was part of it; for he knew how they had counted the days to his return at Sagamore Hill, and now an hour or two—then he should see them.

THEODORE ROOSEVELT

His eyes fairly danced as he sat down to tell
me of the trip. There was so much, he said,
that it would take a month. And then, as in
mind he went back over the thousands of miles
he had traveled, the Sunday quiet of a little
Kansas prairie town, and a picture from the
service that brought the farmers in from fifty
miles around, stood out among all the rest.
The children came to his car to take him to
church, and when the people had all been
seated two little girls for whom there was no
room stood by his pew. He took them in
and shared his hymn-book with them, and the
three sang together, they with their clear girl-
ish voices, he with his deep bass. They were
not afraid or embarrassed; he was just their
big brother for the time. And there was the
tenderness in his voice I love to hear as he
told me of them.

"You should have seen their innocent little
faces. They were so dainty and clean in their
starched dresses, with their yellow braids
straight down their backs. And they thanked
me so sweetly for sharing the book with them
that it was a hardship not to catch them up
in one's arms and hug them then and there."

CHILDREN TRUST HIM

Some of the party told me of the reception that followed, and of the little fellow who squirmed and squirmed in the grasp of the President's hand, twisting this way and that, in desperate search of something, until Mr. Roosevelt asked him whom he was looking for.

"The President," gasped the lad, twisting harder to get away, for fear he would lose his chance. And then the look of amazed incredulity that came into his face when the man who still had him by the hand said that he was the President. He must have felt as I did when I first met King Christian in Copenhagen, and learned who the man in the blue overcoat was, with whom I had such a good time telling him all about my boyish ambitions and my father and home, while we climbed the stairs to the picture exhibition in the palace of Charlottenborg. The idea of a real king in an overcoat and a plain hat! I had had my doubts about whether he took off his crown when he went to bed at night.

That is the boy of it, I suppose; and they are all alike. If any, you would think the precocious youngster from the East-side Jewry would be excepted; but he is not. I have a fairly representative specimen in mind, who wrote home from his vacation in Maine, " Tom Reed has seen me twice." But when at last the privilege was vouchsafed to President Roosevelt, speech and sense forsook our East-sider, and he stood and looked on, gaping, the fine oration he had committed to memory clean gone out of his head. He explained his break after the President was gone.

" Why," he gasped, " he was just like any other plain-clothes man! "

A ribbon or sash, at least, with a few stars and crosses, a fellow might have expected. And, when you come to think of it, it is not so strange. Look at the general of the army in gala suit, and at the President, his commander-in-chief. Which makes me think again of Mr. Cleveland, who, when he was governor, togged out his staff in the most gorgeous clothes ever seen, and when heading it on his way to a public function, himself in plain black, was stopped by an underling, who took one glance at the procession and waved it back.

" The band goes the other way," he said.

Long years after, Mr. Cleveland had not stopped laughing at the recollection of the look that sat upon the faces of the gold-laced company of distinguished citizens.

But I was thinking of President Roosevelt's affection for children. It is just the experience of an unspoiled nature that reaches out for what is pure and natural. I remember that the day we were making the trip of the tenement-house sweat-shops together, we came, in one of the Italian flats, upon a little family scene. A little girl was going to confirmation, all dressed in white, with flowers and veil. She stood by her grandmother's chair in the dingy room, a radiant vision, with reverently bowed head as the aged hand was laid in trembling benediction upon her brow. The Governor stopped on the threshold and surveyed the scene with kindling eyes.

"Sweet child," he said, and learned her name and age from the parents, who received us with the hospitable courtesy of their people. "Tell them," to the interpreter, "that I am glad I came in to see her, and that I believe she will be always as good and innocent as she is now, and a very great help to her mother and her venerable grandmother." That time I did get a chance to tell them who it was that had come to the feast, so that it might add to the pleasure of the day for them. I just sneaked back and told them.

The children usually take to him, as he to them, in the same perfect good faith. We saw it in Mulberry Street, after he had gone, when two little tots came from over on the East Side asking for " the Commissioner," that they might obtain justice. I can see them now: the older a little hunchback girl, with her poor shawl pinned over her head and the sober look of a child who has known want and pinching poverty at an age when she should have been at play, dragging her reluctant baby brother by the hand. His cheeks were tear-stained, and his little nose was bruised and bloody, and he was altogether an unhappy boy, in his rôle of " evidence," under the scrutiny of the big policeman at the door. It was very plain that he would much rather not have been there. But the decrees of fate were no more merciless than his sister's grasp on him as she marched him in and put the case to the policeman. They had come from Allen Street, then the Red Light District. Some doubtful " ladies " had moved into their tenement, she explained, and

the other tenants had " made trouble " with the
police. The " ladies," locating the source of
the trouble in their flat, had seized upon the
child and " punched " his nose. They had
even had to send for a doctor. She unrolled
a bundle and showed a bottle of medicine in
corroboration. Her brother had suffered and
the household had been put to expense. Seeing
which, she had collected her evidence and come
straight to Police Headquarters to " see the
Commissioner." Having said it, she waited
calmly for directions, sure that when she found
the Commissioner they would get justice.

And they did get it, though Roosevelt was
no longer there. It was for him they had come.
Nothing that happened in all that time showed
better how deep was the mark he left. It was
his legacy to Mulberry Street that the children
should come there seeking justice, and their
faith was not to be put to shame.

In those days he would sometimes slip away
with me from Headquarters for an hour with
the little Italians in the Sullivan Street Industrial School, or some other work of the Children's Aid Society, in which his father had
borne a strong hand. It was after the first

McKinley election that we surprised Miss
Satterie's school (in Sullivan Street) at their
Christmas-tree. They were singing " Children
of the Heavenly King," and the teacher, with
the pride in her pupils that goeth before a
fall, according to the proverb, held up the
singing without warning, and asked:

" Children, who is this heavenly King? "

It was not a fair question, with a small bat-
talion of pink-robed dolls nodding from the
branches of the tree, and ice-cream being
brought in in pails. Heaven enough in Sullivan Street for them. just then. There was a
dead silence that was becoming painful when
a little brown fist shot up from a rear bench.

" Well, Vito! " said the teacher, relieved,
" who is he? "

" McKinley," piped the youngster. He had
not forgotten the fireworks and the flags and
the brass bands. Could anything be grander?
And all in honor of McKinley. What better
proof that he must be the King—of Sullivan
Street anyway, where heaven had just found
lodgment?

When Roosevelt had been elected governor,
we went over together for the last time; for

it was getting to be hard for him to go around without gathering a crowd, and I saw that he did not like it. In one of his letters not long ago he spoke of the old days, and our expeditions, and of how he wished we could do again what we did then, for he had ever a great desire to get close to the real life of the people. It was a natural sympathy for his honest but poorer neighbor, for whom he had battled ever since life meant more to him than play. His errand being one of friendly interest, and not of mere curiosity, there was never any danger of his seeming to patronize by his presence, though, if he thought he detected the signs of it, he quickly took himself out of the way. With the children there was, of course, never any peril of that, and they were chums together without long introduction. " I suppose we could not even go among them nowadays without their having to call out the police reserves," he complained in his letter. Though he was followed by a cheering crowd on our last visit to the Sullivan Street School, it had not yet quite come to that. He pulled his coat collar up about his face, and we escaped around the corner.

THEODORE ROOSEVELT

The big brown eyes of the little lads grew bigger and darker yet that day as he told them of his regiment, and of his Italian bugler who blew his trumpet in their first fight, telling the Rough-Riders to advance under cover, or to charge, until a Spanish bullet clipped off the two middle fingers of the hand that held the bugle. Then he went and had it dressed and came back and helped carry in the wounded, all through the rest of the fight, with his damaged hand. He told them of his standard-bearer who carried the flag right through a storm of bullets that tore it to shreds; of how his men were such good fighters that they never gave back an inch, though a fourth of them all were either killed or wounded; and yet no sooner was the fighting over than they all gave half of their hardtack to the starving women and children who came out of Santiago. And he showed them that true manhood and tenderness toward the weak go always together, and that the boy who was good to his mother and sister and little brother, decent and clean in his life, would grow up to be the best American citizen, who would always be there when he was wanted. They almost for-

got to applaud when he stopped, so breathlessly
had they hung upon every word. But they
made good their omission. Talk about rousing the military spirit which some of my good
friends so dread—I think he kindled something that day in those little hearts, whom,
unthinking, we had passed by, that will tell for
our country in years to come. I should not be
afraid of rousing any amount of the fighting
spirit that is bound to battle for the weak and
the defenseless and the right. And that is the
kind he stirs wherever he goes.

Sometimes, when I speak of the children of
the poor, some one says to me,—once it was the
great master of a famous school,—" Yes, they
have their hardships; but God help the children
of the rich who have none! " And he is right.
In his life Theodore Roosevelt furnishes the
precise antidote for the idleness and the sel-
fishness that threaten to eat the heart out of
theirs. His published writings fairly run over,
from the earliest day, with the gospel of work,
and surely he has practised what he preaches
as few have. " Theodore Roosevelt, a bright
precocious boy, aged twelve," wrote a distinguished New York physician of him, in his

THEODORE ROOSEVELT

" case-book," thirty-odd years ago; and added
to his partner, " He ought to make his mark
in the world but for the difficulty that he has
a rich father" ; so he told me after Roosevelt
had become Governor. It *was* a difficulty,—
is with too many to-day. It is not Roosevelt's
least merit that he has shown to those how to
overcome it. But I own that my heart turns
to him as the champion of his poorer brother,
ever eager and ready to give him a helping
hand. When I read, in the accounts of his
journey in the West, of the crowd that besieged his train, and how he picked out a little
crippled child in it, and took it up in his arms,
then I knew him as I have seen him over and
over again, and as I love him best. I knew him
then for the son of his big-hearted father, to
whom wrong and suffering of any kind, anywhere, appealed with such an irresistible claim
that in his brief lifetime he became the greatest of moral forces in my city.

Then I see him as he stood that day on the
car platform at Greenport, shaking hands with
the school children that came swarming down
just as the train was going to pull out. I see
him spy the forlorn little girl in the threadbare

coat, last among them all, who had given up in dumb despair, for how should she ever reach her hero through that struggling crowd, with the engineer even then tooting the signal to start? And I see him leap from the platform and dive into the surging tide like a strong swimmer striking from the shore, make a way through the shouting mob of youngsters clear to where she was on the outskirts looking on hopelessly, seize and shake her hand as if his very heart were in his, and then catch the moving train on a run, while she looked after it, her pale, tear-stained face one big, happy smile. That was Roosevelt, every inch of him, and don't you like him, too?

People laugh a little, sometimes, and poke fun at his " race suicide," but to him the children mean home, family, the joy of the young years, and the citizenship of to-morrow, all in one. And I do not think we have yet made out to the full what the ideal of home, held as he holds it, means to us all in a man whose life is avowedly given to public affairs, and whose way has led him clear to the top. After all, we sum up in the one word all that is worth working for and fighting for. With that gone, what were left? But it has seemed in this generation as if every influence, especially in our big cities, were hostile to the home, and that was one reason why I hailed the coming of this plain man of old-time ideals into our people's life, and wanted him to be as close to it as he could get. His enemies never understood either the one or the other. I remember when in the Police Department they had him shadowed at night, thinking to catch him " off his guard." He flushed angrily when he heard it.

" What! " he cried, " going home to my babies?."

But his anger died in a sad little laugh of pity and contempt. That was their way. They could not understand. And to-day he is the beloved Chief of the Nation; and where are they?

When he came home, his first errand, when the children were little, was always to the nursery. Nowadays they are big enough to run to meet him—and they do, with a rush. I came home with him one day when he was in the Navy Department, and he tempted me to go up with him to see the babies.

" But not to play bear," said Mrs. Roosevelt, warningly; "the baby is being put to sleep."

No, he would not play bear, he promised, and we went up. But it is hard not to play bear when the baby squirms out of the nurse's arms and growls and claws at you like a veritable little cub; and in five minutes Mrs. Roosevelt, coming to investigate the cause of the noise in the nursery, opened the door upon the wildest kind of a circus, with the baby screaming his delight. I can recall nothing more amusing than that tableau, with the silent shape upon the threshold striving hard to put on a look of great sternness, and him, meekly apologetic, on the floor with the baby, explaining, " Well, Edith, it was this way—" We never found out which way it was, for the humor of the situation was too much for us, —and the baby was thoroughly awake by that time, anyway. I say I can think of nothing funnier, unless it be Kermit taking his pet rat out of his pocket at the breakfast-table in the White House, and letting it hop across for my inspection. It was a kangaroo-rat, and it nibbled very daintily the piece of sugar the

President gave it. But it was something new to me then. I have heard of all sorts of things in a boy's pocket,—fish-hooks and nails and bits of colored glass. But a live rat, never!

Kermit was along, last summer, when the President and Mrs. Roosevelt went down in the *Sylph* to Twin Island, to visit the summer home of my people in Henry Street.[1] He is n't a bit awed by the Presidency.

" U-ugh! " he said, with a look of comic concern, as the President leaped into the launch, " something heavy went over then."

That was the day the children of the East Side will remember to the last day of their lives. They absolutely deserted their dinner when word was brought that the *Sylph* had hove to outside the rocks, and with a wild rush made for the shore, where they stood and waved their flags and shouted their welcome. " Three cheers for the red, white, and blue! " And his foot had hardly touched the shore before there were from six to a dozen youngsters hanging to each hand, and plying him with questions as they danced up the jungle-path to the house,

[1] The Fresh Air Home of the Jacob A. Riis House in Henry Street is on Twin Island in Pelham Bay Park.

every one trying to look into his face while they skipped and talked, so that at least half of them were walking backward on the toes of those next to them all the while. No fear of patronizing there. They were chums on the minute. If anything, they did the patronizing, the while their mothers were escorting Mrs. Roosevelt with simple dignity, proud of their guest, and touched in their innermost hearts by her coming among them.

" Was that your ship what was all lit up out there last night? " I heard one of the youngsters ask the President; and another, who had hold of the skirt of his coat, took in the island with one wide sweep of his unclaimed hand: " Ain't it bully? "

And it was. Not a sign "Keep off the grass" on the whole island; free license to roam where they pleased, to wade and to fish and to gather posies, or to sit on the rocks and sing. The visitors went from the woods to the house, saw the big bedrooms,—so big that when the trees outside waved their branches in the patch of moonlight on the floor, the children at first huddled together, frightened, in a corner. They felt as if they were outside in a strange country. The whole tenement flat in the stony street could easily have been packed into one of those rooms. They saw them eat and play and skip about in happiness such as their life had been stranger to before,—these children of few opportunities; and the President turned to me with a joyous little laugh:

" Oh, Jacob! what monument to man is there of stone or bronze that equals that of the happiness of these children and mothers? "

That was a great day, indeed. Twin Island, the home of wealth and fashion till the city made a park alongshore and gave us the use of the deserted mansion, never saw its like.

The Christmas bells are ringing as I write this, and they take me back to that holiday season, half a dozen years ago, when I was mistaken for Mr. Roosevelt with startling results. It happened once or twice, when he was Police Commissioner, that people made that mistake. They could not have been very discerning; but, whether or no, it did me no harm. I was glad of the compliment. This time I had gone to see the newsboys in the Duane Street lodging-house get their Christmas dinner. There were six or seven hundred of them, and as they marched past to the long tables where the plates of roast turkey stood in expectant rows, with a whole little mince-pie at each plate, the little shavers were last in the line. They were just as brimful of mischief as they could be,—that was easy to see. The superintendent pulled my sleeve as they went by, with a "Watch out now and you 'll see some fun." What he meant I did n't know then. I saw only a swift movement of their hands as they went by the table,—too swift for me to follow. I found out when they sat down and eight grimy little hands shot up and eight aggrieved little voices piped:

" Mister, I ain't got no pie! "

" What! " said the superintendent, with another wink to me; " no pie! There must be; I put it there myself. Let 's see about that."

And he went over and tapped the first and the smallest of the lads on the stomach, where his shirt bulged.

" What 's that? " he said, feeling of the bulge.

" Me pie," said the lad, unabashed. " I wuz afeard it w'd get stole on me, and so I—"

They had " swiped " the pies in passing.

"Never mind," said the superintendent,—
"never mind, we'll forgive and forget. It's
Christmas! Go ahead, boys, and eat." And
six hundred pairs of knives and forks flashed,
and six hundred pairs of jaws and six hundred
tongues wagged all at once, until you could n't
hear yourself think.

But one of the lads, who had not taken his
eyes from me, suddenly saw a light. He
pointed his knife straight at me and piped
out so that they all heard it:

"I know you! I seen yer pitcher in the
papers. You 're a P'lice Commissioner.
You 're—you 're—Teddy Roosevelt!"

If a bomb had fallen into the meeting, I
doubt if the effect would have been greater.
A silence fell, so deep that you would have
heard a pin drop—where, a moment before, the
noise of a dray going over the pavement would
have been drowned in the din. Glancing down
the table where the little shavers sat, I saw a
stealthy movement under cover, and the eight
stolen pies appeared with a common accord
over the edge and were replaced as suddenly
as they had gone!

He laughed, when I told him of it, as I had

THE WHITE HOUSE

PHOTOGRAPH BY ARTHUR HEWITT

seldom seen him laugh, and said it was a great compliment. And so it was: it was evidence of the respect he was held in as Police Commissioner. Twin Island told the other end of the story, and it was even better.

XV

THE PRESIDENT'S POLICIES

—

XV

THE PRESIDENT'S POLICIES

I SAID I would not meddle with the President's policies, and neither will I from the point of view of statecraft; for of that I know less than nothing. But how now, looking at them through the man I have tried to show you? Do his " policies " not become the plain expression of his character, of the man? Ask yourself and answer the question whether he has " made good " the promise which any one not wilfully blind could see. Lots of people were uneasy when he became President. It was natural, in the excitement over the murder of President McKinley. Roosevelt was young, he was hot-headed, hasty, things were going to be upset—that was what we heard. Perhaps they looked back and saw that no Vice-President had ever succeeded who did not dismiss the cabinet of his dead chief and set up for himself. But this President did not let the day pass, upon which he took the oath, without asking McKinley's advisers to stay and be his, all of them. It was politically wise, for it allayed the unrest. But it was something beside that: it was the natural thing for Roosevelt to do. He knew the cabinet, and what they could do.

"You know well enough," he said once, when we were speaking of it, "that I am after the thing to be done. It is the fitness of the tool to do the work I am concerned about, not my inventing of it. What does that matter?"

He found in Attorney-General Knox, for instance, a corporation lawyer whose very experience as such had made him see clearly the unwisdom, to look at it merely from the point of view of their own security, of the arrogance that lay ill concealed at the bottom of the dealings of organized wealth with the rest of mankind. And splendidly has he battled for the rights of us all—theirs and ours. The utter mystery to me is that corporate wealth has not long before this made out that there can be no worse misfit and no greater peril to itself in a government of the people than to have the feeling grow that money can buy unfair privilege. "But it is true, and always has been," says my Wall Street neighbor who has the courage of his convictions. Then, if that be so, is he so blind that he cannot see the danger of it, since the very soul of the Republic is in the challenge that it shall not be true forever; that, with every just premium on honest industry, men shall have somewhere near a fair chance at the start; that they shall not be damned into economic slavery any more than into political slavery? Is he so blind that he cannot see that the irrepressible conflict cannot be sidetracked by any subterfuge, by the purchase of delegations, the plotting of politicians, the defeat of Presidents? I used to think that the great captains of industry must be the wisest of men, and so indeed they need be in their special fields. But where is their common sense that they cannot see so plain a thing?

Unless, indeed, they think that the Republic is a mere fake, government by the people and of the people and for the people a fad, a phrase behind which to plot securely for a hundred years more,—life with no other mean-

ing than to fill pockets and belly while they
last! In which case I pity them from the bottom of my heart. For what a meaning to read
into life, one little end of which lies within
our ken, with the key to all the rest, as far as
we are able to grasp it here, in fair dealing
with the brother!

I have said that I speak for myself in these
pages; but for once you may take it that I
speak for Theodore Roosevelt too. That is
what he thinks. That is the underlying thought
of his oft-expressed philosophy, that the poorest plan for an American to act upon is that
of "some men down," and the safest that of
"all men up." For, whether for good or ill, up
we go or down, poor and rich, white or black,
all of us together in the end, in the things
that make for real manhood. And the making
of that manhood and the bringing of it to the
affairs of life and making it tell there, is the
business of the Republic.

How, so thinking, could he have taken any
other attitude than he has on the questions that
seem crowding to a solution these days because there is at last a man at the head who will
not dodge, but deal squarely with them as they

come? How should he have "intended in-
sult" to the South, whose blood flowed in his
mother's veins, when he bade to his table one of
the most distinguished citizens of our day, by
whose company at tea Queen Victoria thought
herself honored because he represents the effort, the hope, of raising a whole race of men
—our black-skinned fellow-citizens—up to the
grasp of what citizenship means? And where
is there a man fool enough to believe that the
clamor of silly reactionists whom history, whom
life, have taught nothing, should move him one
hair's-breadth from the thing he knows is right
—even from " the independent and fearless
course he has followed in his attempt to secure
decent and clean officials in the South "? I
am quoting from the Montgomery (Alabama)
" Times," a manly Democratic newspaper that
is not afraid of telling the truth. I have just
now read the clear, patient, and statesmanlike
answer of Carl Schurz to the question, " Can
the South solve the negro problem? " He
thinks it can if it will follow its best impulses
and its clearest sense, not the ranting of those
who would tempt it to moral and economic ruin
with the old ignorant cry of " Keep the nig-

ger down!" And I know that the South has
no truer and fairer friend in that cause than
the President, who believes in "all men up,"
and who with genuine statesmanship looks
beyond the strife and the prejudice of to-day
to the harvest-time that is coming.

"On this whole question," he sighed, when
we had threshed it over one day, "we are in
a back eddy. I don't know how we are going
to get out, or when. The one way I know that
does not lead out is for us to revert to a condition of semi-slavery. That leads us farther
in, *because it does not stop there."*

Let the South ponder it well, for it is true.
And let it be glad that there is a man in the
White House to voice its better self. "A
nation cannot remain half free and half slave"
or half peon. And it can never throw off its
industrial fetters and take the place to which
it is entitled until it is willing to build upon
the dignity of manhood and of labor, of which
serfdom, by whatever name, is the flat denial.

Truly, the world moves with giant strides
once the policy of postponement is sidetracked
and notice is served that the man at the throttle
is willing to give ear. I wonder now how many

of us, when it comes right down to hard facts, consider government, the Republic, the general scheme of the world, a kind of *modus vivendi* to make sure *we* are not interfered with while we are at the game—never mind the rest? But yesterday the shout arose that the President was inviting " labor men " to break bread at the White House—white men, these. Well, why not labor men, if they are otherwise fit companions for the President of the United States? That these were, no one questioned. It was at that luncheon, I suppose, that one of them made the remark that at last there was a hearing for him and his fellows. I have forgotten the precise occasion, but I remember the President's pregnant answer:

" Yes! The White House door, while I am here, shall swing open as easily for the labor man as for the capitalist, *and no easier.*"

It seems as if it was in the same week that the President had been denounced in labor meetings as " unfriendly " because he would not let union rules supersede United States law in the office of the public printer. Only a little while before, resolutions of organized labor had denounced him as "unfair" because he had opposed mob-rule with rifles in an Arizona mining dispute, and the editors of "organs" that had not yet got through denouncing him as a time-server because of his action in the anthracite coal strike were having a hard and bewildering time of it. How many of their readers they succeeded in mixing up beside themselves, I don't know. Some, no doubt; for even so groundless a lie as this, that President Roosevelt had jumped Leonard Wood over four hundred and fifty veteran soldiers to a major-generalship because he was his friend, found believers when it was repeated day after day by the newspapers that cared even less for the four hundred and fifty veterans than they did for Leonard Wood, merely using him as a convenient screen from behind which to hit Roosevelt. Whereas, the truth is that General Wood was not "jumped" a single number by his friend, but came up for confirmation in the regular routine of promotion by seniority of rank, all the jumping having been done years before by President McKinley for cause, and heartily applauded by the American people. Of all this his defamers were perfectly well aware; and so they must have been of the facts in the labor situation of which they tried to make capital, if I may use so odd a term. It was just as simple as all the rest of President Roosevelt's doings.

"Finance, tariff," he said to me once,— "these are important. But the question of the relations of capital and labor is vital. Your children and mine will be happy in this country of ours, or the reverse, according to whether the decent man in 1950 feels friendly toward the other decent man whether he is a wage-worker or not. 'I am for labor,' or 'I am for capital,' substitutes something else for the immutable laws of righteousness. The one and the other would let the class man in, and letting him in is the one thing that will most quickly eat out the heart of the Republic. I am neither for labor nor for capital, but for the decent man against the selfish and indecent man who will not act squarely."

To a President of that mind came the coal-strike question in October, 1902, with its demand for action in a new and untried field— a perilous field for a man with political aspirations, that was made clear without delay. Then, if ever, was the time for the policy of postponement, had his personal interests weighed heavier in the scale than the public good. To me, sitting by and watching the strife of passions aroused all over the land, it brought a revelation of the need of charity for the neighbor who does not know. From the West, where they burn soft coal, and could know nothing of the emergency, but where they had had their own troubles with the miners, came counsel to let things alone. Men who thought I had the President's ear sent messages of caution. " Go slow," was their burden; " tell him not to be hasty, not to interfere." While from the Atlantic seaboard cities, where coal was twelve dollars a ton, with every bin empty and winter at the door, such a cry of dread went up as no one who heard it ever wants to hear again. From my own city, with its three million toilers, Mayor Low telegraphed to the President:

I cannot emphasize too strongly the immense injustice of the existing coal situation to millions of innocent people. The welfare of a large section of the country imperatively demands the immediate resumption of anthracite coal mining. In the name of the City of New York I desire to protest through you, against the continuance of the existing situation, which, if prolonged, involves, at the very least, the certainty of great suffering and heavy loss to the inhabitants of this city, in common with many others.

Governor Crane of Massachusetts came on to Washington to plead the cause of the Eastern cities, whose plight, if anything, was worse. The miners stood upon their rights. Organized capital scouted interference defiantly, threatening disaster to the Republican party if the President stepped in. The cry of the cities swelled into a wail of anguish and despair, and still the mines were idle, the tracks of the coal roads blocked for miles with empty cars. In the midst of it all the " hasty " man in the White House wrote in reply to my anxious inquiry:

" I am slowly going on, step by step, working within my limited range of powers and endeavoring neither to shirk any responsibilities nor yet to be drawn into such hasty and violent action as almost invariably provokes reaction."

Long after it was over, Secretary of the Navy Moody told me of what was happening then in Washington.

" I remember the President sitting with his

game leg in a chair while the doctors dressed it," he said (it was after the accident in Massachusetts in which the President's coach was smashed and the secret service man on the driver's seat killed). " It hurt, and now and then he would wince a bit, while he discussed the strike and the appeals for help that grew more urgent with every passing hour. The outlook was grave; it seemed as if the cost of interference might be political death. I saw how it tugged at him, just when he saw chances of serving his country which he had longed for all the years, to meet—this. It was human nature to halt. He halted long enough to hear it all out: the story of the suffering in the big coast cities, of schools closing, hospitals without fuel, of the poor shivering in their homes. Then he set his face grimly and said:

" ' Yes, I will do it. I suppose that ends me; but it is right, and I will do it.'

"I don't agree with labor in all its demands," added the Secretary. " I think it is unreasonable in some of them, or some of its representatives are. But in the main line it is eternally right, and it is only by owning it and helping it to its rights that we can successfully choke off the exorbitant demands." And in my soul I said amen, and was glad that with such problems to solve the President had found such friends to help.

Many times, during the anxious days that followed, I thought with wonder of the purblind folk who called Roosevelt hasty. For it seemed sometimes as if the insolence of the coal magnates were meant to provoke him to anger. But no word betrayed what he felt, what thousands of his fellow-citizens felt as they read the reports of the conferences at the White House. The most consummate statesmanship steered us safely between reefs that beset the parley at every point, and the country was saved from a calamity the extent and consequences of which it is hard to imagine. Judge Gray, the chairman of the commission that settled the strike, said, when it was all history, that the crisis confronting the President "was more grave and threatening than any since the Civil War, threatening not only the comfort and health, but the safety and good order of the nation." And he gave to the President unstinted praise for what he did. The London "Times," speaking for all Europe in hailing the entrance of government upon a new field full of great possibilities, said editorially, " In the most quiet and unobtrusive manner, President Roosevelt has done a very big thing, and an entirely new thing."

He alone knew at what cost. Invalid, undergoing daily agony as the doctors scraped the bone of his injured leg, he wrote to the Governor of Massachusetts, who sent him " the thanks of every man, woman, and child in the country ":

" Yes, we have put it through. But, heavens and earth! it has been a struggle."

It was the nearest I ever knew him to come to showing the strain he had been under.

The story of the strike, and of how it was settled by the President's commission, none of us has forgotten. That commission did not make permanent peace between capital and labor, but it took a longer stride toward making a lasting basis for such a peace than we had taken yet; and I can easily understand the President's statement to me that, if there were nothing else to his credit, he would be content to go out of office upon that record alone. For it was truly a service to render. I had sup-

posed that we all understood until I ran up
against a capitalistic friend of the " irreconcilable " stripe. He complained bitterly of the
President's mixing in; had he kept his hands
off, the strike would have settled itself in a very
little while; the miners would have gone back
to work. I said that I saw no sign of it.

No, he supposed not; but it was so, all the
same. " We had their leaders all bought," said
he.

He lied, to be plain about it, for John Mitchell and his men had proved abundantly that
they were not that kind. And, besides, he could
not speak for the mine-operators; he was not
one of them. But the thing was not for whom
he spoke, but what it was he said, with such
callous unconcern. Think of it for a moment and tell me which was, when all is said
and done, the greater danger: the strike, with
all it might have stood for, or the cynicism
that framed that speech? The country might
outlive the horrors of a coal-famine in midwinter, but this other thing would kill as sure
as slow poison. Mob-rule was not to be feared
like that.

There comes to my mind, by contrast, something John Mitchell said to the Southwestern miners' convention, after the strike, that shows the quality of the man and of his leadership.

" Some men," he said, " who own the mines think they own the men, too; and some men who work in the mines think they own them. Both are wrong. The mines belong to the owners. You belong to yourselves."

Upon those who said that the President had surrendered the country, horse, foot, and dragoons, to organized labor, his action a few months later, in sending troops within the hour in which they were demanded to prevent violence by miners in Arizona, ought to have put a quietus. But it did not; they gibbered away as before. The reason is plain: they did not themselves believe what they said. The Miller case followed hard upon it, with no better effect. But the Miller case is so eloquent both of the President's stand upon this most urgent of all questions in our day, and of his diplomacy,—which is nothing else than his honest effort, with all the light he can get upon a thing, to do the right as he sees it,—that it is worth setting down here as part of his record, and a part to be remembered.

THE PRESIDENT'S POLICIES

Miller was an assistant foreman in the government bookbindery. He was discharged by the public printer, upon the demand of organized labor, on charges of " flagrant non-unionism," he having been expelled from Local Union No. 4 of the International Brotherhood of Bookbinders. His discharge was in defiance of the civil service laws, and the matter having come before the President, he ordered that he be reinstated. In doing so he pointed to this finding of the anthracite coal strike commission which organized labor had accepted:

It is adjudged and awarded that no person shall be refused employment or in any way discriminated against on account of membership or non-membership in any labor organization, and that there shall be no discrimination against or interference with any employé who is not a member of any labor organization by members of such organization.

" It is, of course," was the President's comment, " mere elementary decency to require that all the government departments shall be handled in accordance with the principle thus clearly and fearlessly enunciated." But there are people who do not understand, on both sides of the line. Seventy-two unions in the

Central Labor Union of the District of Columbia " resolved " that to reinstate Miller was " an unfriendly act." The big leaders, including Mr. Gompers and Mr. Mitchell, came to plead with the President. Miller was not fit, they said.

That was another matter, replied the President. He would find out. As to Miller's being a non-union man, the law he was sworn to enforce recognized no such distinction. " I am President," he said, " of all the people of the United States, without regard to creed, color, birthplace, occupation, or social distinction. In the employment and dismissal of men in the government service I can no more recognize the fact that a man does or does not belong to a union as being for or against him than I can recognize the fact that he is a Protestant or a Catholic, a Jew or a Gentile, as being for or against him."

The newspapers did not tell us that the White House rang with applause, as did Clarendon Hall on that other occasion when he met the labor men as a police commissioner. I do not know whether it did or not, for I was not there. But if in their hearts there was no response to that sentiment, they did not represent the best in their cause or in their people; for of nothing am I better persuaded than that, as the President said in his Labor Day speech at Syracuse, " Our average fellow-citizen is a sane and healthy man who believes in decency and has a wholesome mind." And that was the gospel of sanity and decency and wholesomeness all rolled into one.

Well, these are his policies. Can any one who has followed me so far in my effort to show what Theodore Roosevelt is, and why he is what he is, conceive of his having any other? And is there an American worthy of the name who would want him to have any other? Cuba is free, and she thanks President Roosevelt for her freedom. But for his insistence that the nation's honor was bound up in the completion of the work his Rough-Riders began at Las Guasimas and on San Juan hill, a cold conspiracy of business greed would have left her in the lurch, to fall by and by reluctantly into our arms, bankrupt and helpless, while the sneer of the cynics that we were plucking that plum for ourselves would have been justified. The Venezuela imbroglio that threatened the peace of the world has added, instead, to the prestige of The Hague Court of Arbitration through the wisdom and lofty public spirit of the American President. The man who was called hasty and unsafe has done more for the permanent peace of the world than all the diplomats of the day. The Panama Canal is at last to be a fact, with benefit which no one can reckon to the commerce of the world, of our land, and most of all to the Southern States, that are trying to wake up from their long sleep. I confess that the half-hearted criticism I hear of the way of the administration with Panama provokes in me a desire to laugh; for it reminds me of the way the case was put to me by a man, than whom there is no one in the United States who should know better.

" It is just," he said, " as if a fellow were to try to hold you up, and you were to wrench the gun away from him, so "—with an expressive gesture; " and then some bystander should cry out, ' Oh, the poor fellow! you 've taken away his gun! Maybe he would n't have shot at all; and then it is his gun, anyway, and you such a big fellow, and he so small. Oh, shame!' "

We can smile now, but Assistant Secretary

of State Loomis lifted the curtain enough, the other day, to give us a glimpse of what might have been, had the Colombian plot to confiscate the French canal company's forty millions of property, when the concession lapsed in another year, been allowed to hatch. Half the world might have been at war then. I think we may all well be glad, as he truly said, that " there was in Washington, upon this truly fateful occasion, a man who possessed the insight, the knowledge, the spirit, and the courage to seize the opportunity to strike a blow, the results of which can be fraught only with peace and good to the whole world."

I am not a jingo; but when some things happen I just have to get up and cheer. The way our modern American diplomacy goes about things is one of them. You remember, don't you, when the captains were conferring at Tientsin about going to the relief of the ministers there that were besieged in their embassies, and the little jealous rivalries of the powers would not let them get anywhere, the French and Russians pulling one way, the Germans another, the British another, and so on, how Captain McCalla got up and said:

THEODORE ROOSEVELT

" Well, gentlemen, you have talked this matter over pretty thoroughly and have come to no decision. And now I will tell you what I am going to do. My minister is in danger, and I am going to Peking." Wherefore they all went.

I had to cheer then, and I have to give a cheer off and on yet for the man at the helm, and to thank God that he sent me over the sea to cast in my lot with a country and with a people that do not everlastingly follow worm-eaten precedent, but are young enough and strong enough and daring enough to make it when need be.

" But about his financial policy, about his war upon the trusts, the corporations, which they say is going to defeat him for reëlection, you have said nothing. You have offered no defense." Well, good friend, if you have found nothing in these pages that answers your question, I am afraid there is little use in my saying anything now on the subject. Defense I have not offered, because, in the first place, I am quite unable to see that there is need of any. If there were, I should think the coal strike experience, or, later yet, the disclosures

in the ship-building trust case as to what it is
that ails Wall Street, would have given everybody all the information he could wish. The
President is not, Congress is not, making war
upon corporations, upon capital. They are
trying to hold them—through publicity, by
compelling them to obey the laws their smaller
competitors have to bow to, and in any other
lawful and reasonable way—to such responsibility that they shall not become a power
full of peril to the people and to themselves.
For that might mean much and grave
mischief,—would mean, indeed, unless the
people were willing to abdicate, which I think
they are not. That mischief I should like to
see averted.

" It is not designed to restrict or control the
fullest liberty of legitimate business action,"—
I quote from the President's last message,—
and none such can follow. " Publicity can do
no harm to the honest corporation. The only
corporation that has cause to dread it is the
corporation which shrinks from the light,
and about the welfare of such we need not be
over-sensitive. The work of the Department
of Commerce and Labor has been conditioned

upon this theory, of securing fair treatment alike for labor and capital."

That is all, and nothing has been done that is not in that spirit. Perhaps it is natural that a corporation like the Standard Oil Company, which has amassed enormous wealth through a monopoly that enabled it to dictate its own freight rates to the utter annihilation of its competitors, should object to have the government step in and try to curtail unfair profits. Perhaps it is natural for it to object to the anti-rebate law, though it comes too late to check its greed.

Perhaps it is natural for some speculating concerns to wish to keep their business to themselves; but it seems to me we have seen enough swindling exposed, to be plain about it, these last few months, to make a good many people wish there had been some way of finding out the facts before it was too late. That, again, is all there is to that. Nobody is to be hurt, nobody can be hurt, except the one that deserves to be. I have faith enough in the American people to believe that the time has not yet come, and will not soon come, when the speculators can defeat a man running for the Presi-

THE PRESIDENT'S POLICIES

dency on the platform of an equal chance to all and special favors to none. If they can, it is time we knew it.

And, in the next place, I have not the least idea in the world that the men who are plotting against the President do, or ever did, seriously question the fairness of his policy. It is him they do not want. Let a witness that is certainly on the inside tell why. I quote from an editorial in the " Wall Street News "—another newspaper that dares to tell the truth, it seems:

It is not because President Roosevelt is antagonistic to capital, or a partner in that hatred of wealth which is so odious and so threatening, that certain financial interests, expert in the manipulation of the markets, are scheming to prevent his election to a second term. They know very well that he is no enemy to capital. They know that by birthright, by education and by long political training he is a supporter of sound money, an advocate of a protective tariff, a firm upholder of the rights of property. They know that he is the last man in the world to lead in an assault on capital lawfully applied to the development of the commercial enterprises of the country. They have no fear that he will be led by ambition or impulse into paths of socialism, or that he will, for one moment, give the authority of his name and

office to the aid of organized labor in any movement
to crush out competition, and thus to establish a monopoly more destructive to the interests of the country than even the most corrupt, oppressive, and pow-
erful trust.

What, then, is the reason why these financial interests are scheming to defeat him? The answer is
plain.

They cannot control him.

All efforts to control him through his ambition
have failed. Any attempt to control him by grosser
forms of bribery would, of course, be useless. Effort to move him by sophistical arguments framed
by clever corporation lawyers into departure from
the paths of duty and law have not succeeded. He
is a friend of capital. He is a friend of labor. But
he is no slave of either.

And so those Wall Street interests have decided that he is to be driven out of office. They
will prevent his renomination, if they can. If
not, they will try to beat him at the polls with
money. "All the money is to be on the other
side this year." They made the beginning in
New York this last fall. It is no secret that
enormous amounts of money were thrown into
the campaign in the last two weeks to turn the
election. Low and reform were sacrificed.

PRESIDENT ROOSEVELT AT HIS DESK IN THE
EXECUTIVE OFFICE

THE PRESIDENT'S POLICIES

Next it is to be Roosevelt. " Money talks," is their creed. Other arguments are wasted.

Well, as to that, we shall see. There is still the American people to hear from.

XVI
A YOUNG MEN'S HERO
—

XVI

A YOUNG MEN'S HERO

I HAVE told you what Theodore Roosevelt is like as I see him. I have told of the man, the friend, the husband and father, because back of his public career, of his great office, I see himself always; and to my mind so it must be that you will take him to your heart as the President, also, and find the key to all he is and stands for. Knowing him as he really is, you cannot help trusting him. I would have everybody feel that way toward him who does not do so already; for we are facing much too serious times, you and he and all of us, to be honestly at odds where we should pull together. As for the others who are not honestly at odds with him, who are " working for their own pockets all the time," who are kin to the malefactors who burned up four thousand Christmas-trees in Philadelphia the other day to reduce the supply and force up the price of the remaining ones—what sweet Christmas joys must have been theirs!—I care nothing for them. I would as lief have them all in front and within fighting reach from the start. They belong there, anyhow.

And now, what does it all mean? Why have I written it? Just to boom Roosevelt for the Presidency in the election that comes soon? No, not that. I shall rejoice to see him elected, and I shall know that never was my vote put to better use for my country than when I cast it for him. To have him beaten by the Christmas-tree cabal would argue an unpreparedness, an unfitness to grapple with the real problems of the day, that might well dishearten the patriot. But this not because of himself, much as I like to hear the whole country shout for the friend I love, but because of what he stands for. It matters less that Theodore Roosevelt is President, but it matters a good deal that the things prevail which he represents in the nation's life. It never mattered more than at this present day of ours—right now. Yester-

A YOUNG MEN'S HERO

day I spoke in a New England town, a pros-
perous, happy town, where the mills were all
running, property booming, the people busy;
but there was a fly in the ointment, after all.
It came out when I expressed my pleasure at
what I had seen.

" Yes," they said, " we are all that; and we
would be perfectly happy but for the meanest
politics that ever disgraced a town."

When I settled into my seat in the train to
think it over, this paragraph from a sermon on
" Money-madness " stared me in the face—
curiously, it was preached by the pastor of the
biggest money-king of them all, so the paper
said:

In these days there is such a hunt after wealth that
the efforts of our best men are withdrawn from the
public service. The men of the stamp of Jefferson, of
Washington, who gave themselves to their country,
are not now to be found in legislative halls; they are
corporation lawyers.

And before I had time to run over in my
mind the shining exceptions I knew, the Roots,
the Tafts, the Knoxes, the Garfields, and the
rest of them, and who only brought out more

sharply the truth of the general statement, in comes my neighbor with whom just now I fought shoulder to shoulder against Tammany in New York, as good and clean and honest a fellow as I know, and tells me it is all over. Clean discouraged is he, and he will never spend his time and money in fighting for decency again.

" What 's the use? " says he. ' It is all waste and foolishness; and, after all, how do I lose by some one getting what he wants and paying for it? I know this blackmailing business, a wide-open town, and all that,—I know it is wrong when you come to high principle; but we live in a practical, every-day world. Let us live and let live. I get what I want, the other fellow gets what he wants; and if it is worth my paying the price to get it, how am I hurt? Is n't it better than all this stew for nothing? Tammany 's in and back, and we will never win again. I am done with reform."

He is not; I know it, for I know him. He is just tired, and he will get over it. But he speaks for a good many who may not get over it so easily, and that is exactly what Tammany banks upon. It is what the enemy hopes

A YOUNG MEN'S HERO

for in all days: that he may tire out the good,
convince them that the game is n't worth the
candle. And right here is the immense value
of the man whom you cannot tire out, who
will stand like a rock for the homely virtues,
for the Ten Commandments, in good and evil
report, and refuse to budge. For, though men
sneer at him and call him a grand-stand player,
as they will, the time will come when he will
convince them that there is something more
important than winning to-day or to-morrow,
where a principle is at stake; that the function
of the Republic, of government of the people,
shall, please God, yet be to make high principle the soul and hope of the practical every-
day world, even if it takes time to do it; and
that it is worth losing all our lives long, with
the lives thrown in, if that be necessary, to have
it come true in the end. The man who will do
that, who will take that stand and keep it, is
beyond price. That is Theodore Roosevelt
from the ground up. And now you know why
I have written of him as I have.

There was never a day that called so loudly
for such as he, as does this of ours. Not that
it is worse than other days; I know it is better.

THEODORE ROOSEVELT

I find proof of it in the very fact that it is as if the age-long fight between good and evil had suddenly come to a head, as if all the questions of right, of justice, of the brotherhood, which we had seen in glimpses before, and dimly, had all at once come out in the open, craving solution one and all. A battle royal, truly! A battle for the man of clean hands and clean mind, who can think straight and act square; the man who will stand for the right " because it is right "; who can say, and mean it, that " it is hard to fail, but worse never to have tried to succeed." A battle for him who strives for " that highest form of success which comes, not to the man who desires mere easy peace, but to him who does not shrink from danger, from hardship or from bitter toil, and who out of these wins the splendid ultimate triumph." I am but quoting his own words, and never, I think, did I hear finer than those he spoke of Governor Taft when he had put by his own preferences and gone to his hard and toilsome task in the Philippines; for the whole royal, fighting soul of the man was in them.

" But he undertook it gladly," he said, " and

he is to be considered thrice fortunate; for in this world the one thing supremely worth having is the opportunity coupled with the capacity to do well and worthily a piece of work the doing of which is of vital consequence to the welfare of mankind."

There is his measure. Let now the understrappers sputter. With that for our young men to grow up to, we need have no fear for the morrow. Let it ask what questions it will of the Republic, it shall answer them, for we shall have men at the oars.

This afternoon the newspaper that came to my desk contained a cable despatch which gave me a glow at the heart such as I have not felt for a while. Just three lines; but they told that a nation's conscience was struggling victoriously through hate and foul play and treason: Captain Dreyfus was to get a fair trial. Justice was to be done at last to a once despised Jew whose wrongs had held the civilized world upon the rack; and the world was made happy. Say now it does not move! It does, where there are men to move it,—I said it before: men who believe in the right and are willing to fight for it. When the children of poverty and want came to Mulberry Street for justice, and I knew they came because Roosevelt had been there, I saw in that what the resolute, courageous, unyielding determination of one man to see right done in his own time could accomplish. I have watched him since in the Navy Department, in camp, as Governor, in the White House, and more and more I have made out his message as being to the young men of our day, himself the youngest of our Presidents. I know it is so, for when I speak to the young about him, I see their eyes kindle, and their hand-shake tells me that they want to be like him, and are going to try. And then I feel that I, too, have done something worth doing for my people. For, whether for good or for evil, we all leave our mark upon our day, and his is that of a clean, strong man who fights for the right *and wins.*

Now, then, a word to these young men who, all over our broad land, are striving up toward the standard he sets, for he is their hero by right, as he is mine. Do not be afraid to own it. The struggle to which you are born, and in which you are bound to take a hand if you would be men in more than name, is the struggle between the ideal and the husk; for life without ideals is like the world without the hope of heaven, an empty meaningless husk. It is your business to read its meaning into it by making the ideals real. The material things of life are good in their day, but they pass away; the moral remain to bear witness that the high hopes of youth are not mere phantasms. Theodore Roosevelt *lives his ideals;* therefore you can trust them. Here they are in working shape: " Face the facts as you find them; strive steadily for the best." " Be never content with less than the possible best, and never throw away that possible best because it is not the ideal best." Maxims, those, for the young man who wants to make the most of himself and his time. Happily for the world, the young man who does not is rare.

Perhaps I can put what is in my mind in no better shape than by giving you his life-rules, to which I have seen him live up all these years, though I have not often heard him express them in so many words. Here is one:

" It is better to be faithful than famous."

Look back now upon his career as I have sketched it, and see how in being steadfastly

one he has become both. What better character
could you or I or anybody give our day, which
the croakers say worships only success? Put
it the other way, that we refuse to accept the
goodness that is weak-kneed and cowardly,
that we demand of the champion of right that
he shall believe in his cause enough to fight
for it, and you have it. Look at him in every
walk of life, from boyhood, when by sheer will-
power he conquered his puny body that he
might take his place among men and do a man's
work, and see how plain, straightforward manliness won its way despite the plotters. See him
going on his way, bearing no grudges, nursing
no revenge,—you cannot afford those things if
you want to make the most of yourself,—be-
lieving no evil, but ever the best, of his neighbor, and craving his help for the best. The
secret of the ages which the wise men sought
with toil and trouble and missed, he found in his
path without seeking. The talisman that turns
dross to gold is your own faith in your fellow-man. Whatever you believe him to be,
with the faith that makes you love your neighbor in spite of himself, that he will become. He
will come up or come down to it, as you make

your demand. Appeal to the animal, and watch the claws come out; appeal to the divine in him, and he will show you the heart of your brother. As the days passed in Mulberry Street, Roosevelt seemed to me more and more like a touchstone by rubbing against which the true metal of all about him was brought out: every rascal became his implacable enemy; the honest, his followers almost to a man.

When, then, you have a bird's-eye view of Theodore Roosevelt's career, cast your eye down it once more and mark its bearings as a " pathway to ruin." That, you remember, was what the politicians called it, from the early years in Albany down to the present day, — honestly enough, after their fashion, for they are the keepers of the husk I spoke of, and of the power of the ideal they have, can have no conception. Study their " path to ruin " carefully, and note whither it led, despite the " mistakes " with which it was thickly strewn.

Mistakes! Roosevelt is no more infallible than you or I, and no doubt he has made his mistakes, though they were not the ones the politicians picked out. There is a use for mistakes in his plan of life: they are made to

learn from. Here is another of his maxims:
" The only man who makes no mistakes is the
man who never does anything." He has made
fewer than most people, because he has taught
himself from the very start to think quick and
straight. He makes sure he is right and then
goes ahead. The snags, if there be any in the
way, do not trouble him. Dodge them he never
does, but shoulders the responsibility and goes
ahead. That is one reason why he has been
able to do so much in his brief life: he never
has to be on the defensive, to cover his retreat,
but is ever ready to go ahead, to attack.

He is always fair. That is a cardinal virtue
in a fighter of Anglo-Saxon blood, for we all
have the love of fair play in us. He never hits
a man below the belt. Even to the policemen
whom he searched out at night in the old days
when as Commissioner he made a roundsman of himself, he gave a fair show. He was
not out to " make a case " against them, but
to see that they did their duty. Of every man
he demands the best that is in him, no more,
no less. For himself, there is nothing that is
worth doing at all that is not worth doing as
well as it can be done. When he was a boy the

wonders of electricity aroused his interest, and
he pelted a friend, a medical practitioner, with
questions concerning it. " Other boys asked
questions," the doctor said, recalling the experience; " but Theodore wanted to know the
nature of the force." There he came to the
limit of knowledge. But it was so with everything. What he knows he knows thoroughly,
because he has learned all he could learn about
it; and so he is able to give points to his opponent and win. For just as in boxing it is
science, not slugging, that wins, so in life it is
the man who knows who carries off the prizes
worth having. He gets all the rewards, the
other fellow the hard knocks.

When the work in hand has been done he
believes in having a good time. No man has
a better. He put it in words once in my hearing: " Have all the fun you honestly and de-
cently can; it is your right." It is part of the
perfect balance that gets things done, and done
right. Above all, his conception of life is a
sane, common-sense one. It is the view which
leaves the fun out that makes all the trouble.
Somewhere I have told of my experience in
Denmark, my old home, where they make but-

ter for a living. I had been away more than
twenty years, and many things had changed.
I found the country divided into two camps,
in matters of religious practice, when in my
childhood we were one. Now there were the
" happy Christians," and the " hell-preachers "
who saw only the wrath to come. Speaking
with an old friend about the dairy industry, he
gave me, quite unconsciously, directions that
were good beyond the borders of the Danish
land: " If you want good butter," said he,
" go to the happy Christians. They make the
best." Of course they do. They make the
world go round. It is the honest fun that
keeps life sane and sweet, butter and all.

One more of his life-rules, and this one you
may fairly call his motto: " Be ready! " Ammunition fixed, canteen filled, knapsack slung,
watch for the opportunities of life that come,
and seize them as they pass. They are for the
one who is ready for them. Lose no time; a
man can lose a fortune and make another; but
the time that is lost is lost forever. It does
not come back. Waste no time in grumbling.
Roosevelt never does. The man who is busy
helping his neighbor has no time to growl.

A YOUNG MEN'S HERO

Growling holds up progress and never helps anything. Be ready, and when the order comes fall in. Fighting for the things worth while, hit the hardest licks you know how and never count the odds against you. They have nothing to do with it. If you are right, just fight on, "trying to make things better in this world, even if only a little better, because you have lived in it." Let that be your watchword, and all will come out right.

My story stops here. There is nothing in it, as I have shown you Roosevelt and his life, that is beyond the reach or strength of any one who will make the most of himself with determined purpose. "He stands," some one has said, "for the commonplace virtues; he is great on lines along which each one of us can be great if he wills and dares!" It is for that reason above all significant that he should be the young man's President, the type and hero of the generation that is to shape the coming day of our Republic as it is entering upon its world-mission among the nations. When Theodore Roosevelt first came into my life, he "came to help." How he has helped me I can never tell. He made my life many times richer for his coming. Of how he has helped all of us we heard the echo in the resolution that instructed the delegates of Luzerne County, Pennsylvania, the first to be chosen anywhere to the National Convention of the Republican party, to vote for him for President.

"We admire the courage," it ran, "that prompts him to do right to all men, without respect to race, color, or condition. We trust that he may long be spared to stand as an example of virile American manhood, fearing nothing but failure to do his duty toward God and man."

When that can be truly said of a man, the rest matters little. To him apply the words of Washington, which will never die:

"Let us rear a standard to which the wise and the honest may repair. The event is in the hands of God."

XVII

ROOSEVELT AS A SPEAKER AND WRITER

—

XVII

ROOSEVELT AS A SPEAKER AND WRITER

PRESIDENT ROOSEVELT speaks as he writes. That tells the story. He makes no pretense to being an orator. Critics sometimes say that his books are not "literature," by which they apparently mean words strung together to sound well. They are not. But what he writes no one can misunderstand, and the style seems to the reader unimportant, though it is notably direct, terse and vigorous. When he speaks, there is not often much applause, and when there is, he often raises his hand with a warning gesture to stop it. Both his hearers and he are much too interested in the thing he says to pay great heed to the way he says it. But when it is

over, his hearers go away, thinking. They
know exactly what he meant, and, for the best
of reasons—*he* did. I cannot think of a better
prescription for speechmaking of the present
day that is meant to convince. And no one
ever winks when he speaks.

Another thing: he is all the time growing.
The man who does not grow in the White House
is not fit to be there. "A full-grown man who is
growing still," an Eastern newspaper that is
not exactly a champion of Roosevelt called him
after his Chamber of Commerce speech in New
York. One of the brightest of the newspaper
men who went with him on his long Western
trip said to me, when they were back East:
" I don't think any sane man could be with him
two weeks without getting to like him; but
the thing that struck me on that trip was the
way he grew; the way an idea grew in his
mind day by day as he lived with it until it took
its final shape in speech. Then it was like a
knock-down blow."

Then they express *the man*. Phrases like
this: " It is the shots which hit that count," and
to the boys of his country: " Hit the line hard;
don't foul and don't shirk, but hit the line

hard," are Theodore Roosevelt all over. From
time to time I have made notes from his
writings and speeches. I am going to set
down a few of the extracts here. Very likely
they are not the ones that would appeal to
many of my readers. They did to me; that
was why I wrote them down. And Roosevelt
is in them all, every one. Let the first one be
the extract from his speech at the opening of
the New York Chamber of Commerce, on
November 11, 1902. It has been called " The
Roosevelt Doctrine ":

" It is no easy matter to work out a system
or rule of conduct, whether with or without the
help of the lawgiver, which shall minimize that
jarring and clashing of interests in the industrial world which causes so much individual
irritation and suffering at the present day, and
which at times threatens baleful consequences
to large portions of the body politic. But the
importance of the problem cannot be over-
estimated, and it deserves to receive the careful
thought of all men. There should be no yield-
ing to wrong; but there should most certainly
be not only desire to do right, but a willingness
each to try to understand the viewpoint of his

fellow, with whom, for weal or for woe, his own fortunes are indissolubly bound.

" No patent remedy can be devised for the solution of these grave problems in the industrial world; but we may rest assured that they can be solved at all only if we bring to the solution certain old-time virtues, and if we strive to keep out of the solution some of the most familiar and most undesirable of the traits to which mankind has owed untold degradation and suffering throughout the ages. Arrogance, suspicion, brutal envy of the well-to-do, brutal indifference toward those who are not well-to-do, the hard refusal to consider the rights of others, the foolish refusal to consider the limits of beneficent action, the base appeal to the spirit of selfish greed, whether it take the form of plunder of the fortunate or of oppression of the unfortunate—from these and from all kindred vices this nation must be kept free if it is to remain in its present position in the forefront of the peoples of mankind.

" On the other hand, good will come, even out of the present evils, if we face them armed with the old homely virtues; if we show that we are fearless of soul, cool of head, and kindly of heart; if, without betraying the weakness that cringes before wrongdoing, we yet show by deeds and words our knowledge that in such a government as ours each of us must be in very truth his brother's keeper.

" At a time when the growing complexity of our social and industrial life has rendered inevitable the intrusion of the state into spheres of work wherein it formerly took no part, and when there is also a growing tendency to demand the illegitimate and unwise transfer to the government of much of the work that should be done by private persons, singly or associated together, it is a pleasure to address a body whose members possess to an eminent degre the traditional American self-reliance of spirit which makes them scorn to ask from the government, whether of state or or nation, anything but a fair field and no favor—who confide not in being helped by others, but in their own skill, energy, and business capacity to achieve success.

" The first requisite of a good citizen in this republic of ours is that he shall be able and willing to pull his weight; that he shall not be a mere passenger, but shall do his share in the work that each generation of us finds ready to hand; and, furthermore, that in doing his work he shall show, not only the capacity for sturdy self-help, but also self-respecting regard for the rights of others."

Here are some observations of the President on national duties and expansion:

" Nations that expand and nations that do not expand may both ultimately go down, but the one leaves heirs and a glorious memory, and the other leaves neither."

" We are strong men and we intend to do our duty."

" We cannot sit huddled within our own borders and avow ourselves merely an assemblage of well-to-do hucksters who care nothing for what happens beyond. Such a policy would defeat even its own ends; for as the nations grow to have ever wider and wider interests and are brought into closer and closer contact, if we are to hold our own in the struggle for naval and commercial supremacy, we must build up our power within our own borders."

" We have but little room among our people

for the timid, the irresolute and the idle; and it is no less true that there is scant room in the world at large for the nation with mighty thews that dares not to be great."

" It is not possible ever to insure prosperity merely by law."

" This government is not and never shall be a plutocracy. This government is not and never shall be ruled by a mob."

" Woe to us all if ever as a people we grow to condone evil because it is successful."

" The wilfully idle man, like the wilfully barren woman, has no place in a sane, healthy and vigorous community."

" Success comes only to those who lead the life of endeavor."

" Our interests are at bottom common; in the long run we go up or go down together."

" No prosperity and no glory can save a nation that is rotten at heart."

" Ultimately no nation can be great unless its greatness is laid on foundations of righteousness and decency. We cannot do great deeds as a nation unless we are willing to do the small things that make up the sum of greatness, unless we believe in energy and thrift, unless we believe that we have more to do than to simply accomplish material prosperity; unless, in short, we do our full duty as private citizens, interested alike in the honor of the state."

" A nation's greatness lies in its possibility of achievement in the present, and nothing helps it more than consciousness of achievement in the past."

" Boasting and blustering are as objectionable among nations as among individuals, and the public men of a great nation owe it to their sense of national self-respect to speak courteously of foreign powers, just as a brave and self-respecting man treats all around him courteously."

The famous phrase, " the strenuous life," is from his speech to the Hamilton Club, in Chicago, in 1899. This was the sentence in which it occurred:

" I wish to preach, not the doctrine of ignoble ease, but the doctrine of the strenuous life, the life of toil and effort, of labor and strife; to preach that highest form of success which comes, not to the man who desires mere easy peace, but to the man who does not shrink from

THEODORE ROOSEVELT AND HIS FAMILY AT OYSTER BAY

danger, from hardships, or from bitter toil, and who out of these wins the splendid ultimate triumph."

On practical politics and Christian citizenship he has this to say:

" I am a loyal party man, but I believe very firmly that I can best render aid to my party by doing all that in me lies to make that party responsive to the needs of the state, responsive to the needs of the people, and just so far as I work along those lines I have the right to challenge the support of every decent man, no matter what his party may be."

" I despise a man who surrenders his conscience to a multitude as much as I do the one who surrenders it to one man."

" If we wish to do good work for our country we must be unselfish, disinterested, sincerely desirous of the well-being of the commonwealth, and capable of devoted adherence to a lofty ideal; but in addition we must be vigorous in mind and body, able to hold our own in rough conflict with our fellows, able to suffer punishment without flinching, and, at need, to repay it in kind with full interest."

" You can't govern yourselves by sitting in your studies and thinking how good you are. You've got to fight all you know how, and you'll find a lot of able men willing to fight you."

" A man must go into practical politics in order to make his influence felt. Practical politics must not be construed to mean dirty politics. On the contrary, in the long run the politics of fraud and treachery and foulness is unpractical politics, and the most practical of all politicians is the politician who is clean and decent and upright."

" The actual advance must be made in the field of practical politics, among the men who are sometimes rough and coarse, who sometimes have lower ideals than they should, but who are capable, masterful and efficient."

" No one of us can make the world move on very far, but it moves at all only when each one of a very large number does his duty."

" Clean politics is simply one form of applied good citizenship."

" A man should be no more excused for lying on the stump than for lying off the stump."

" It is a good thing to appeal to citizens to

work for good government because it will better their state materially; but it is a far better thing to appeal to them to work for good government because it is right in itself to do so."

" Morally, a pound of construction is worth a ton of destruction."

ON EXPEDIENCY: " No man is justified in doing evil on the ground of expediency. He is bound to do all the good possible. Yet he must consider the question of expediency, in order that he may do all the good possible, for otherwise he will do none. As soon as a politician gets to the point of thinking that to be ' practical ' he has got to be base, he has become a noxious member of the body politic. That species of practicability eats into the moral sense of the people like a cancer, and he who practices it can no more be excused than an editor who debauches public decency in order to sell his paper."

ON CYNICISM: " Cynicism in public life is a curse, and when a man has lost the power of enthusiasm for righteousness it will be better for him and the country if he abandons public life."

ON LABOR (from the President's Labor Day speech at Syracuse, 1903) : " No man needs sympathy because he has to work, because he has a burden to carry. Far and away the best prize that life offers is the chance to work hard at work worth doing."

" We can keep our government on a sane and healthy basis, we can make and keep our social system what it should be, only on condition of judging each man, not as a member of a class, but on his worth as a man. It is an infamous thing in our American life, and fundamentally treacherous to our institutions, to apply to any man any test save that of his personal worth, or to draw between two sets of men any distinction save the distinction of conduct, the distinction that marks off those who do well and wisely from those who do ill and foolishly. There are good citizens and bad citizens in every class, as in every locality, and the attitude of decent people toward great public and social questions should be determined, not by the accidental questions of employment or locality,

AS A SPEAKER AND WRITER

but by those deep-set principles which represent the innermost souls of men."

" The average American knows not only that he himself intends to do about what is right, but that his average fellow-countryman has the same intention and the same power to make his intention effective. He knows, whether he be business man, professional man, farmer, mechanic, employer or wage-worker, that the welfare of each of these men is bound up with the welfare of all the others; that each is neighbor to the other, is actuated by the same hopes and fears, has fundamentally the same ideals, and that all alike have much the same virtues and the same faults.

" Our average fellow-citizen is a sane and healthy man, who believes in decency and has a wholesome mind."

ON CORPORATIONS (in speech to the City Club, New York, when he was Governor): " I hope no party will make a direct move against corporations. . . . Make the man who says he is for the corporation see to it that he doesn't give those corporations undue protection, and let the man who is against corporative wealth remember that he has no right to pillage a corporate treasury."

From the President's Message, January, 1904: "Every man must be guaranteed his liberty and his right to do as he likes with his property or his labor, so long as he does not infringe the rights of others. No man is above the law and no man is below it; nor do we ask any man's permission when we require him to obey it. Obedience to the law is demanded as a right, not asked as a favor."

ON IMMIGRATION: "We cannot have too much immigration of the right kind, and we should have none at all of the wrong kind. The need is to devise some system by which undesirable immigrants shall be kept out entirely, while desirable immigrants are properly distributed throughout the country."

ON BRIBERY: "There can be no crime more serious than bribery. Other offences violate one law, while corruption strikes at the foundation of all law. The stain lies in toleration, not in correction."

AS A SPEAKER AND WRITER

On Fellowship (in address to New York State Conference on Church Federation): "People make an unspeakable mistake when they quarrel about the boundary line between them. They have a common enemy to face, who demands united attention and united action."

On How to Help a Neighbor: "In charity the one thing always to be remembered is that while any man may slip and should at once be helped to rise to his feet, yet no man can be carried with advantage either to him or to the community."

"If a man permits largeness of heart to degenerate into softness of head he inevitably becomes a nuisance in any relation of life."

"If, with the best of intentions, we can only manage to deserve the epithet of 'harmless,' it is hardly worth while to have lived in the world at all."

On Success in Life (in speech at La Crosse, Wis., 1903): "If you want your children to be successful, you should teach them the life that is worth living, is worth working for. What a wretched life is that of a man who seeks to shirk the burdens laid on us in the world. It is equally ignoble whether he be a man of wealth or one who earns his bread in the sweat of his brow."

ON LYNCHING: " The worst enemy of the colored race is the colored man who commits some hideous wrong, especially if that be the worst of all crimes: rape; and the worst enemy of the white race is the white man who avenges that crime by another crime, equally infamous. . . . Shameless deeds of infamous hideousness should be punished speedily, but by the law, not by another crime."

Two things which Mr. Roosevelt did when Governor of New York, among the countless minor details of his official life, always seemed to me so characteristic of him that I have kept the record of them.

When Mrs. Place was to be executed for the murder of her step-daughter, after a period of great public excitement, he wrote to the warden of Sing Sing: " I particularly desire that this solemn and awful act of justice shall not

be made an excuse for the hideous sensational-
ism which is more demoralizing than anything
else to the public mind."

A bill had passed the Assembly, giving
directions as to the wearing of gowns by attor-
neys practicing in the Supreme Court. Governor Roosevelt returned it without his approval, but with this endorsement:

" This bill is obviously and utterly unneces-
sary. The whole subject should be left and
can safely be left where it properly belongs—
to the good sense of the judiciary."

I shall set down last the closing words of
the speech in which Theodore Roosevelt sec-
onded the nomination of William McKinley,
whom so soon he was to succeed, at the Philadelphia Convention, in June, 1900. They
contain his prophecy of

THE NEW CENTURY.

" We stand on the threshold of a new century, a century big with fate of the great
nations of the earth. It rests with us to decide
whether in the opening years of that century
we shall march forward to fresh triumphs, or
whether at the outset we shall deliberately crip-

ple ourselves for the contest. Is America a weakling to shrink from the world-work to be done by the world powers? No! The young Giant of the West stands on a continent and clasps the crest of an ocean in either hand. Our nation, glorious in youth and strength, looks into the future with fearless and eager eyes, and rejoices as a strong man to run a race. We do not stand in craven mood, asking to be spared the task, cringing as we gaze on the contest. No! We challenge the proud privilege of doing the work that Providence allots us, and we face the coming years high of heart and resolute of faith that to our people is given the right to win such honor and renown as has never yet been granted to the peoples of mankind."

XVIII

THEODORE ROOSEVELT'S FATHER

—

XVIII

THEODORE ROOSEVELT'S FATHER*

ON the rocky point of Lake Wah-waskesh, across from where I have been idling in my canoe all morning, angling for bass, there stood once a giant pine, a real monarch of the forest. The winter storms laid it low, and its skeleton branches harass the inlet, reaching half-way across. Perched on the nearest one, a choleric red squirrel has been scolding me quite half an hour for intruding where I am not wanted. But its abuse is wasted; my thoughts were far away. From among the roots of the fallen tree a sturdy young pine has sprung, straight and shapely, fair to look at. The sight of the two, the dead and the living, made me think of two

*Written in camp, in Canada, when Mr. Roosevelt was a candidate for the Vice-Presidency.

at home who loved the wildwood well. Father and son, they bore but one name, known to us all—Theodore Roosevelt. There came to my mind the pronunciamento of some one which I had read in a New York newspaper, that Theodore Roosevelt's day was soon spent, and other less recent deliverances to the same effect. And it occurred to me that these good people had probably never heard the story of the other Theodore, the Governor's father, or else had forgotten it. So, for the benefit of the prophetic souls who are always shaking their heads at the son, predicting that he will not last, I tell the story here again. They will have no trouble in making out the bearing of it on their pet concern. And they will note that the father " lasted " well, which was giving the community in which he lived a character to be proud of. He did more. " He grew on us continually," said one who had known him well, " until we wondered with a kind of awe for what great purpose he had been put among us." The people " resolved " at his untimely death that it " involved a loss of moral power and executive efficiency which no community can well spare."

THEODORE ROOSEVELT'S FATHER

Theodore Roosevelt was a glass importer in Maiden Lane, having taken over the business after his father, Cornelius. The Roosevelts had always borne an honored name in New York. Two of the sons of Jacob Roosevelt, who in the early part of the last century bought land " in the swamp near the cripple bush " and had the street that still bears the family name cut through, were Aldermen when the office meant something. Isaac Roosevelt sat in the Constitutional Convention with Alexander Hamilton. He had been the right-hand man of Governor Moore in organizing the New York hospital corporation, and President of the Board of Governors. Organizers they ever were, doers of things, and patriots to a man. It was a Roosevelt who started the first bank in New York and was its first president. Theodore came honestly by the powers which he turned to such account for his city when it needed him. He had in him the splendid physical endurance, the love of a fight in the cause of right, and the clear head of his Dutch ancestors, plus the profound devotion that " held himself and all he had at the service of humanity." With such an equipment a college education matters little. Theodore's father thought it might spoil his boys, and took no chances. But exclusion of college did not mean to them loss of culture. That was their birthright.

The war came, with its challenge to the youth of the land. I fancy that Theodore Roosevelt fought and won a harder fight in staying home than many a one who went. There were reasons why he should stay, good reasons, and he stayed. But if he could not fight for his country, he could at least back up those who did. He set himself at once to develop practical plans of serving them. He helped raise and equip regiments that went out—the first colored one among them; he joined in organizing the Union League Club, the strong patriotic center of that day; he worked with the Loyal Publication Society, which was doing a great educational work at a time when there was much ignorance as to the large issues of the conflict; he had a hand in the organization of the sanitary commission that saw to the comfort of the soldiers in the field. And when he had made sure that they were well fed and cared for, he turned his attention to those they had left behind. It was then he did the work for which he and his colleagues received the thanks of the Legislature of the State in joint session, much to its own credit.

Many of the soldiers' families were suffering for bread, while they wasted it by the cart-load in the army. The Government paid millions each month to the men, only to see the money squandered in riotous living at the sutlers' tents. Very little of it, if any, ever reached home. There were enough to offer to start it out, but the chances were greatly against its getting there. The sutler who sold forbidden rum in hollow loaves or imitation Bibles was not one to stop at a little plain robbery. The money was lost or wasted, the families starved, and the morale of the army suffered. Mr. Roosevelt drafted a bill to establish "allotment commissions," and took it to Washington. It was a plain measure authorizing commissioners appointed for each State to receive such a proportion of the soldier's pay as he wished to send home, and to forward it without cost or risk to him. He simply gave notice how much he wanted the wife to have, for instance; the general Government handed the amount to them, and they saw that she got it. But it was not plain sailing to get the bill passed. The men who were robbing the soldier denounced it as a swindle. Congressmen rated it a " bankers' job," unable to understand why any one should urge a bill at much personal inconvenience when " there was nothing in it " for him. The bill provided for unsalaried commissioners. But Mr. Roosevelt persisted. In the end, after three months of hard work, he got his bill through. President Lincoln, who understood, appointed Theodore Roosevelt, William E. Dodge, and Theodore B. Bronson the commissioners from New York. They went to work at once.

It was midwinter. During the first three months of 1862 they traveled from camp to camp, visiting the eighty regiments New York had in the field, and putting the matter to them personally. In the saddle often all day, they stood afterward in the cold and mud sometimes half the night, explaining and persuading, bearing insults and sneers from many of those they wished to benefit. The story of that winter's campaign is a human document recommended to the perusal of the pessimists and the head-shakers of any day. They had soon

to give up the plea that they received no pay
for their services, "because it aroused only suspicion." But they did not quit on that account.
There was this thing to be done, by such means
as they could. They learned, when any one
asked how they benefited by it, to tell them that
it was none of their business. "The money
does not come out of your pocket; if we are
satisfied, what is it to you?" They won their
fight, as they were bound to, saved thousands
of homes, and raised the tone of the army, in
spite of snubs and predictions of failure. Even
their own city sent rival commissioners into the
field at one time, discrediting their work and
their motives.

Other States heard of the great things done
in New York, and followed suit. Great good
resulted. In New York alone the amount
saved to those in dire need of it ran up in the
millions. It is recorded of Theodore Roosevelt
that through it all he never lost his temper or
his sunny belief in his fellow-men whom he had
set out to serve. Conscious zeal did not sour
him. It is easy to believe the statement that it
was he who, with a friend, persuaded President
Lincoln to replace Simon Cameron with Stan-

ton in the War Department. That lonely man had few enough of his kind about him. At a time when the camps were gloomy and the outlook dark, it was Roosevelt who got up the— I came near saying the round-robin to his countrymen; it is not always an easy thing to keep the two Theodores apart. But that was not what was wanted at that time; it was a message of cheer from home, and it came in the shape of a giant Thanksgiving dinner sent from the North to the Army of the Potomac. Veterans remember it well, and how it revived flagging spirits and put heart into things, though grumblers were not wanting to dub it fantastical. Mr. Roosevelt got that up. He collected the funds, and, with his marvelous faculty for getting things done, made it the rousing success it was. Perhaps it is not a great thing to give a dinner; but just then it was the one thing to be done, and he did it. Then, when the fight was over, he had a hand in organizing the Protective War Claims Association, which collected the dues of crippled veterans and of the families of the dead without charge, and saved them from the fangs of the sharks. It was at Mr. Roosevelt's house that the Soldiers'

Employment Bureau was organized, which did
so much toward absorbing into the population
again the vast army of men who were in danger of becoming dependent, and helped them
preserve their self-respect.

That issue was not so easily met, however.
The heritage of a great war was upon the land.
The community was being rapidly pauperized.
Vast sums of money were wasted on ill-con-
sidered charity. Fraud was rampant. Mr.
Roosevelt set about weeding it out by organizing the city's charities. We find him laboring
as a member of a " committee of nine," with
Protestants, Jews, and Roman Catholics, to
ferret out and arraign the institutions " existing only to furnish lazy managers with a living." He became the Vice-President of the
State Charities' Aid Association, a member of
the Board of United Charities, and finally the
head of the State Board of Charities, for the
creation of which he had long striven. Wherever there was a break to be repaired, a leak to
be stopped, there he was. He founded a hospital and dispensary for the treatment of hopeless spine and hip diseases. He pleaded, even
on his death-bed, for rational treatment of the

unhappy lunatics in the city's hospitals; for a farm where the boys in the House of Refuge might be fitted for healthy country life; for responsible management of the State's Orphan Asylums, for decent care of vagrants, for improved tenements. In all he did he was sensibly practical and wholesomely persistent. When he knew a thing to be right, it had to be done, and usually was done. With all that, he knew how to allow for differences of opinion in others who were as honest as he. Those who were not, expected no quarter and got none.

Mr. Roosevelt's good sense showed him early that the problem of pauperism with which he was battling could not be run down. It had to be headed off if the fight was to be won. So he became Charles Loring Brace's most energetic backer in his fight for the children. He was a trustee of the Children's Aid Society, and never in all the years missed a Sunday evening with the boys in the Eighteenth Street lodging-house which was his particular charge. He knew them by name, and was their friend and adviser. And they loved him. When he lay dying, they bought rosebuds with their spare pennies and sent

them to his house. Many a time he had come
from the country with armfuls of flowers
for them. The little lame Italian girl for
whom he had bought crutches wrote him with
infinite toil a tear-stained note to please get
well and come and see her. His sympathy with
poverty and suffering was instinctive and instant. One day of the seven he gave, however
driven at the office, to personal work among
the poor, visiting them at their homes. It was
not a penance with him, but, he used to say, one
of his chief blessings.

He was rich and gave liberally, but always
with sense. He was a reformer of charity
methods, as of bad political methods in his own
fold. For that cause he was rejected by a
Republican Senate, at the instance of Roscoe
Conkling, when President Hayes appointed
him Collector of the Port. Mr. Roosevelt had
accepted with the statement that he would
administer the office for the benefit, not of the
party, but of the whole people. That meant
the retirement of the Custom-House influence
in politics, and civil service reform, for which
the time was not ripe. It was left to his son
to carry out, as was so much else he had at

heart. So far as I know, that was the elder Roosevelt's only appearance in politics, as politicians understand the term. Always a Republican, he had gone to the Cincinnati Convention, which nominated Mr. Hayes, as a representative of the Reform League.

Church, Mission, and Sunday-school had in him a stanch supporter. He was a constant contributor with counsel and purse to the work of the Young Men's Christian Association. I like to think that the key to all he was and did is in the answer he gave his pastor when once the latter said that he liked his name Theodore, with its meaning, " a gift of God." " Why may we not," replied Mr. Roosevelt, " change it about a bit and make it ' a gift to God ' ? " No man could have said it unless he meant just that. And, meaning it, his life must be exactly what it was.

This is the picture we get of him: a man of untiring energy, of prodigious industry, the most valiant fighter in his day for the right, and the winner of his fights. Mr. Brace said of him that it would be difficult to mention any good thing attempted in New York in twenty years in which he did not have a hand.

THEODORE ROOSEVELT, SR.
FROM THE PORTRAIT BY DANIEL HUNTINGTON

With it all he enjoyed life as few, and with
cause: he never neglected a duty. He drove
a four-in-hand in the Park, sailed a boat, loved
the woods, shared in every athletic sport, and
was the life and soul of every company. At
forty-six he was as strong and active as at
sixteen, his youthful ideals as undimmed. I
have had to suffer many taunts in my days on
account of my hero of fiction, John Halifax,
from those who never found a man so good.
I have been happier than they, it seems. But
perhaps they did not know him when they saw
him. Some of them must have known Theodore Roosevelt, and he was just such a one.
He would go to a meeting of dignified citizens
to discuss the gravest concerns of the city or of
finance, with a sick kitten in his coat-pocket,
which he had picked up in the street and was
piloting to some safe harbor. His home life
was what you might expect of such a man.
His children worshiped him. A score of times
I have heard his son sigh, when, as Governor
or Police Commissioner, he had accomplished
something for which his father had striven and
paved the way, " How I wish father were here
and could see it! " His testimony of filial love

completes the picture. " Father was," he said
to me, " the finest man I ever knew, and the
happiest."

His power of endurance was as extraordinary as his industry. In the last winter of his
life, when he was struggling with a mortal
disease, his daily routine was to rise at 8:30,
and after the morning visit to his mother, which
he never on any account omitted, to work at the
office till six. The evening was for his own
and for his friends until eleven o'clock, after
which he usually worked at his desk until 1 or
2 A.M. Several years before, he had had to
give up his father's business to attend to the
many private trusts that sought him as his
influence grew in the community. A hundred
public interests demanded his aid besides. He
helped to organize the Metropolitan Museum
of Art and the Museum of Natural Sciences,
and kept a directing hand upon them up to his
death. When mismanagement of the American department at the Vienna Exhibition
caused scandal and the retirement of the direc-
tors, it was Mr. Roosevelt who straightened out
things. Were funds to be raised for a charity,
he was ever first in demand. His champion-

ship of any cause was proof enough that it was good. His sunny temper won everybody over. " I never saw him come into my office," said a friend about him, " but I instinctively took down my check-book." He surrendered at sight.

The news of his death, on February 9, 1878, came home to thousands with a sense of personal bereavement. Though he was but a private citizen, flags flew at half-mast all over the city. Rich and poor followed him to the grave, and the children whose friend he had been wept over him. In the reports of the meetings held in his memory one catches the echo of a nature rarely blending sweetness with strength. They speak of his stanch integrity and devotion to principle; his unhesitating denunciation of wrong in every form; his chivalric championship of the weak and oppressed wherever found; his scorn of meanness; his generosity that knew no limit of sacrifice; his truth and tenderness; his careful, sound judgment; his unselfishness, and his bright, sunny nature that won all hearts. The Union League Club resolved " that his life was a stirring summons to the men of wealth, of culture, and of leisure in the community, to a more active participation in public affairs " as a means of saving the State.

Four years later his son Theodore was elected to the Assembly, and entered upon the career of public service which, by his exercise of the qualities that made his father beloved, set him in the Governor's Chair of his State. Other monument the people have never built to the memory of the first Theodore; but I fancy that they could have chosen none that would have pleased him more; and I am quite sure that he is here to see it.

This is the story, not of a people in its age-long struggle for righteousness, but of a single citizen who died before he had attained to his forty-eighth year, and it is the material out of which real civic greatness is made. I know of none in all the world that lasts better, prophets of evil and pessimists generally to the contrary notwithstanding. I have been at some pains to tell it to this generation, out of charity to the prophets aforesaid. Let them compare now the son's life as they know it, as we all know it, with the father's, point for point, deed for deed, and tell us what they think of it.

THEODORE ROOSEVELT'S FATHER

The truth, mind; for that, with knowledge of what has been, is, after all, the proper basis for prophecy as to what is to be. Or else let them come squarely out and declare that they have lived in vain, that ours is a worse country, every way, than it was twenty years ago, and not fit for a decent man to live in. That is the alternative, as they will see—unless, indeed, they prefer to do as the squirrel does, just sit and scold.

THE ROOSEVELT CHRONOLOGY

THE ROOSEVELT CHRONOLOGY

(FROM CONGRESSIONAL DIRECTORY)

Born in New York City - - Oct. 27, 1858
Entered Harvard College - - - - 1876
Graduated from Harvard - - - - 1880
Studied law.
Elected to New York Legislature - - 1881
Re-elected to New York Legislature - 1882
Re-elected to New York Legislature - 1883
Delegate to State Convention - - - 1884
Delegate to National Convention - - 1884
Ranching in West - - - - - 1884-1886
Nominated for Mayor of New York - 1886
Appointed member of United States Civil
    Service Commission - - - May, 1889
Appointed President New York Police
    Board - - - - - - - - May, 1895
Appointed Assistant Secretary of the
    Navy, - - - - - - - April, 1897

THE ROOSEVELT CHRONOLOGY

Appointed Lieutenant-Colonel of First
    Volunteer Cavalry - - - May 6, 1898
Promoted to Colonel of First Volunteer
    Cavalry - - - - - - - July 11, 1898
Mustered out with Regiment at Montauk
    Point - - - - - - September, 1898
Elected Governor of New York,
                    November, 1898
Unanimously nominated Vice-President,
                        June, 1900
Elected Vice-President - - November, 1900
Succeeded to Presidency - - Sept. 14, 1901

BOOKS BY
THEODORE ROOSEVELT

—

BOOKS BY THEODORE ROOSEVELT

COMPILED FROM THE CATALOGUE OF
THE CONGRESSIONAL LIBRARY

In each case the date given is of the first published edition. For complete editions see at the end of this bibliography.

THE NAVAL OPERATIONS OF THE WAR BETWEEN GREAT BRITAIN AND THE UNITED STATES—1812-1815. G. P. Putnam's Sons, New York. 1 Vol. . 1882

HUNTING TRIPS OF A RANCHMAN. G. P. Putnam's Sons, New York. 1 Vol. 1886

LIFE OF THOMAS HART BENTON. (Vol. 14 of American Statesmen Series.) Houghton, Mifflin & Co., Boston. Cloth 1887

LIFE OF GOUVERNEUR MORRIS. (American Statesmen Series.) Houghton, Mifflin & Co., Boston 1888

RANCH LIFE AND HUNTING TRAIL. The Century Co., New York . . . 1888

BOOKS BY THEODORE ROOSEVELT

ESSAYS ON PRACTICAL POLITICS. (Questions of the Day Series.) G. P. Putnam's Sons, New York. (Reprinted in "American Ideals.") 1888

NEW YORK CITY: A HISTORY. Longmans, Green & Co., New York . . 1891
(With postscript to date.) 1895

AMERICAN BIG-GAME HUNTING. (Book of the Boone and Crockett Club.) Forest and Stream Publishing Company, New York 1893

LIBER SCRIPTORUM. A shot at a bull-elk; Roosevelt; pp. 484-487 1893

THE WILDERNESS HUNTER. G. P. Putnam's Sons, New York 1893

HERO TALES FROM AMERICAN HISTORY. H. C. Lodge and Theodore Roosevelt. The Century Co., New York . . . 1895

HUNTING IN MANY LANDS. (The book of the Boone and Crockett Club.) Forest and Stream Publishing Company, New York 1895

WINNING OF THE WEST. G. P. Putnam's Sons, New York. 4 Vols. . 1896

BOOKS BY THEODORE ROOSEVELT

AMERICAN IDEALS, AND OTHER ESSAYS.
G. P. Putnam's Sons, New York . . 1897

BOOKS BY THEODORE ROOSEVELT

AMERICAN IDEALS, AND OTHER ESSAYS
CONTINUED

Social Evolution. North American
Review 1895
The Law of Civilization and De-
cay. Forum 1897

TRAIL AND CAMP-FIRE. (The book of
the Boone and Crockett Club.) Forest and Stream Publishing Company,
New York 1897

HISTORY OF THE ROYAL NAVY OF ENG-
LAND. (6 vols.) From the earliest
times to the present day. By W. L.
Clowes, assisted by Sir C. Markham,
Captain A. T. Mahan, H. W. Wilson,
Theodore Roosevelt, L. C. Langton
and others. (Mr. Roosevelt wrote part
of the sixth volume on the War of
1812.) Little, Brown & Co., Boston . 1898

BIG GAME HUNTING IN THE ROCKIES
AND ON THE GREAT PLAINS. (Including " Hunting Trips of a Ranchman "
and " The Wilderness Hunter.") G.
P. Putnam's Sons, New York . . 1899

ROUGH RIDERS. Charles Scribner's Sons,
New York 1899

EPISODES FROM THE "WINNING OF THE
WEST." (The Knickerbocker Litera-
ture Series.) G. P. Putnam's Sons,
New York 1900

BOOKS BY THEODORE ROOSEVELT

THE STRENUOUS LIFE. The Century
Co., New York. 225 pp. 1900

CONTENTS

The Strenuous Life. Speech.
Hamilton Club, Chicago, April
10 1899
Expansion and Peace. Independ-
ent, Dec. 21 1899
Latitude and Longitude of Re-
form. Century, June . . . 1900
Fellow Feeling a Political Factor.
Century, Jan. 1900
Civic Helpfulness. Century,
Oct. 1900
Character and Success. Outlook,
March 31 1900
Eighth and Ninth Command-
ments in Politics. Outlook,
May 12 1900
The Best and the Good. Church-
man, March 17 1900
Promise and Performance. Out-
look, July 28 1900
The American Boy. St. Nicholas,
May 1900
Military Preparedness and Un-
preparedness. Century, Nov. . 1899
Admiral Dewey. McClure's, Oct. 1899
Grant. Speech at Galena, Ill.,
April 27 1900
The Two Americas. Buffalo,
N. Y., May 20 1901
Manhood and Statehood. Colo-
rado Springs, August 2 . . 1901

BOOKS BY THEODORE ROOSEVELT

THE STRENUOUS LIFE
CONTINUED

Brotherhood and the Heroic Virtues. Vermont, Sept. 5 . . . 1901
National Duties. Minnesota, Sept. 2 1901
Christian Citizenship. New York Y. M. C. A., Dec. 30 . . . 1900
Labor Question. Chicago, Sept. 3 1900
(Character and Success is issued by the Philadelphia Institution for the Blind in raised letters.)

CAMERA SHOTS AT BIG GAME. By Allen Grant Wallihan; introduction by Theodore Roosevelt. Doubleday, Page & Co., New York 1901

OLIVER CROMWELL. Charles Scribner's Sons, New York. (Also in French.) 1901

LA VIE INTENSE, &c. (19 essays.) E. Flammarion, Paris 1902

THE DEER FAMILY. By T. Roosevelt, T. S. Van Dyke, D. G. Elliot and A. J. Stone. (The Deer and Antelope of North America, by Mr. Roosevelt.) Macmillan & Co., New York . . . 1902

THE PHILIPPINES: THE FIRST CIVIL GOVERNOR. By Theodore Roosevelt. CIVIL GOVERNMENT IN THE PHILIPPINES. By William H. Taft. The Outlook Company, New York . . . 1902

BOOKS BY THEODORE ROOSEVELT

MAXIMS OF THEODORE ROOSEVELT. The
Madison Book Co., Chicago . . . 1903

THE WOMAN WHO TOILS. By Mrs. Van
Vorst and Marie Van Vorst. (Ex-
perience of two ladies as factory
girls.) Introduction by Theodore
Roosevelt, in which occurs the famous
Race Suicide phrase. Doubleday,
Page & Co., New York 1903

COMPLETE EDITIONS

KNICKERBOCKER PRESS EDI-
TION. G. P. PUTNAM'S SONS, New
York. 14 Volumes. American Ideals;
Administration—Civil Service; The
Wilderness Hunter; Hunting the
Grizzly; Hunting Trips of a Ranch-
man; Hunting Trips on the Prairies;
and in the Mountains. Winning of
the West (6 Vols.). Naval War of
1812 (2 Vols.) 1903

SAGAMORE EDITION. G. P.
PUTNAM'S SONS. 15 Volumes. (Same
as Knickerbocker Edition, but including " The Rough Riders.") 1900

STANDARD LIBRARY EDI-
TION. G. P. PUTNAM'S SONS.
(Same volumes as Sagamore Edi-
tion.) 1900

BOOKS BY THEODORE ROOSEVELT

UNIFORM EDITION. GEBBIE &
Co., Philadelphia. 20 Volumes.
                    1902 and 1903
(Same as Knickerbocker Press Edi-
tion, but including besides: Rough
Riders, 2 vols.; New York: A His-
tory; Life of Thomas Benton; Life of
Gouverneur Morris; Hero Tales from
American History.)

INDEX

INDEX

INDEX

INDEX

INDEX

INDEX

INDEX